WITHDRAWN FROM
THE LIBRARY

UNIVERSITY OF
WINCHESTER

D1336686

To be

KA 0359953 1

GREAT WRITERS ON ORGANIZATIONS

To our parents and to our professional forebears

GREAT WRITERS ON ORGANIZATIONS
THE THIRD OMNIBUS EDITION

Derek S. Pugh and David J. Hickson

UNIVERSITY OF WINCHESTER LIBRARY

ASHGATE

© Derek S. Pugh, David J. Hickson and C. R. Hinings, 1964, 1971, 1983.
Fourth, fifth and sixth editions copyright © Derek S. Pugh and David J. Hickson, 1989, 1996, 2007.
Omnibus edition copyright © Derek S. Pugh and David J. Hickson, 1993.
Second omnibus edition copyright © Derek S. Pugh and David J. Hickson, 2000.
Third omnibus edition copyright © Derek S. Pugh and David J. Hickson, 2007.

All rights reserved. No part of this publication may be reproduced, stored in a retrieval system or transmitted in any form or by any means, electronic, mechanical, photocopying, recording or otherwise without the prior permission of the publisher.

Derek S. Pugh and David J. Hickson have asserted their moral right under the Copyright, Designs and Patents Act, 1988, to be identified as the authors of this work.

Published by
Ashgate Publishing Limited
Gower House
Croft Road
Aldershot
Hampshire GU11 3HR
England

Ashgate Publishing Company
Suite 420
101 Cherry Street
Burlington, VT 05401-4405
USA

Ashgate website: http://www.ashgate.com

British Library Cataloguing in Publication Data
Pugh, Derek Salman
    Great writers on organizations. - 3rd omnibus ed.
    1. Organizational sociology 2. Industrial management
    I. Title II. Hickson, David John
    302.3'5

Library of Congress Cataloging-in-Publication Data
Pugh, Derek Salman.
    Great writers on organizations / by Derek S. Pugh and David J. Hickson. -- 3rd omnibus ed.
        p. cm.
    Includes bibliographical references and indexes.
    ISBN 978-0-7546-7056-8
    1. Organizational sociology. I. Hickson, David John. II. Title.

HM786.P84 2007
302.3'5--dc22

ISBN 978-0-7546-7056-8

2007002019

UNIVERSITY OF WINCHESTER

302.
35
PUG

0359445 31

Printed and bound in Great Britain by MPG Books Ltd, Bodmin, Cornwall.

Contents

Introduction to the Third Omnibus Edition

It is more than 40 years since the first edition of *Writers on Organizations* appeared. Since that time it has been in gratifyingly continuous demand, having now reached its sixth edition. One of the attractions of the book is that it remains a relatively slim volume. This means that we have had to balance the addition of new writers with the omission of others. The contributions of those dropped, however, continues to form part of the flow of concepts and theories which illuminate organizational issues.

We are therefore very pleased to have this opportunity of presenting a third omnibus edition which contains a description of the work of every writer included in all the previous editions of the book. This gives a more comprehensive picture of organizational writing which is such an important input to managerial effectiveness.

It is a commonplace of discussion among managers and administrators that all organizations are different. Even so it is important to study these differences and to classify them. Something useful can thus be said about various kinds of organizations, the ways in which they function and the behaviour of members within them. This book describes the contributions that many prominent writers have made to the understanding of organizations and their management.

These writers have a variety of different backgrounds. Some draw upon their expertise as practising managers, some on their knowledge of national and local government administration, some on the findings of their research work. All are modern in that the influence of their work is currently being felt. All have attempted to draw together information and distil theories about how organizations function and how they should be managed.

In presenting these contributions, our aim has remained the same over the years. It is to give a direct introductory exposition of the views of leading authors whose ideas are currently the subject of interest and debate. We conceive of this work as a resource tool giving a general overview of the field, and so we have not essayed critical analysis which would be a quite different task. It is our hope that readers will bring their own critical appraisal to each contribution. Even so we are conscious of the very considerable selection and compression involved in presenting a writer's work in a few pages. Some distortions must inevitably result. We can only plead the best of intentions in that our hope is to entice the reader to explore the richness and complexity of the original sources which we list in each case. A companion volume *Organization Theory: Selected Readings* (edited by Derek S. Pugh, fifth edition, Penguin Books, 2007) presents extracts from the work of many of the writers summarized here.

We are grateful to Bob Hinings who was a co-author with us of early editions, to our publishers, Ashgate, for their support, and to Marjorie Hickson who first planted the idea of an omnibus volume. As always, she and Natalie Pugh, our wives, suffered in the cause.

Derek S. Pugh
Open University
Business School

David J. Hickson
University of Bradford
Management School

1 The Structure of Organizations

The decisive reason for the advance of bureaucratic organization has always been its purely technical superiority over any other form of organization.
MAX WEBER

It would be entirely premature, then, to assume that bureaucracies maintain themselves solely because of their efficiency.
ALVIN W. GOULDNER

It may not be impossible to run an effective organization of 5000 employees non-bureaucratically but it would be so difficult that no one tries.
THE ASTON GROUP

The danger lies in the tendency to teach the principles of administration as though they were scientific laws, when they are really little more than administrative expedients found to work well in certain circumstances but never tested in any systematic way.
JOAN WOODWARD

The managers are mainly conduits of causation, adding little independently in the causal sense, since the structural outcome has already been shaped by the contingencies.
LEX DONALDSON

The organization and control of bureaucracy can be designed so as to ensure that the consequential effects on behaviour are in accord with the needs of an open democratic society, and can serve to strengthen such a society.
ELLIOTT JAQUES

The visible hand of managerial direction has replaced the invisible hand of market mechanisms in coordinating flows and allocating resources in major modern industries.
ALFRED D. CHANDLER

Transaction cost economizing is, we submit, the driving force that is responsible for the main institutional changes [in corporations].
OLIVER E. WILLIAMSON

Adhocracy [the innovative configuration] is the structure of our age.
HENRY MINTZBERG

Increasingly your corporations will come to resemble universities or colleges.
CHARLES HANDY

The task [of the transnational organization] is not to build a sophisticated matrix structure, but to create a 'matrix in the minds of managers'.
CHRISTOPHER BARTLETT AND SUMANTRA GHOSHAL

Where modernist organization is rigid, postmodern organization is flexible.
STEWART CLEGG

All organizations have to make provision for continuing activities directed towards the achievement of given aims. Regularities in activities such as task allocation, supervision and coordination are developed. Such regularities constitute the organization's structure and the fact that these activities can be arranged in various ways means that organizations can have differing structures. Indeed, in some respects every organization is unique. But many writers have examined a variety of structures to see if any general principles can be extracted. This variety, moreover, may be related to variations in such factors as the objectives of the organization, its size, ownership, geographical location and technology of manufacture, which produce the characteristic differences in structure of a bank, a hospital, a mass-production factory or a local-government department.

The writers in this section are concerned to identify different forms of organizational structures and to explore their implications. Max Weber presents three different organizational types on the basis of how authority is exercised. He views one of these types – bureaucracy – as the dominant modern form. Alvin W. Gouldner also examines the bureaucratic type and shows that, even in one organization, three variants can be found. Derek Pugh and the Aston Group suggest that it is more realistic to talk in terms of dimensions of structures rather than types. Joan Woodward argues that production technology is the major determinant of the structure of manufacturing firms. Lex Donaldson examines the factors which lead an organization to a particular structure fitting to its needs.

Elliott Jaques examines the psychological nature of the authority relationships in a bureaucratic structure, and Alfred Chandler shows how the management structure flows from the company strategy. Oliver E. Williamson points to the way in which the pressures on the organization to process its information efficiently leads to the type of relationship – market or hierarchical – which is developed. Henry Mintzberg describes a range of types of modern organizations and their effectiveness. Charles Handy identifies some established structures of organization, but suggests that a distinctively different new form is coming into being. Christopher Bartlett and Sumantra Ghoshal argue that, for multinational firms to be successful in the current global market environment, they must develop an innovative new structure and culture of working. Stewart Clegg looks forward to a new relationship between superiors and subordinates in the 'post-modernist organization'.

All the contributors to this section suggest that an appropriate structure is vital to the efficiency of an organization and must be the subject of careful study in its own right.

Max Weber

Max Weber (1864–1920) was born in Germany. He qualified in law and then became a member of the staff of Berlin University. He remained an academic for the rest of his life, having a primary interest in the broad sweep of the historical development of civilizations through studies of the sociology of religion and the sociology of economic life. In his approach to both of these topics he showed a tremendous range in examining the major world religions such as Judaism, Christianity and Buddhism, and in tracing the pattern of economic development from pre-feudal times. These two interests were combined in his classic studies of the impact of Protestant beliefs on the development of capitalism in Western Europe and the US. Weber had the prodigious output and ponderous style typical of German philosophers, but those of his writings which have been translated into English have established him as a major figure in sociology.

Weber's principal contribution to the study of organizations was his theory of authority structures which led him to characterize organizations in terms of the authority relations within them. This stemmed from a basic concern with why individuals obeyed commands, why people do as they are told. To deal with this problem Weber made a distinction between *power*, the ability to force people to obey, regardless of their resistance, and *authority*, where orders are obeyed voluntarily by those receiving them. Under an authority system, those in the subordinate role see the issuing of directives by those in the superordinate role as legitimate. Weber distinguished between organizational types according to the way in which authority is legitimized. He outlined three pure types which he labelled 'charismatic', 'traditional' and 'rational-legal', each of which is expressed in a particular administrative apparatus or organization. These pure types are distinctions which are useful for analysing organizations, although any real organization may be a combination of them.

The first mode of exercising authority is based on the personal qualities of the leader. Weber used the Greek term 'charisma' to mean any quality of individual personality by virtue of which the leader is set apart from ordinary people and treated as endowed with supernatural, superhuman or at least specifically exceptional powers or qualities. This is the position of the prophet, messiah or political leader, whose organization consists of a set of disciples: the disciples have the job of mediating between the leader and the masses. The typical case of this kind is a small-scale revolutionary movement, either religious or political in form, but many organizations have had charismatic founders, such as Henry Ford or Richard Branson. Because the basis of authority lies in the characteristics of one person and because commands are based on that person's inspiration, however, this type of organization has a built-in instability. The question of succession always arises when the leader dies and the authority has to be passed on. Typically, in political and religious organizations, the movement splits, with the various disciples claiming to be the 'true' heirs to the charismatic founder. Thus, the process is usually one of fission. The splitting of Islam into Sunni and Shia sects on the death of the founding prophet Mohammed, exemplifies the problem. Even if the leader nominates a successor, that person will not necessarily be accepted. It is unlikely that another charismatic leader will be present, and so the organization must lose its charismatic form, becoming one of the two remaining types. If the succession becomes hereditary, the organization becomes traditional in form; if the succession is determined by rules, a bureaucratic organization develops.

The bases of order and authority in *traditional* organizations are precedent and usage. The rights and expectations of various groups are established in terms of taking what has always happened as sacred; the great arbiter in such a system is custom. Leaders have authority by virtue of the status that they have inherited, the extent of their authority being fixed by custom. When charisma is traditionalized by making its transmission hereditary, it becomes part of the role of the leader rather than being part of the founder's personality. The actual organizational form under a traditional authority system can take one of two patterns. There is the *patrimonial* form where officials are personal servants, dependent on the leader for remuneration. Under the *feudal* form the officials have much more autonomy, with their own sources of income and a traditional relationship of loyalty towards the leader. The feudal system has a material basis of tithes, fiefs and beneficiaries all resting on past usage and a system of customary rights and duties. Although Weber's examples are historical, his insight is equally applicable to modern organizations. Managerial positions are often handed down from one generation to the next as firms establish their own dynasties based on hereditary transmission. Selection and appointment may be based on kinship rather than expertise. Similarly, ways of doing things in many organizations are justified in terms of always having been done that way *as a reason in itself*, rather than on the basis of rational analysis.

The concept of rational analysis leads to Weber's third type of authority system, the rational-legal one, with its bureaucratic organizational form. This Weber sees as the dominant institution of modern society. The system is called rational because the means are expressly designed to achieve certain specific goals (that is, the organization is like a well-designed machine with a certain function to perform, and every part of the machine contributes to the attainment of maximum performance of that function). It is legal because authority is exercised by means of a system of rules and procedures through the office which an individual occupies at a particular time. For such organizations, Weber uses the name 'bureaucracy'. In common usage, bureaucracy is synonymous with inefficiency, an emphasis on red tape, and excessive writing and recording. Specifically, it is identified with inefficient public administrations. But in terms of his own definition, Weber states that a bureaucratic organization is technically the most efficient form of organization possible. 'Precision, speed, unambiguity, knowledge of files, continuity, discretion, unity, strict subordination, reduction of friction and of material and personal costs – these are raised to the optimum point in the strictly bureaucratic administration.' Weber himself uses the machine analogy when he says that the bureaucracy is like a modern machine, while other organizational forms are like non-mechanical methods of production.

The reason for the efficiency of the bureaucracy lies in its organizational form. As the means used are those which will best achieve the stated ends, it is unencumbered by the personal whims of the leader or by traditional procedures which are no longer applicable. This is because bureaucracies represent the final stage in depersonalization. In such organizations there is a series of officials, whose roles are circumscribed by written definitions of their authority. These offices are arranged in a hierarchy, each successive step embracing all those beneath it. There is a set of rules and procedures within which every possible contingency is theoretically provided for. There is a 'bureau' for the safekeeping of all written records and files, it being an important part of the rationality of the system that information is written down. A clear separation is made between personal and business affairs, bolstered by a contractual method of appointment in terms of technical qualifications for office. In such an organization authority is based in the office and commands are obeyed because the rules state that it is within the competence of a particular office to issue such commands. Also important is the stress on the appointment of experts. One of the signs of a developing bureaucracy is the growth of professional managers and an increase in the number of specialist experts with their own departments.

For Weber this adds up to a highly efficient system of coordination and control. The rationality of the organization shows in its ability to 'calculate' the consequences of its action. Because of the hierarchy of authority and the system of rules, control of the actions of individuals in the organization is assured; this is depersonalization. Because of the employment of experts who have their specific areas of responsibility and the use of files, there is an amalgamation of the best available knowledge and a record of past behaviour of the organization. This enables predictions to be made about future events. The organization has rationality: 'the methodical attainment of a definitely given and practical end by means of an increasingly precise calculation of means'.

This is where the link between Weber's interest in religion and organizations occurs. Capitalism as an economic system is based on the rational long-term calculation of economic gain. Initially for this to happen, as well as for world markets to expand, a particular moral outlook is needed. Weber saw this as being supplied by the Protestant religion after the Reformation, with its emphasis on this world and the need for individuals to earn their salvation through their industry on earth. Thus, economic activity gradually became labelled as a positive good rather than as a negative evil. Capitalism was launched on its path; this path was cleared most easily through the organizational form of bureaucracy which supplied the apparatus for putting economic rationality into practice. Providing it does so with efficiency and regularity bureaucratic administration is a necessity for any long-term economic calculation. Thus with increasing industrialization, bureaucracy becomes the dominant method of organizing. So potent is it that it becomes characteristic of other areas of society such as education, government, politics and so on. Finally, the bureaucratic organization becomes typical of all the institutions of modern society.

Most studies of the formal, structural characteristics of organizations over the past five decades have started from the work of Max Weber. His importance lies in having made the first attempt to produce systematic categories for organizational analysis.

BIBLIOGRAPHY

GERTH, H. H. and MILLS, C. W. (eds), *From Max Weber: Essays in Sociology,* Routledge & Kegan Paul, 1948.
WEBER, M., *The Protestant Ethic and the Spirit of Capitalism,* Allen & Unwin, 1930.
WEBER, M., *The Theory of Social and Economic Organization,* Free Press, 1947.

Alvin W. Gouldner

Alvin W. Gouldner (1920–1980) was an American sociologist who held the Max Weber Chair of Social Theory at Washington University, St Louis. He conducted research into social problems for the American Jewish Committee and worked on industrial organization, including consulting for the Standard Oil Company of New Jersey. In the last two decades of his life he was particularly concerned with the development of sociological theory and with the role of knowledge in society.

Gouldner has applied Weber's concept of bureaucracy and its functioning to modern industrial organizations. Weber's analysis was based on the assumption that the members of an organization will in fact comply with the rules and obey orders. He asked on what basis do the rule-promulgators and the order-givers obtain their legitimate authority. He paid no attention to the problem of establishing the legitimacy of authority in the face of opposition and a refusal to consent on the part of the governed. This is a situation frequently met, for example, when a bureaucratic authority attempts to supplant a traditionalistic one, or when the rule of the expert or the rational legal wielder of power is faced with resistance.

On the basis of a very close study of this type of situation in an American gypsum mine, Gouldner has described the effects of the introduction of bureaucratic organization in the face of opposition. The previous management system of the mine was based on 'the indulgency pattern'. The rules were ignored or applied very leniently; the men were only infrequently checked on and were always given a second chance if infringements came to light. There was a very relaxed atmosphere and a favourable attitude of the workers to the company. Into this situation came the new mine manager who set about seeing that the rules were enforced, that the authority structure functioned effectively, and in general that an efficient rational-legal organization was operated. But this also resulted in a great drop in morale and increased management-worker conflict – including a wildcat strike.

In his analysis of this situation Gouldner was able to distinguish three patterns of bureaucratic behaviour: mock, representative and punishment-centred – each with its characteristic values and conflicts.

In *mock bureaucracy* the rules are imposed on the group by some outside agency; for example, a rule laid down by an insurance company forbidding smoking in a shop, or official returns required outside the organization on the activities of members. Neither superiors nor subordinates identify themselves with or participate in the establishment of the rules, nor do they regard them as legitimate. Thus the rules are not enforced, and both superiors and subordinates obtain status by violating them. Smoking is allowed unless an outside inspector is present;

purely formal returns are made, giving no indication of the real state of affairs. The actual position differs very much from the official position and people may spend a lot of time going through the motions. This behaviour pattern of mock bureaucracy corresponds with the common conception of bureaucratic red tape administration which is divorced from reality. However, in such a system, as Gouldner points out, morale may be very high since the informal values and attitudes of all participants are bolstered by the joint violation or evasion of the rules in order to get on with the real job.

In *representative bureaucracy* Gouldner takes up and develops one strand of Weber's concept, the situation in which rules are promulgated by experts whose authority is acceptable to all the members of the organization. Superiors and subordinates support the rules which fit in with their values and confer status on those who conform. For example, pressure may come from both management and workers to develop a safety programme; a high quality of workmanship may be expected and achieved. In this situation rules are enforced by superiors and obeyed by subordinates, perhaps with some tension but with little overt conflict. As the values are held in common by all, deviations are explained by well-intentioned carelessness or ignorance, since it would not be thought possible to dispute the values themselves. The joint support for the rules is buttressed by feelings of solidarity and participation in a joint enterprise. This behaviour pattern of representative bureaucracy corresponds very closely to the ideal forms of organization strongly advocated by such writers as Taylor and Fayol (see Chapter 4) in which authority is based not on position but on accepted knowledge and expertise.

In the third type of bureaucracy, *punishment-centred*, rules arise in response to the pressures of *either* management *or* workers. The attempt is made to coerce the other side into compliance. For example, management may introduce stricter control on production, clocking-in procedures and fines. This type of bureaucracy emphasizes the elements of authority and command-hierarchy in Weber's concept; although as Gouldner points out, there can be a power struggle in which the solidarity of the subordinates imposes rules on the management – for example job demarcation rules, overtime bans or rigid redundancy procedures. Either superiors or subordinates consider the rules legitimate but not both. If conformity leads to a gain in status for one side, this involves a loss in status for the other. Deviation from the rules is not explained away as in representative bureaucracy, but is regarded as wilful disobedience. Such a situation clearly entails much conflict and tension.

The patterns of behaviour characteristic of these three types of bureaucracy may coexist in different degrees in any one organization, and they are perhaps better described as 'modes of bureaucratic functioning'. The punishment-centred mode, which is the most frequently used, is intended to produce an efficient organization working in conformity with rationally designed rules and procedures. It emphasizes the use of general and impersonal rules, which decrease the emphasis on the personal power of those in authority. This in turn leads to a reduction in interpersonal tension which promotes efficiency and reinforces the use of impersonal bureaucratic rules. This is the strength of bureaucracy, as Weber pointed out.

But Gouldner maintains that there are unanticipated consequences of bureaucratic functioning which Weber left out of account. General and impersonal rules, by their very nature, define what is *not* allowed and thus increase people's knowledge of what is the minimum acceptable behaviour which tends to become the standard behaviour. This lowers efficiency and, in a punishment-centred bureaucracy, leads to increased closeness of supervision to see that the rules are carried out; consequently there is increased emphasis on authority and greater interpersonal tension. This results in the continued issue of formal impersonal rules to deal with the conflicts, and the cycle then begins again. Thus both the anticipated and unanticipated consequences of bureaucracy lead to a reinforcement of bureaucratic behaviour. The system is essentially unstable, achieving its goals only at the cost of much interpersonal tension and conflict.

Thus rules have both positive and negative effects, anticipated and unanticipated consequences. An overall aim of rules is to overcome the effect of close supervision which makes power differences too visible and thereby may offend norms of equality. So rules serve as an equivalent for direct orders by providing a statement of the obligations of a particular job (their explicational function). However, in certain circumstances the informal group may provide this function, thereby leading to the unanticipated consequence of conflict. Rules also provide an impersonal way of using authority (their screening function). Along with this, rules enable control to take place at a distance (their remote control function). But here again, the distance may get too great, leading to a mock situation of authority. Rules also constitute a definition of expectation, together with sanctions for non-performance (their punishment-legitimating function). But rules also define minimal standards allowing individuals to work at low levels of commitment (their apathy-preserving function). It is the different possibilities in the operation of rules which provide the dysfunctions of bureaucracy.

Gouldner has also been concerned to distinguish different outlooks among administrators and to show the effects these have upon their attitudes to their jobs, their employing organizations, their professions and their colleagues. This arises from a further criticism of Weber. Gouldner suggests that there is an inherent contradiction in bureaucracy between a system of authority based on the appointment of experts, and authority based on hierarchy and discipline. In the first case authority is legitimized because of superior knowledge; in the second it arises from the office held. This represents a particular incompatibility in those organizations which employ large numbers of professionals who may have more technical knowledge than their hierarchical superiors. Gouldner distinguishes two main categories of administrators: 'cosmopolitans' and 'locals'. Cosmopolitans are administrators with little loyalty to the organization, but high commitment to their specialized skills. They have an extremely professional outlook. They think of themselves primarily as engineers or accountants, for instance. Locals are administrators with great loyalty to the organization, but with little commitment to specialized skills. They think of themselves as 'company people'. Although organizations wish to retain the loyalty of their personnel (and therefore, for example, to promote by seniority from within), they also have a basic rational orientation towards efficiency (which requires appointment by skill and competence from wherever it is obtainable). This built-in dilemma is another major cause of tension in the modern organization.

Gouldner has contrasted mechanical systems with natural systems such as societies, institutions and organizations. People within natural systems are not just empty shells constrained by the circumstances in which they find themselves; as they operate the system, they have ideas, perceptions and choices to make which shape the organization's structure, often away from the intentions of its designers. For Gouldner social science has the special role in society of offering an explanatory and critical approach to organizations and institutions in order to help in this process and thus proclaim the autonomy of the individual.

BIBLIOGRAPHY

GOULDNER, A.W., *Patterns of Industrial Bureaucracy*, Routledge & Kegan Paul, 1955.
GOULDNER, A.W., *Wildcat Strike*, Routledge & Kegan Paul, 1955.
GOULDNER, A.W., 'Cosmopolitans and Locals: Towards an Analysis of Latent Social Roles, 1', *Administrative Science Quarterly, I* (1957), 281–306.
GOULDNER, A.W., 'Organizational Analysis', in R.K. Merton et al. (eds), *Sociology Today,* Basic Books, 1958.

Derek Pugh and the Aston Group, including John Child and David Hickson

In the late 1950s Derek Pugh, now Emeritus Professor of International Management at the Open University Business School, UK, brought to the Birmingham College of Advanced Technology (which became the University of Aston-in-Birmingham) a distinctive view of how to conduct research. His research experience as a social psychologist at the University of Edinburgh had placed him in close contact with researchers in other social sciences. He believed that the scope of empirical investigation and of understanding could be widened by multidisciplinary research, founded on a common commitment to and ownership of results within the research team, and on team management skills.

The Industrial Administration Research Unit at Aston, founded and led by Pugh between 1961 and 1970, included several generations of researchers whose academic origins ranged from psychology, sociology, economics and politics to no specific discipline at all. The names which appear most frequently on publications are John Child, David Hickson, Bob Hinings, Roy Payne, Diana Pheysey and Charles McMillan as the initiator, with David Hickson, of much subsequent international research, but there are many more. It is symptomatic of the nature of the group that it has not taken on the name of any one individual, even that of Derek Pugh, but is usually known as the 'Aston Group', even though there is no longer any special link with that university. The programme of research dispersed with the members of the group, and they and others in touch with them have pursued its work elsewhere in Britain and in several other countries.

The Aston Programme contributed to organization theory by blending some of the research methods and assumptions of psychology with conceptions of organizations and their workings from sociology and economics. Its approach has three essential elements. First, because organizations and their members are changing and complex, numbers of their *attributes should be studied together and as matters of degree*, not as 'either/or' phenomena – a multi-variate approach to a changing world of greys, rather than blacks and whites. This also implies that there will be no single reason for the way in which an organization is set up and run, but many possible influences (that is, multivariate causal explanations). What happens cannot be due to an organization's size alone, nor for that matter to its technology alone, but must in some degree be due to a number of these and other factors all acting together.

Second, because organizations outlast the comings and goings of individuals, it is *appropriate to study their non-personal or institutional aspects* using information on their divisions of work, their control systems and their formal hierarchies. For this, individuals can be interviewed as informants who describe these aspects, rather than being asked to indicate how they experience the organization personally, which they would be if asked to respond to questionnaires about themselves.

Third, because organizations are working wholes, they and their members *should be seen from more than one perspective* to give the fullest possible view. 'The response to the recurring conundrum "does man make organization or does organization make man?" must be to assume that both are happening all the time.' Therefore, the Aston Programme aimed to link:

- organizational structure and functioning;
- group composition and interaction;
- individual personality and behaviour.

Early ambitions to include features of the surrounding society were not realized initially, but began to be included later, when research extended beyond Britain to organizations in other societies.

The Programme commenced with a project in the Birmingham area in England, from which has grown all further research. It focused on the organizational level by studying a highly diverse sample of 46 organizations: private sector and public sector, from manufacturers of cars and chocolate bars to municipal departments, public services and chain stores. Their formal structures were analysed in terms of their degrees of:

- *specialization* of functions and roles;
- *standardization* of procedures;
- *formalization* of documentation;
- *centralization* of authority;
- *configuration* of role structure.

These concepts reflect prevalent ideas about bureaucratization and how to manage, which can be found in the work of Weber (see earlier in this chapter) and Fayol (in Chapter 4).

A very large number of ways of measuring these aspects of structure were devised, which have been employed variously by many researchers since. The most distinctive kind of measure used, an innovation in research on organizations, was based on demonstrating that, for example, the number of functions (such as finance or public relations) that an organization had specialized out of a set of possible specialisms could validly be added to give it a specialization score, and similarly with standardization, formalization and centralization. This enabled one organization to be compared with another in these terms for the first time.

Despite the range and ramifications of this research, its salient results took on a relatively simple outline. First, the measures of specialization, standardization and formalization were simplified into a combined score for each organization. To distinguish this from its three constituents it was called 'structuring of activities'. An organization with highly structured activities has many specialized sections such as buying, training, work study and so on, and many routine procedures and formal documents, the total effect being that what has to be done is marked out or structured. Second, centralization of decision making and the autonomy of an organization's decision making from any owning organization were together termed 'concentration of authority'. An organization with concentrated authority not only has most of its decisions taken at the top of its own hierarchy but has many decisions taken for it, over its head, by the management of another organization of which it is a wholly or partly owned subsidiary or subordinate section.

Thus, at its simplest, the Aston Group isolated two primary elements of any organization, how far the activities of its personnel are structured and how far its decision-making authority is concentrated at the top, which between them sum up much of what an organization is like. Know them and you know it, to a large extent, for they are its two fundamentals.

Although the Aston Programme's approach assumes that organizations are what they are for many reasons, these first results were also relatively simple in the principal explanations that they suggested. A series of features of the organizational context, including its purpose, ownership, technology, size and dependence, were examined for any correlation with the extent to which an organization had structured its activities or concentrated its authority. It was found that ownership (whether private or public, dispersed in thousands of shareholdings or in the hands of a family) made little difference to structuring and concentration; as did technology, which was reflected in only a few aspects of structure.

What did and does matter much more for the form taken by an organization is its *size* and its degree of *dependence upon other organizations*. The larger it is, the more likely its employees are to work in very specialized functions, following standardized procedures and formalized documentation; that is, it will score highly on structuring of activities and have many of the appearances of bureaucracy. The more it is dependent upon only a few owning, supplier or customer units, or even just one – total dependence is where an organization is wholly owned by another which supplies all its needs and takes all its outputs – the less autonomy it will have in its own decision making, and even those decisions that are left to it are likely to be centralized within itself rather than decentralized.

Casting its results into an empirically derived taxonomy of forms of organization structure, the Aston Group put forward from its first project a view of the forms prevalent in contemporary industrialized society, in Britain and probably elsewhere too. Large firms and big businesses are typically *workflow bureaucracies*, highly structured but not as highly concentrated in authority as some. Public service organizations of local and central government are *personnel bureaucracies*, not very structured but with highly concentrated authority and procedures focused on the hiring, promoting and firing of personnel. Smaller units within large private or public groups are full bureaucracies, with the high structuring of the workflow type and the highly concentrated authority of the personnel type. Smaller firms in personal ownership have neither of these features to any great extent, being *non-bureaucracies* (or implicitly structured). There are other types, but these four main ones can be depicted as in the figure below.

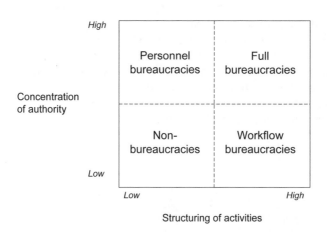

Structuring of activities

The progression of the Aston Group into research on group and role characteristics and on the individual's experience of organizational 'climate', in accordance with their Programme of linking organizational, group and individual levels analysis, is not so well known. Its results are not so clear cut. If any construction can be placed on them overall, it is that they lift from bureaucracy the pall of gloom laid over it by widespread assumptions of its uniformly stifling and dreary nature. It may be like that, but if it is, then it is for those in the lowest-level jobs and not necessarily for those higher in the hierarchy. Life for them differs from one bureaucratic organization to another.

Through a mixture of surveys and of intensive case studies with batteries of methods, Aston researchers showed that, while structuring of activities does tend to be associated with greater formality at the group interaction level, and concentration of authority does tend to be associated with less autonomy for individuals and with greater conventional attention to rules, nevertheless a uniformly bureaucratic-type firm can be effective and its personnel can like working in it. At least, this was so in their case study of a small firm owned by a large international corporation, a 'small effective bureaucracy' which they code-named 'Aston'.

In organizations that showed both high structuring and high concentration of authority, which were loosely equated with bureaucracies, there was no evidence of less attractive climates (in terms of the way in which authority was exercised, of interest in work, of routine and of personal relationships). At the top, such organizations tended to have managers who were younger and better qualified, with more flexible and challenging attitudes. And firms with younger managers tended to show faster growth in sales and assets (though whether youth caused growth or growth attracted younger personnel is an unanswered question). So those managing more bureaucratic-type firms were unlikely themselves to be cautious and conformist, and were most likely to seek innovation and risk.

Greater confidence is shown in the Aston Programme's achievements at the organizational level of analysis, however. On issues such as the presence or absence of procedures, documents, defined authority and control systems, the Programme demonstrated that significant comparisons can be made between organizations of virtually any kind. (But it must be remembered that the data do not tell how far these means are then used.) The Aston Programme provides concepts and measures of organizational structure that have withstood use and re-use by researchers beyond the original team in a way that rarely happens.

In later work Pugh with Hickson and others went on to investigate national cultural differences and their effect on the processes of management in different countries.

BIBLIOGRAPHY

EBSTER-GROSZ, D. and PUGH, D., *Anglo-German Business Collaboration: Pitfalls and Potentials*, Macmillan, 1996.

HICKSON, D.J. and PUGH, D.S., *Management Worldwide: Distinctive Styles Amid Globalization*, 2nd edn., Penguin Books, 2001.

PUGH, D.S., 'The Measurement of Organization Structures: Does Context Determine Form?', *Organizational Dynamics* (Spring 1973), 19-34; reprinted in D.S. Pugh (ed.), *Organization Theory*, 5th edn, Penguin, 2007.

PUGH, D.S. (ed.), *The Aston Programme*, Vols 1, 2 and 3, Ashgate(Dartmouth), 1998.

JOHN CHILD

John Child, now Professor of Commerce at the University of Birmingham, England, joined Pugh at Aston in using the same methods to replicate the results in contrasting industries – stable compared to fast-changing.

Most significantly, he made explicit what had remained implicit in the thinking behind the Aston Programme. He highlighted *strategic choice* by emphasizing that all aspects of organizations were in some sense chosen by their managements; they did not just happen. Size, for example, does not 'cause' specialization just like that. Growth in size enables, or pressures, managers who want to have effective organizations to add more specialist departments so that work can be divided clearly between more people, who thus acquire more specialized expertise. It is the managers who choose what to do. More than that, they choose the growth in size to begin with. They decide to expand output, add a new marketing department, or whatever, and so they increase the numbers of employees. Strategic choice by managers affects both context and structure.

But *one choice constrains another*: each choice (for example of size) constrains the options open for the next (for example of the degree of structuring to be adopted).

A major instance of this is that the choice of how far to develop either of the two primary elements, structuring and concentration, is likely to limit to some extent what can be done with the other, for there is a small negative relationship between them; that is, more of one probably means somewhat less of the other, and to that extent they are alternative means of controlling an organization – not mutually exclusive alternatives (since all organizations use both) but alternative emphases.

Later Child spent some years in China during the transition from Maoist rule. In some of the first ever independent empirical research in that nation's industries, he and Chinese colleagues exposed the problems of devolving a centrally planned system. Decentralization was uneven and only partially effective. Central and local government kept capital investment in their own hands, and formal delegation to managements of decisions on, for instance, purchasing and recruiting meant little if in practice managers had to go to state agencies to find sources of goods and personnel.

Child also studied the operation of US multinational corporations which had established joint ventures in China. He found that, in general, they were prepared to de-centralize certain decisions to their affiliate companies concerning local issues such as choice of suppliers or of markets aimed for. But they retained control of decisions on issues which could have corporate implications such as modifications of the product, and they imposed their standard quality and financial reporting regimes.

BIBLIOGRAPHY

CHILD, J., "Organizational Structures, Environment, and Performance: The Role of Strategic Choice," *Sociology, 6,* (1972), 2-22. Reprinted in PUGH, D.S. (ed.) *The Aston Programme,* Vol. 1, Ashgate (Dartmouth), 1998.

CHILD, J., *Management in China During the Age of Reform,* Cambridge University Press, 1994.

CHILD, J., *Organization: Contemporary Principles and Practice,* Blackwell, 2005.

CHILD, J., FAULKNER, D. and PITKETHLY, R. *The Management of International Acquisitions,* OUP, 2001.

DAVID HICKSON

David Hickson, now Emeritus Professor of International Management at the University of Bradford Management School, England, who was with the Aston Group from the beginning, shared with Pugh a particular responsibility for extending its work beyond Britain. Over the years, Aston-based projects took place in many nations worldwide, including the US and Canada, Western Europe, together with Poland and Sweden, the Middle East and Israel, India, Hong Kong and Japan. Among the differences which have been found are notably high centralization of organizations under state central planning in Poland, high structuring (specialization and formalization) in Japanese companies which have adopted contemporary Western forms of organization and management, and comparatively less structuring in paternalistic Hong Kong firms.

Hickson with C. R. Hinings (now of the University of Edmonton, Alberta, Canada) and other colleagues put forward a culture-free hypothesis, which originated from a comparison of manufacturing firms in Britain, Canada and the US. As they saw it, this stated the 'boldest' possibility, namely: 'Relationships between the structural characteristics of work organizations and variables of organization context will be stable across societies.' Greater size, for instance, would consistently go with greater specialization and greater formalization, in any country, West or East. Lex Donaldson (see later in this chapter) tested this hypothesis using the published results of studies in 13 countries across the world and found that it was supported. There were indeed stable relationships, especially with size of organizations. Everywhere bigger organizations are not only likely to be more structured, but also less centralized (the latter relationship may be weaker in the East). In other words, once jobs and procedures are set up, top managers can delegate more because people know what they should do, and simultaneously they ask to be allowed to do it. This finding suggests, not that all organizations are the same, but that managers in all nations have similar constraints upon their choices, which show up as a repeated pattern of relationships between size, and dependence, and structural features.

Again with Hinings, and with other colleagues in the Faculty of Business at the University of Alberta, Canada, Hickson went on to examine which managers most influence these choices, and why. They proposed a *strategic contingencies theory of intraorganizational power*, building up the ideas of Crozier (Chapter 5), and verified it by studying departmental influence in firms in Canada and the US. The theory gives three reasons why some departmental managers are powerful and others weak. These are how far they *cope with uncertainty, are centrally situated* and are *not substitutable*. If their department can cope with uncertainty, then the rest of the organization can function with fewer difficulties, as when a marketing department evens out erratic fluctuations in customer demands by astute advertising, so that production can be more stable year-round. If their department is central to the flows of work around the organization, then more of the others who feed work to it and wait upon its work are dependent upon it, as when a finance department receives estimates and allocates budgets. If this department cannot be substituted for, since no one else in the organization nor any external agency can do what it does, then it holds a monopoly-like position. Should there be an alternative, as when some of the work of a purchasing department could be contracted out to a buying agent, that position is fragile.

Departmental managers whose personnel is strong in all three respects have an overall *control of strategic contingencies* within their organization that gives them more influence over decisions than anyone else has, even over decisions outside their departmental concerns. Pfeffer and Salancik (see Chapter 2) used this same idea in their theory about an organization's external relationships.

Hickson, together with colleagues at Bradford Management Centre (now the University of Bradford Management School), then investigated how these managerial decisions, particularly the major ones, came to be made. Comparing

150 histories of decisions in 30 organizations in England, they found three prevalent ways of making such decisions. Decisions could be arrived at by a process that was *sporadic*, 'informally spasmodic and protracted'; or *fluid*, 'steadily paced, formally channelled, speedy'; or *constricted*, 'narrowly channelled'.

Which type of process occurred depended more on what was being decided than on the kind of organization, manufacturer, hospital, utility or whatever it might be, in which it was being decided. The most complex and political matters (which could be new products or major reorganizations, for example) most often gave rise to a sporadic process; those that were still complex but less political (which could be a big share issue, for example) were likely to go through a smoother, fluid process; whilst those that were still political but less complex (which could be the organization's corporate budget and business plan) were likely to go through a tighter, constricted process. As the Bradford researchers put it, 'the matter for decision matters most'.

Together with his colleagues, Hickson therefore draws attention to three of the more crucial features of what managers have to work with. First, wherever in the world they may be, there will be consistent constraints, one decision upon another, in the structural features – as defined by the Aston Programme – that characterize organizations. Second, they must expect differing patterns of influence in different organizations: marketing may have great say in one firm but little in another, for instance. Third, by contrast, they will be able to recognize what is going on when big decisions are made in organizations other than their own, easily fitting in if they change jobs; a similarly complex and political matter is likely to engender much the same process wherever it occurs.

In later work Hickson with Pugh and others extended the investigation of national cultural differences and their effect on the processes of management in different countries.

BIBLIOGRAPHY

HICKSON, D. J., BUTLER, R. J., CRAY, D., MALLORY, G. R. and WILSON, D. C., *Top Decisions: Strategic Decision-Making in Organizations*, Blackwell and Jossey-Bass, 1986.

HICKSON, D. J., BUTLER, R. J., CRAY, D. and WILSON, D. C. (eds.), *The Bradford Studies of Strategic Decision Making*, Ashgate, 2001.

HICKSON, D. J., HININGS, C. R., LEE, C. A., SCHNECK, R. E., and PENNINGS, J. M., 'A Strategic Contingencies Theory of Intraorganizational Power', *Administrative Science Quarterly*, 16/2, 1971, 216-229.

HICKSON, D. J., and McMILLAN, C. J. (eds.), *Organization and Nation: The Aston Program IV*, Gower, 1981.

HICKSON, D. J. and PUGH, D. S., *Management Worldwide: Distinctive Styles Amid Globalization*, 2nd edn., Penguin Books, 2001.

HININGS, C. R., HICKSON, D. J., PENNINGS, J. M. and SCHNECK, R. C., 'Structural Conditions of Intraorganizational Power', *Administrative Science Quarterly*, 19/1, 1974, 22-44.

Joan Woodward

Joan Woodward (1916–1971) was Professor of Industrial Sociology at the Imperial College of Science and Technology, University of London. She began her research career at the University of Liverpool, but is best known for her subsequent work on technology and organization in manufacturing firms as director of the Human Relations Research Unit at the South-East Essex Technical College. She and her colleagues at Imperial College broadened and deepened this line of research.

From 1953 to 1957 Woodward led the South-East Essex research team in a survey of manufacturing organizations in that area (see Woodward 1958, 1965). In all, 100 firms participated, but because the amount of information obtained on them varied from firm to firm, the published information is on smaller numbers. Firms ranged in size from 100 employees to over 1000; some were the main establishments of their companies while others were branch factories. The survey was supplemented by intensive studies of selected firms.

Woodward does not use sweeping classifications of organizations by types (such as those suggested by Weber – charismatic, traditionalistic, bureaucratic; or by Burns – organismic, mechanistic). Rather than attempt in this way to summarize whole ranges of characteristics of organizations, she investigates specific features such as the number of levels of authority between top and bottom, the span of control or average number of subordinates per supervisor, the clarity or otherwise with which duties are defined, the amount of written communication, and the extent of division of functions among specialists.

Woodward finds that firms show considerable differences in features such as these. Foremen may have to supervise anything from a handful to 80 or 90 workers; the number of levels of management in production departments may be anywhere from two to eight; communication can be almost entirely verbal or largely written. Why should these differences occur?

Woodward's team compared firms of different sizes and examined differences in historical background, without finding any answer. But when differences in technology were studied, relationships were seen with many organizational features. It is not claimed as a result that technology is the only influence upon a firm's organization nor that individual managers make no impression, but that technology is a major factor.

Woodward finds that the objectives of a firm – what it wishes to make and for what markets –determine the kind of technology it uses. For example, a firm building novel prototypes of electronic equipment could not do so by the techniques of mass production which dominate vehicle manufacture. Production systems differ in their degree of technical complexity, from unit (jobbing) and small batch production, through large batch and mass production to the most complex, namely process production.

These three broad categories are subdivided into nine sub-categories of production systems (see Woodward 1958, for an earlier and slightly different version) from least to most complex:

UNIT AND SMALL BATCH

1. Production of units to customers' requirements.
2. Production of prototypes.
3. Fabrication of large equipment in stages.
4. Production of small batches to customers' orders.

LARGE BATCH AND MASS PRODUCTION

1. Production of large batches.
2. Production of large batches on assembly lines.
3. Mass production.

PROCESS PRODUCTION

1. Intermittent production of chemicals in multi-purpose plant.
2. Continuous flow production of liquids, gases and crystalline substances.

Some firms used more than one of these production systems and so were placed in additional 'combined system' categories. A distinguishing feature of process systems is that they manufacture products measured by dimensions of weight or volume (for example liquids) rather than counted as series of integral units (for example numbers of vehicles or packaged goods).

In general, the higher the category the more it is possible to exercise control over the manufacturing operations because performance can be predetermined. In a continuous-flow plant such as a chemical installation, the equipment can be set for a given result; capacity and breakdown probabilities are known. But in batch production, full capacity may not be known; even well-developed production control procedures represent a continuing attempt to set fresh targets in face of the many uncertainties of day-to-day manufacture. In unit production of prototypes, for example, it is almost impossible to predict the results of development work.

These differences in technology account for many differences in organization structure. In process technologies where equipment does the job, taller hierarchies are found with longer lines of command, but managed through committees rather than by instruction down the line. Such hierarchies include more trained university graduates, and since the proportion of personnel working directly on production is low, the hierarchy of administrative and managerial personnel comprises a comparatively large proportion of total employees.

Despite the complex administrative hierarchy of specialist staff and control departments common in large batch and mass production technologies, these have shorter lines of command and proportionately fewer managers and clerks. Their salient characteristic is large numbers of direct production operatives.

Unit and small batch production typically has an even shorter hierarchy where no manager is very far from the production work itself. This relies relatively heavily upon the production personnel themselves without extensive administrative controls.

Some organizational characteristics do not differ in the same order straight along the nine technology categories. On some, large batch and mass production are often distinctive, while unit and process production have much in common with each other. The large numbers of semi-skilled workers on which mass production is based mean that the span of control of supervisors is very wide, and since results are obtained through the pressure exerted by bosses upon subordinates, human and industrial relations may be strained. Typical of both unit and process production are comparatively small groups of skilled workers with closer personal relationships with their supervisors.

Similarly, the complex production control problems of large batch and mass systems are reflected in their larger numbers of staff specialists, greater paperwork, and attempted clear-cut definition of duties, leading to more 'mechanistic' organizations as Burns (see Chapter 2) has called them.

A rough assessment of the firms on both financial and market performance and on reputation showed that the apparently more successful firms had organizational characteristics near the median or average for their category of technology. Perhaps there is one form of organization most appropriate to each system of production. Successful process firms must have taller, more narrowly based organization pyramids; successful unit production firms must have relatively short pyramids, and so on.

Certainly more prolonged case-studies carried out by Woodward and her colleagues to test out the results of the initial survey showed that a change of technology category seems to force changes in organization. This in itself may bring conflict among those whose interests are affected, especially if the change is into batch type production. Firms were studied which moved from unit to batch, attempts being made to rationalize and increase the scale of production; and from process to batch where, for example, a firm began to package a product previously sold in bulk. In such cases, middle managers and supervisors found that in batch production their days disappeared in a confusion of calls and contacts with other people, that this subjected them to greater personal stress, and that their responsibility for production overlapped with that of new planning and control departments.

Indeed, such changes in technology may alter the overall status of the several functions in a firm. This is because the cycle of manufacture places development, production and marketing in a different order in different technologies. In unit or jobbing systems, marketing precedes development and production follows last, since not until a customer requires a product and it is designed can production occur. In large batch and mass systems, the development and production of a new line precedes its mass marketing. In process systems, development of a possible product and marketing to assured customers must precede commitment of capital to special-purpose plant to produce it. In each system, the most critical function is the central one upon which success most heavily depends. That is, in unit systems, development has most importance and status; in mass systems it is production; in process systems it is marketing.

Woodward and her colleagues carried out further detailed case studies of managerial control in its various forms as the link between the technology of manufacture and organizational structure and behaviour. In *Industrial Organization: Behaviour and Control*, Reeves and Woodward focus upon two dimensions of managerial control systems: first, the extent to which control varies between being personal and impersonal; secondly, the degree to which control is fragmented.

Along the first dimension, there is a range of control systems from completely personal hierarchical control at one extreme, as operated by an owner-employer, to completely impersonal mechanical control at the other, as operated by measurement mechanisms and the automatic control of machine tools. In the middle of the range come the impersonal control processes which are based on administrative procedures, such as production planning and cost systems. Firms may be compared along this dimension, which is associated with characteristic effects upon structure and behaviour. The most important effect is that movement towards impersonal control involves a separation between the planning and execution stages of the work process.

At the personal end of the scale there is almost total overlap between planning and execution; with impersonal administrative control processes, there is considerable separation but the planning departments (such as production control, quality control and cost control) are involved in the execution of the work; at the mechanical end of the scale there can be total separation, the control designers and planners being totally unconcerned with the operations since they have already built in correction mechanisms at the planning stage. Indeed the planning and design stages at the mechanical control end of the scale may be the concern of a separate organization, as when a chemical engineering firm undertakes the design and erection of an automated continuous-flow chemical plant complete with mechanical control processes, which is then handed over to the contracting organization.

The second dimension of control systems studied by Reeves and Woodward was the extent to which control was fragmented, ranging from a single integrated system of control at one extreme to multisystem fragmented control at the other. To obtain a single integrated system, a firm would continuously attempt to relate the standards set for various departments to the performance and adjustment mechanisms associated with them. At the other end of the scale, a firm might have a number of control criteria operating independently which are continuously reconciled by the supervisor or the production operative. A job has to be done by a particular date as set by production control, to a particular standard as set by quality control, to a cost limit as set by cost control, by particular methods as set by work study and so on. An inevitable result of having a multiplicity of systems with fragmented control is conflict: in attempting to satisfy one particular control criterion, supervisors jeopardize their performance on the others.

The two dimensions of control processes are used together to generate a four-fold typology of systems in a developmental sequence. Four categories are outlined:

1. Firms with unitary and mainly personal controls, such as an entrepreneurial firm, where the owner would personally relate time and quality to cost. This type is characteristic of unit and small batch production.
2. Firms with fragmented and mainly personal controls, such as a firm where more individuals are involved in setting control criteria.
3. Firms with fragmented and mainly impersonal administrative or mechanical controls, such as a firm where the control criteria are impersonally set by functional departments. Most large batch and mass production firms fall here or in category 2.
4. Firms with unitary and mainly impersonal administrative or mechanical controls, such as a firm controlling the total manufacturing process to a master plan, perhaps using a computer for information processing and process control. This type is characteristic of process production.

The basic assumption and conclusion of Woodward's work are that meaningful explanations of differences in organization and behaviour can be found in the work situation itself. The technology of this work situation should be a critical consideration in management practice. There is no one best way. She warns against accepting principles of administration as universally applicable. The same principles can produce different results in different circumstances; many principles derive from experience of large batch or mass production only and are not likely to apply to other technologies. Careful study of the objectives and technology of a firm is required.

Woodward's study was pioneering both in terms of empirical investigation and in setting a fresh framework of thought. Prior to it, thinking about organization depended on the apt but often overgeneralized statements of experienced managers and on isolated case studies of particular firms. Woodward showed the possibilities of comparisons of large numbers of firms so that generalizations might be securely based and their limits acknowledged.

She thus forced thinking away from the abstract elaboration of principles of administration to an examination of the constraints placed on organization structure and management practice by differing technologies and their associated control systems.

BIBLIOGRAPHY

WOODWARD, J., *The Dock Worker*, Liverpool University Press, 1955.

WOODWARD, J., 'Management and Technology', *Problems of Progress in Industry,* 3, *HMSO,* 1958.

WOODWARD, J., *The Saleswoman: A Study of Attitudes and Behaviour in Retail Distribution,* Pitman, 1960.

WOODWARD, J., *Industrial Organization: Theory and Practice,* Oxford University Press, 1965; *2nd edn,* 1980.

WOODWARD, J.(ed.), *Industrial Organization: Behaviour and Control,* Oxford University Press, 1970.

Lex Donaldson

Lex Donaldson is Professor of Organizational Design at the Australian Graduate School of Management in Sydney. Originally from Liverpool in England, his undergraduate degree is from the University of Aston, Birmingham, and his PhD was gained at the London Business School. His research books and papers have established him as a major advocate of a scientific 'positivist' approach to how organizations are structured and why they change. He has put forward a carefully argued explicit theory of continual cycles of change, which explains, among other things, why high performance may not be all to the good. He has robustly defended his position and given detailed critical assessments of possible alternative approaches.

Donaldson crystallizes his position in his SARFIT model of organizational change. SARFIT stands for *structural adaptation to regain fit*. He argues that if good performance is to be attained, the principal structural features of an organization have to be constantly adjusted to fit the main factors that bear upon it. If its performance is suffering because it is out of alignment with such factors, then structural adaptation will bring it into fit and performance will improve.

If, for example, a firm has concentrated on making a certain range of products for its own home market, it is likely to have a functional structure. That is, it will be differentiated, or divided, into functions such as finance and sales and human resources, and production units each making some of the parts of the finished items, all reporting up the same line to the same top management. But if the firm diversifies, say, into making not one but three product ranges each aimed at different markets, then this structure will be strained. Too much will be loaded on to the management apex, and responsibilities and priorities will become confused. There will be misfit between task and structure. So performance will suffer.

Based on empirical study, Donaldson showed that the large majority of failing firms in this situation moved from a functional to a divisional structure, with each division responsible for only one of the product ranges. Each division had its own management structure with sales and HRM departments, and so on. This structural adaptation restored fit between task and structure, and performance recovered. Similarly, a firm that becomes a multinational corporation may have to divide into several divisions each covering a geographical area in order to recover fit. But SARFIT does not happen overnight: it may take years. Task and market strategy lead to structure, but only slowly.

The approach underlying SARFIT applies more widely, but Donaldson focuses the model on two main features of structure, and three main contingencies affecting structure which have all been established by much empirical research. To do so, he draws, among others, on the work of Pugh and the Aston Group (see earlier in this chapter), Burns (see Chapter 2) and March (see Chapter 5).

The two structural features of the model are:

- bureaucracy
- differentiation;

and the three contingencies are:

- organization size
- task uncertainty
- task interdependence.

Of the structural features, *bureaucracy* has three principal constituents, namely specialization (narrowly defined jobs), formalization (rules) and centralization/decentralization (of authority). *Differentiation*, or grouping of activities, refers primarily to the contrasting functional and divisional structures.

A contingency is any variable that moderates the effect of an organizational characteristic on organizational performance. The first is *organization size*, that is, the number of employees. Of the two Task contingencies, there can be greater or lesser *task uncertainty* about what to do, when, and for how long, and greater or lesser *task interdependence* between activities, some having to wait upon what is done elsewhere whilst others are comparatively unconstrained by activities in other parts of the organization.

These three features are contingencies for an organization because if any of them alter, then there will be misfit, or misalignment, between them and its structure, and performance is likely to decline. In the SARFIT model, size and task moderate the effect of structure on performance. The model holds that rearranging structure with the intention of improving performance will not work unless the structural changes fit what the new size or task uncertainty or task interdependence require. This is because the potentially positive effect of organizational reform on performance is contingent on, that is, affected by, those variables.

With size this is because taking on more employees and growing larger requires an increase in bureaucracy if performance is not to decline. Without clearly defined bureaucratic structure, more people will be doing ill-defined jobs, poorly coordinated, and duplicating effort, which will be costly. Organization size and bureaucratization are positively related: the larger the organization the more bureaucratic it will be and should be.

Taking on new work which is not yet fully understood creates more *task uncertainty*, which requires more flexibility in organization if performance is not to decline. There must be decentralization with a looser, more organic structure. *Task interdependence* may require something similar when linked work requires flexible organizing.

Of these three broad contingencies that cause structural forms, size, Donaldson argues, is the more basic cause for it lies behind the two task contingencies and can alter them. For instance, to spur innovation in manufacturing more design staff may be recruited. These extra staff then increase task uncertainty as they redesign plant or product.

SARFIT, like the wider contingency paradigm of which it is part, is a theoretical model of change. The statistical correlations on which it is based are not themselves inherently static, as they are sometimes thought to be. They show the likely directions of change. The model is a theory of performance-driven change. It shows that change in the structural features of organizations is predominantly a response to changes in performance. Low performance, due to a change in a contingency variable that causes misfit between contingency and structure, prompts reorganization. This brings structure into a new fit with the contingencies and so performance improves. This process is a functional one of adaptation, making changes so that the organization will perform better.

The idea of 'fit' is central to Donaldson's thinking. An organization initially may be in fit. If it then changes its level of a contingency variable while retaining its existing structure, it thereby becomes a misfit with its new contingency level. This misfit leads to lower performance, and the organization then tries to make an adaptive change to a new fit which could restore high performance. The difficulty for management is that they are unlikely to know exactly where fit will be. How much adjustment, in what, will achieve fit? But they are likely to recognise in which direction fit lies and to move towards it by trial and error, through one or more stages of 'quasi-fit', until fit is attained.

Organizations typically function at a 'satisficing' level of performance (see Simon, Chapter 5). Performance could be better perhaps, but it is good enough. So usually change is not provoked until performance drops below a satisficing level. (Donaldson acknowledges that performance-induced change is not the only kind of change in organizations.)

What then causes performance to fluctuate and set off the cycle of change? To explain this, Donaldson takes from finance the notion of a portfolio. In finance, a portfolio is a bundle of varied investments. An 'organizational portfolio' contains key corporate factors, both internal and external, which can cause performance to vary. There are eight of these. Four of them lead to adaptive change, namely: business cycle, competition, debt and divisional risk. The other four factors, namely: diversification, divisionalization, divestment and directors, are more likely to lead to a lack of adaptive change.

The first factor leading to adaptive change is the business cycle of economic activity, boom and recession, which can cause fluctuations in the performance of a commercial firm. The firm will need to change if the economic situation depresses performance but also if it enhances performance. This is because better performance leads to growth in size, and that too, as has been described, brings the misfit that triggers adaptation. The second factor, competition, has similar diverse effects. Though competition may depress performance, ineffective competition, from competitors themselves in misfit, could allow easier growth. Thirdly, debt may reduce profit or alternatively it may provide resources for growth. As for divisional risks, these will differ between the different products and markets of an organization's divisions, causing the results of particular divisions to fluctuate, so affecting corporate performance overall.

First among the four portfolio factors which counter the need to change is diversification. Diversifying into a wider range of products or services can moderate oscillations in overall corporate performance as the results of one offset the results of another, averaging out. So there is less need to change. Divisionalization, which is likely to accompany diversification, works in the same way, spreading the risks. Thirdly divestment, selling off low-performing divisions or subsidiaries, also stabilizes the overall performance. Finally, directors who are non-executive can damp down the risks that might otherwise be taken by full-time directors and so avoid performance failures. They have been shown to exert a restraining influence in the boardroom because of their experience elsewhere. These latter four factors, by reducing the chances of changes in performance, make adaptive change less needful. It is also possible that two or more of these portfolio factors cancel each other out. Competition may be keen enough to force down profits, for example, but a simultaneous upswing in the business cycle could offset this by increasing sales. So performance is unaffected.

If, however, the combined effects of the portfolio factors do leave the performance of an organization which is in fit quite steady, then what? Why ever change? Why not just stand still? Conventional contingency theory does not have an answer to that, and would leave the organization in infinite equilibrium.

Donaldson's answer is to take a further theoretical step to develop his SARFIT model into a *neo-contingency theory*. Upward changes in any of the three SARFIT contingencies, he says, need more resources. Greater size would need funds to pay more personnel. The new equipment that increases task uncertainty and task interdependence requires capital. And so on. These resources are most readily generated by an organization that is in fit and high performing. They enable it to make these sorts of improvements. Yet these are the sorts of improvements that change its contingencies. Those changes then shift it out of fit into misfit. Thus high performance feeds back to cause an organization to move from fit into misfit.

Neo-contingency theory is therefore a dynamic theory of disequilibrium, predicting continual change. It predicts that organizations in misfit will move into fit *and* also that organizations in fit will move into misfit. Change in one factor leads to change in others, which feeds back to cause further change in the first factor, thus causing recurrent change.

Throughout his writings, Donaldson espouses the philosophical position of positivism, and defends it from its critics. Contingency theory, and neo-contingency theory, are positivist since like the natural sciences they seek general causal relationships shown in law-like regularities. Organizations are to be explained by scientific laws in which the shape taken by organizations is determined by material factors such as the elements of the SARFIT model. These laws hold across organizations of all types and national cultures.

Critics of positivism see it as downplaying voluntaristic action, that is, failing to allow for such capability as the members of an organization have to act of their own accord in ways not determined in a rather mechanical manner by contingencies.

Donaldson does not deny these views in themselves. He sees them as tenable within the wider structural contingency view, but lacking the systematic generalizations it offers. They are confined to lower-level descriptions of employee behaviour, unable to offer a conception of an organization as a whole that can illuminate practical action.

For example, the conception of *strategic choice*, originated by Child (see earlier in this chapter), argues that the contingency theory of organizations is incomplete. That is because it is impersonal and does not recognize the scope that managers have to *choose* both the contingencies (they decide to increase size, for example) and the structure (they create specialist departments, or divisionalize). Against this, while Donaldson accepts that there is choice, he sees it as highly circumscribed. He points out that the research data show that contingency variables account for most of the variation in structure, substantially more than half. The preferences and choices of managers make little independent contribution. Moreover, those preferences themselves are limited by the situation in which the managers work. Although it is appealing to think of managers as freely making decisive choices, they typically select the right structure because they are 'conduits of causation'. The situational imperatives mean that they do not have a free strategic choice. Their room for manoeuvre is limited.

To those who, like Mintzberg (see later in this chapter), prefer *typologies* to shades of difference on many variables, Donaldson responds that though types are easy to remember they are unrealistic. Evidence that organizations in general fall into distinct types is lacking, whereas there is ample evidence of fine differences and similarities in numerous characteristics that do not add up to simply being this type or that type.

Population ecology theory (see Hannan and Freeman, Chapter 2) puts forward a very distinctive explanation of change. Change is brought about more by the 'death' of organizations that become outmoded and are squeezed out by new organizations with innovative ways, than it is by reforming existing organizations. Donaldson contends that evidence of misfitting organizations dying out is lacking. There is much more evidence that organizations are adaptive. Most often corporations do change strategy and structure and so do survive.

To Donaldson, a pervasive problem of other theories in organizational study is that they are value driven, that is, they are based not on supporting evidence but on how people might like the world to be. But, he says, 'sound theorizing is not wishful thinking'; it is based on clearly seeing the world as it is. The positivist thinking on which contingency theory and the SARFIT model rest is unrivalled in the understanding it gives of organizations, based as it is on empirical research.

BIBLIOGRAPHY

DONALDSON, L. *In Defence of Organization Theory: A Reply to the Critics*, Cambridge University Press, 1985.

DONALDSON, L. *American Anti-Management Theories of Organization: a Critique of Paradigm Proliferation*, Cambridge University Press, 1995.

DONALDSON, L. *For Positivist Organization Theory: Proving the Hard Core*, Sage, 1996.

DONALDSON, L. *Performance-Driven Organizational Change: the Organizational Portfolio*, Sage, 1999.

DONALDSON, L., *The Contingency Theory of Organizations*, Sage, 2001.

HILMER, F. G. and DONALDSON, L., *Management Redeemed: Debunking the Fads that Undermine our Corporations*, Free Press, 1996.

Elliott Jaques and the Glacier Investigations

Elliott Jaques (1917–2003) was a Canadian who graduated in psychology at the University of Toronto and later in medicine at the Johns Hopkins Medical School. After service in the Royal Canadian Army Medical Corps, he joined the staff at the Tavistock Institute of Human Relations where, over a period of years, he led a study of worker and management activities in the Glacier Metal Company – an engineering factory in London whose managing director was Wilfred Brown, himself a well-known writer on management issues (see Chapter 3). The Glacier Investigations may well come to bear comparison with the Hawthorne Studies for their impact on management thinking. For this work Jaques was awarded a Doctorate of Philosophy in the Department of Social Relations at Harvard University. He was a qualified Kleinian psychoanalyst and worked as a psychotherapist and as a 'social therapist' to the Glacier Company. Jaques was Professor of Social Science and Director of the Institute of Organization and Social Studies at Brunel University and worked with the National Health Service, the Church of England and with many commercial and public organizations in Europe and America.

Jaques and his collaborators in the Glacier Investigations use the technique of 'action research'. Working in collaboration with members of the firm, they have several aims: to study psychological and social forces affecting group behaviour, to develop more effective ways of resolving social stress and to facilitate agreed and desired social change.

The problems they tackle are those on which particular groups in the organization request their help. Thus Jaques's book *The Changing Culture of a Factory* describes, for example, studies of problems of payment and morale in the Service Department, worker-management cooperation in the Works Committee and executive leadership at the Divisional Managers' meeting. The method used consists of the 'working-through' (by the investigator and the group together) of current problems and their possible solutions. The investigator attends meetings of the group, interpreting for its members the social and personal factors at play in an attempt to increase the social and psychological insight of the group. This also promotes a more rational attitude to social change.

The working-through process usually leads to the discovery that the apparent problems of the group are only symptoms of more basic and long-term difficulties; these are then examined. What began as an issue of wages and methods of payment in the Service Department, for example, soon developed into the complex ramifications of inter-group stresses so often associated with wage questions. As a result of the working-through of management and worker differences at a series of meetings of representatives of both sides (which was facilitated by the investigator's interpretations), not only was the changeover to a new system of payment accomplished, but in the new situation created by these discussions it was possible to institute a Shop Council as a continuing mechanism through which members could take part in setting policy for the department.

One of the most important findings to come out of the Glacier Investigations is people's felt need to have their role and status clearly defined in a way which is acceptable both to themselves and to their colleagues. Where there is some confusion of role boundaries, or where multiple roles occupied by the same person are not sufficiently distinguished, insecurity and frustration result. The study of the Divisional Managers' meeting showed that it functioned sometimes as an executive management committee taking decisions for the London factory, sometimes as a group for non-decision-making discussions with the Managing Director, and sometimes as a concealed Board of Directors for the whole company (including the Scottish factory). In this mixture of different functions, the same group had different powers over the affairs of the organization, depending on the particular capacity in which it was functioning. But the fact that these powers were not clear was personally disturbing to the members.

Even when a role has been defined it may contain elements which the individual finds unacceptable or difficult to fill. In an organization committed to consultative management, a superior may become increasingly unwilling to exercise authority. Jaques describes some mechanisms by which responsibility and authority may be avoided. One is the exercise of a consultative relationship only. Thus the Managing Director, failing to perceive that he also held a role as chief executive of the London factory, adopted only a consultative Managing Director's role to the Divisional Managers. This left a gap in the executive hierarchy. Another mechanism is the misuse of the process of formal joint consultation. This often provides an escape route from accepting responsibility for immediate subordinates by making possible easy and direct contact between higher management and workers' representatives. To make consultative management work, the consultation must follow the chain of command, otherwise conflict arises from those bypassed. Yet another evasive possibility is pseudo-democracy; for instance, a superior asserting 'I'm just an ordinary member of this committee' while being in fact the most senior person present, or a superior avoiding a leadership role by excessive delegation. One of the most important conclusions is that there is a distinctive leadership role in groups that members expect to be properly filled, and groups do not function well unless it is.

At the conclusion of these Tavistock studies, Jaques changed his position, becoming, with the consent of the workers' representatives, a part-time employee of the firm. He still retained his independent position, however, and continued his role as social analyst, working on problems of wages and salaries. Since previous discussion had revealed continuous problems arising from supposed unfair differences in pay, the task was to determine the appropriate payment and status of individuals; in other words, how to establish what will generally be accepted as the right level of pay for a given job, particularly in relation to other jobs.

Work was divided by Jaques into its prescribed and its discretionary content. Prescribed work is specified in such a way as to leave nothing to the judgement of the individual doing it. But all jobs have some content, however small, which requires the individual to use discretion. From this developed the concept of the 'time-span of discretion' – the idea that the main criterion by which the importance of a job is implicitly evaluated is the length of time which expires before decisions taken by an individual are reviewed and evaluated. At the lowest level what the individual does is frequently checked, but at the highest level it might take several years before the effectiveness of a decision shows up. This approach is developed by Jaques in *The Measurement of Responsibility*.

Jaques finds that there is not a continuous increase in range of timespans of discretion as one goes up the organization; in fact, the changes go in steps. He identifies seven major strata (although there are substeps within each) up to three months, up to one year, two years, five years, ten years, twenty years, more than twenty years. These are generally recognized as clear differences of level, worthy of differences in payment. Those working in level one accept that those with level two discretion should be paid more and all would feel it inequitable if they were not. Differentials in 'felt-fair pay' – what people think they and others should earn – are very highly correlated (0.9 in the Glacier Metal Company) with objective measurements of differences in timespan, so that if a payment system is based on the discretion differences between jobs, it will generally be seen as equitable.

A third element is the growth in capacity of the individual to operate with greater discretion. Jaques thus presents earnings progression curves which identify appropriate payments for those capable of, and on their way towards, higher levels of discretion. Individuals function best when working at a level which corresponds to their capacity and for which they obtain equitable payment, but appropriate opportunity must be given for individuals to progress to their maximum timespan capacity.

These arguments are developed in *Free Enterprise, Fair Employment* in which both Keynesian and monetarist economic measures are rejected as inadequate for dealing with self-perpetuating inflationary movements which then cause unemployment. Jaques argues that any nation has as much work as it wants for everyone, regardless of economic conditions. But there is one prime condition for full employment without inflation: the achievement of equitable pay differentials by political consensus based on the equitable work payment-scale appropriate to different time-span levels. Jaques presents evidence that in 1980, for example, the equitable annual wage and salary levels for a timespan of discretion of three months was £7000 in England and $20 500 in the US, whereas for a two-year timespan job it was £19 500 and $60 000. (The actual monetary levels will, of course, change over the years depending upon the rate of earnings inflation.)

The figures are not for the *actual* levels of pay in 1980 but for what people felt was differentially fair at that time. Any systematic policy for wages and salaries must decide (i) what the general level should be in one year compared with the preceding year, and (ii)whether any adjustment of differentials is called for: should the rates for the timespan levels be compressed or expanded, in the whole of the range or part of the range, and so on These are issues for a rational policy which Jaques maintains would be accepted as just and fair as long as the differences in timespan of discretion were objectively determined and recognized.

Levels of timespan of discretion and the individual's work capacity to operate within them are also the keys to Jaques's general theory of bureaucracy. A bureaucracy in Jaques's terms is a hierarchically stratified employment system in which employees are accountable to their bosses for work that they do. This particular definition (which is somewhat different from the usual one – see Weber earlier in this chapter) means that, for example, universities which have collegiate accountability for academic staff, or trade unions which have electoral accountability for full-time officers, are not bureaucracies in this sense. Jaques is insistent that neither his theory of bureaucracy nor his theories of timespan of discretion and equitable payment are intended to apply in such organizations.

In bureaucracies (such as business firms, government agencies, armed services), Jaques has found that ascending the hierarchy involves operating with increasing timespans and that the basic seven strata of timespan correspond with levels of thinking capability – from concrete thinking at the bottom end to abstract modelling and institution-creating at the top. The capacity to operate at longer timespans with higher levels of abstraction in reasoning is the determinant of effectiveness at the higher levels of bureaucracy. The reason why bureaucracies are pyramidal in shape is that this work capacity (which Jaques maintains is innate) is very differentially distributed in human populations. Fewer are capable of the higher abstractions, a fact generally recognized by organization members. It is the consensus which would allow equitable payment based on time-span capacity to operate in economic competition *without* the exploitation of labour.

BIBLIOGRAPHY

BROWN, W. and JAQUES, E., *Glacier Project Papers*, Heinemann, 1965.
JAQUES, E., *The Changing Culture of a Factory*, Tavistock, 1951.
JAQUES, E., *The Measurement of Responsibility*, Tavistock, 1956.
JAQUES, E., *Equitable Payment*, Heinemann, 1961, Penguin, 1967.
JAQUES, E., *A General Theory of Bureaucracy*, Heinemann, 1976.
JAQUES, E., *Free Enterprise, Fair Employment*, Heinemann, 1982.

Alfred D. Chandler

Alfred Chandler (1918–2007) was Professor of Business History in the Graduate School of Business Administration, Harvard University. He was an economic historian whose research work has centred on the study of business history and, in particular, administration. He long argued that this is a much neglected area in the study of recent history. His studies of big business have been carried out with grants from a number of sources including the Alfred P. Sloan Foundation. His work has been internationally recognized, his book *The Visible Hand* being awarded the Pulitzer Prize for History and the Bancroft Prize. Chandler taught at a variety of universities in the US and Europe.

All of Chandler's academic work has been concerned with the theme of the rise and role of the large-scale business enterprise during what he describes as the formative years of modern capitalism. These are the years 1850–1920. He suggests, from his many studies, that during this period a new economic institution was created – the multi-unit firm – controlled by a new class of managers operating within a new system of capitalism. These new managers had to develop strategies different from those of their entrepreneurial predecessors and also be particularly innovative in creating structures to implement those strategies. The reasons for this shift are to be found in changes in demand bringing about mass markets and technological change which allowed high volume production. The new organization structures allowed the integration of mass production with mass distribution.

While Chandler's analysis is historical, he makes general points about organizational change and the relationship between strategy and structure. In particular, from his studies Chandler is clear that the structure of an organization follows from the strategy that is adopted. The distinction between these two is crucial. *Strategy* is the determination of basic long-term goals and objectives together with the adoption of courses of action and the allocation of resources for carrying out those goals. *Structure* is the organization which is devised to administer the activities which arise from the strategies adopted. As such it involves the existence of a hierarchy, the distribution of work and lines of authority and communication. In addition, the concept of structure covers the information and data that flow along those lines.

Once an organization moves away from the small, owner-controlled enterprise towards the modern, multi-unit business enterprise, then the new class of managers appears. This is important for structural developments because the salaried manager is committed to the long-term stability of the enterprise. The managerial hierarchy gives positions of power and authority and as a result becomes a source both of permanence and continued growth. As part of this process the careers of salaried managers become increasingly technical and professional.

The role of management in developing structure is central to Chandler's analysis. As he puts it, 'the visible hand of management has replaced Adam Smith's invisible hand of market forces'. Managers are both products of, and developers of, the multi-divisional, decentralized structure which is the organizational outcome of technological change and rising demand. They become responsible for the administration of the enterprise; that is, coordinating, planning and appraising work, and allocating resources.

The structural arrangements of a large business enterprise have to allow both for the efficient day-to-day operations of its various units and for dealing with the long-run health of the company. The developments which follow from this involve operating with a decentralized structure to deal with day-to-day manufacturing and services, and building up a central office with functional departments to manage the long-run prospects of the company. This is all part of the process of specialization of functions as a major structural device. The key distinctions are between the general office, divisions, departments and field units, each of which has a particular function. One of the basic reasons for the success of this type of structure is that it clearly removes from immediate operations those executives responsible for long-term planning and appraisal. The significance of this separation is that it gives those executives the time, information and psychological commitment for long-term activities.

The introduction of this distinctive organizational structure (with its unique managerial hierarchy) marked the transition from family- or finance-based capitalism to managerial capitalism. But because, in Chandler's view, structure follows strategy, this transition could occur only in response to external pressures. Particularly important was the increasing volume of activity which arose in response to the new national and increasingly urban markets of the late nineteenth century. Together with this was technological change which enabled enterprises to move into high-volume production.

In the face of such pressures, enterprises could adopt either defensive or positive strategies. A *positive strategy* occurs when an enterprise actively looks for new markets and new products to serve those markets. It is organized around product diversification. A *defensive strategy* is where an enterprise acts to protect its current position. The common way of achieving this is to form a vertically integrated company by means of mergers with similar enterprises, suppliers and customers.

Both strategies lead to bigger organizations which have administrative problems. This begins a systematization of techniques for the administration of functional activities. An initial type of organization for achieving this is the centralized, functionally departmentalized structure. It enables the necessary new expert skills to be brought while owners still retain control. But increasing the scale of organizations involves building up capacity and enlarging the resources of people, money and materials at the disposal of an enterprise. A result of this is further and continuing growth to ensure the full use of those resources, a result which emanates from the interests of the new managers rather than the owners. Growth

UNIVERSITY OF WINCHESTER
LIBRARY

becomes internally as well as externally generated and then produces the really innovative structure – multi-unit decentralization.

To illustrate his points in detail and to chart the process of structural innovation, Chandler looks at the cases of four companies: Du Pont, General Motors, Standard Oil of New Jersey and Sears Roebuck. According to Chandler, the general pressures and needs facing these four companies were the same. Also in general terms, the structural outcome was very similar. But the process of diagnosing the issues and introducing the consequent administrative changes was quite different.

The particular structural innovation of Du Pont was to create autonomous divisions. The company reached the beginning of the twentieth century as a loose federation with no central administrative control. The first strategy of the younger Du Ponts was to centralize control and concentrate manufacturing activity in a few larger plants. This was the centralized, functionally departmentalized structure. Important to the operation of the company was the development of new forms of management information and forecasting. The introduction of the multi-unit, decentralized structure came with the need to maintain growth. It was done by basing the structure on a new principle, coordinating related effort rather than like things. This innovative principle meant that different broad functional activities had to be placed in separate administrative units. To operate these units, the executives responsible were given enhanced authority. Eventually these developed into product-based units backed by a central, general office to deal with strategic issues. This left the autonomous units to get on with day-to-day operations.

The General Motors case underlines the need for structure to follow strategy. William Durant, the founder of General Motors, went for a volume strategy with many operating units in an extremely loose federation. There was a crisis in 1920 due to lack of overall control. The response of Alfred P. Sloan, who became the Chief Executive Officer in 1923, was to create a general office to be responsible for broad policies and objectives and to coordinate effort. A line-and-staff structure was developed, allowing the product divisions to ensure good use of resources and a proper product flow, with the headquarters staff appraising divisional performance and plans. The new structure took five years to put in place (see Sloan, Chapter 4).

As with General Motors, Standard Oil of New Jersey was, for Chandler, a case of initial failure to adjust structure to strategy. The channels of authority and communication were insufficiently defined within a partly federated, partly consolidated company. As a result there was a series of crises over inventories and over-production during the 1920s which led to ad hoc responses. The initial development was to build up a central office for resource allocation and coordination. A second stage was to set up a decentralized divisional structure. According to Chandler, the response in Standard Oil was slower and more tentative than in Du Pont or General Motors, partly because the problems were more difficult and partly because of a general lack of concern with organizational problems.

During the 1920s and 1930s, Sears Roebuck underwent the same process in its own particular way, partly planned and partly unplanned. The initial defensive strategy of vertical integration produced a centralized, functionally departmentalized structure. Continued growth produced pressure for decentralized, regional organization and for sorting out the relationships between operating units and functional departments. Contributors to the book edited by Chandler and Daems trace similar processes in French, German and British industry.

For Chandler, both his case studies and his broader work illustrate a number of general points about structural development and organizational innovation. The first is that the market and technological pressures of an urban, industrial society push enterprises in the same structural direction, though the actual process of innovation can be quite different. In this process it is important to distinguish between an adaptive response and a creative innovation. An *adaptive response* is a structural change which stays within the range of current custom and practice, as was the case with functional departments and a central office. A *creative innovation* goes beyond existing practice and procedures, developing decentralized field units for example. The general adoption of a line-and-staff departmental structure meant that delegation of authority and responsibility to field units was possible.

From this process, says Chandler, there arises a new economic function in society, that of administrative coordination and control. To carry out that function, a new species is created, the salaried manager. Thus the modern business enterprise, with its two specific characteristics of the existence of many distinct operating units and their management by a hierarchy of salaried executives, comes into being.

BIBLIOGRAPHY

CHANDLER, A. D., *Strategy and Structure*, MIT Press, 1962.

CHANDLER, A. D.,*The Visible Hand: The Managerial Revolution in American Business*, Harvard University Press, 1977.

CHANDLER, A. D., *Inventing the Electronic Century*, Free Press, 2001.

CHANDLER, A. D., *Shaping the Industrial Century*, Harvard University Press, 2005.

CHANDLER, A. D. and DAEMS, H. (eds), *Managerial Hierarchies: Comparative Perspectives on the Rise of Modern Industrial Enterprises*, Harvard University Press, 1980.

CHANDLER, A. D. and TEDLOW, R. S., *The Coming of Managerial Capitalism*, Irwin, 1985.

Oliver E. Williamson

Oliver Williamson, an American economist, began his working life as a project engineer in US government service, but soon moved into academic life, taking degrees at the Universities of Stanford and Carnegie-Mellon. His career took him through leading American universities, and he is now Professor Emeritus of Business, Economics, and Law at the University of California, Berkeley.

Williamson probes beneath the usual questions about what organizations are like and how their members behave to ask why they are there at all. Why organizations? His answer is because they lower the cost of transactions. He sees society as a network of transactions – contracts in the widest sense of that term – and suggests that a 'transactional paradigm' will yield the reasons for organizations. These reasons are not size – that is, the economies of scale which have been supposed to explain large organizations – nor large-scale technologies, but the information cost of transactions. Size and technology are important not in themselves, but because of the demands they make for information.

Each of the multitude of recurrent transactions which take place in a society can be conducted either in a market or within an organization. Which mode of transacting is used depends upon the information available and the costs to the transacting parties of adding to that information should they require more. As the requirements for information change, transactions may be conducted more in markets, or more and more within organizations. The trend has been for more transactions to be gathered within the boundaries of organizations, and Williamson's discussion is primarily about change in that direction. That is because he has been concerned mainly with societies moving that way, but if the starting point were a society in which central planning and non-market transactions predominated, the analysis could as appropriately deal with the shifting of transactions from within organizations out to markets. Analysis of transaction costs can answer 'why not organizations?' as well as 'why organizations?'

Williamson's point of view joins market economics to organization theory in a form of institutional economics. He looks forward to the possibility that measures of market structure will eventually combine with measures of the internal structure of organizations (see Derek Pugh and the Aston Group, earlier in this chapter).

Markets and *hierarchies* are alternatives for conducting transactions. Thus transactions are brought within the hierarchical structures of organizations when the market mode is no longer efficient. For example, mergers or takeovers bring into a single organization contracting parties whose transactions will then be regulated by the internal rules of a hierarchy and not by the rules of a market.

Additionally, organizations are set up to transact within themselves business that might alternatively have been done by separate parties contracting between themselves in market terms.

Which mode is adopted depends upon the degree of *information impactedness.* This exists when the 'true underlying circumstances' of a transaction are known to one or more parties but not to others. Where there is less than complete trust between the parties, those who lack information can obtain parity only by incurring costs, which may be high, even prohibitive. Thus a buyer who is offered supplies may be unsure whether the quality will be what is required, whether delivery is likely to be on time, or how far the proposed price is more than need be paid. This may be because no one, not even the seller, has adequate information on these matters; or it may be that even if information is available, the buyer cannot trust it because the seller will have interpreted it to favour the selling vantage point.

A market is the most efficacious mode of conducting transactions when all necessary information is conveyed between parties by a price; that is, when this single item of information is sufficient. Transactions are better brought within a hierarchy when much more must be known, when much less is certain, and when there may be 'quasi-moral' elements, for the hierarchy brings the inadequately informed parties to a transaction together under some degree of control.

Transactions will be shifted out of a market and into the hierarchy of a firm or other form of organization when information impactedness is high. That is, when the uncertainties and distrust inherent in transactions become so great that those involved cannot determine acceptable prices. At this point the advantages of a hierarchy outweigh those of a market. First, it extends the bounds on rationality. Though the rationalities of each of the parties within an organization are still restricted, specialization enables each to deal with a part of the overall problem that is small enough to be comprehended, the results of everyone's work being brought together by specialized decision-makers at the apex. More information is exchanged or can be required to be handed over. Common numbering and coding systems and occupational jargon cut down communication costs. Second, sub-sections of an organization can each attend to a given aspect of the uncertainty-complexity of a situation, so making manageable a problem which would in total be too uncertain-complex. Aspects can be attended to as the situation unfolds rather than all at once, and decisions which might otherwise be too complex can be split down into smaller sequential steps (see Lindblom, Chapter 5). Third, a hierarchy curbs opportunism. Pay, promotion and control techniques ensure that the parties work in some degree towards common goals. Confidence may not be complete, but it is greater. Parties cannot use their gains entirely for their own ends, and what they do can be more effectively checked and audited. Should disputes arise, superior hierarchical levels can decide them. Fourth, where there are small numbers – a situation which opportunistic parties are inclined to take advantage of – the hierarchy can overrule bargaining.

In general then, hierarchy more nearly approaches parity of information and, in particular, provides for quasi-moral and reciprocal obligations over and above strictly economic ones.

What then stops hierarchies from taking over more and more transactions indefinitely? The limits begin to appear as firms grow larger and as vertical integration between firms extends. Costs then rise to a level at which the marginal costs of administering the incremental transaction begin to exceed those of completing transactions through a market. The goals of groups or sub-sections within an organization start to outweigh common aims; the proliferation of specialists in control systems to combat this tendency becomes more and more expensive; sunk costs encourage the persistence of existing ways of working even if they would not now be done that way were they to start afresh, and communication is increasingly distorted. Leaders become more distant from those they lead – 'bureaucratic insularity' – and cooperation between those at lower levels becomes perfunctory rather than wholehearted. Coordination and common purpose lapse.

These costs rise in the unitary structure of hierarchy (called 'Uform') when the top management of a single large organization tries to control transactions within it. The U-form is therefore a vanishing breed among large US corporations, although the Reynolds Metal Company and the Quaker Oats Company retained this form throughout the 1960s. Organizational transaction costs can be relatively reduced by the adoption of a multi-divisional structure (called 'M-form') as in the examples described by Chandler (see previous section) of Du Pont, General Motors, Standard Oil of New Jersey and Sears Roebuck, who changed to the M-form in the 1920s and 1930s. To be effective, this form of organization requires the general overall management to concentrate on monitoring the performance of the constituent divisions and on strategic planning. Management can use the multi-divisional structure as a miniature capital market in which funds are moved into the most profitable uses more effectively than by the external capital market. This is so because internally there is more complete information about the firm than parties in the external capital market can gain about comparative investment opportunities.

But if general management gets involved in the day-to-day operation of the divisions, then information costs will again be forced up, in what is called the 'corrupted M-form'. One large corporation is quoted as attempting to move from the corrupted M-form by releasing a total of 5000 non-production personnel. It also reduced corporate staff – people not reporting to profit centres – by over 1300, down to a new total of 132. The aim was to decentralize into true profit centres in which each divisional manager's performance could be accurately evaluated without the allocation of heavy corporate overheads.

If the change from the corrupted M-form cannot be achieved and information costs remain high, then market transactions will become more attractive. Ultimately it is the relative cost of overcoming information impactedness that determines whether transactions in a society are conducted through markets or within organizations. Thus, in Williamson's terms, transaction cost economics determines the mechanisms of organizational governance.

BIBLIOGRAPHY

WILLIAMSON, O. E., *Markets and Hierarchies: Analysis and Antitrust Implications*, Free Press, 1975.
WILLIAMSON, O. E.,*Economic Organization*,Wheatsheaf Books, 1986.
WILLIAMSON, O. E., *The Mechanisms of Governance*, Oxford University Press, 1996.

Henry Mintzberg

Henry Mintzberg is Cleghorn Professor of Management Studies at McGill University, Montreal. He graduated from the Sloan School of Management at the Massachusetts Institute of Technology. Among a variety of consulting assignments and visiting appointments, he has been visiting professor at the University of Aix-en-Provence in France. He has studied what managers actually do as they manage, and what kinds of organization they are managing.

Mintzberg shows a substantial difference between what managers do and what they are said to do. On the basis of work activity studies, he demonstrates that a manager's job is characterized by pace, interruptions, brevity, variety and fragmentation of activities and a preference for verbal contacts. Managers spend a considerable amount of time in scheduled meetings and in networks of contacts outside meetings.

The fragmentary nature of what managers do leads to the suggestion that they have to perform a wide variety of roles. Mintzberg suggests that there are ten managerial roles which can be grouped into three areas: *interpersonal*, *informational* and *decisional*.

Interpersonal roles cover the relationships that a manager has to have with others. The three roles within this category are figurehead, leader and liaison. Managers have to act as *figureheads* because of their formal authority and symbolic position, representing their organizations. As *leaders*, managers have to bring together the needs of an organization and those of the individuals under their command. The third interpersonal role, that of *liaison*, deals with the horizontal relationships which work activity studies have shown to be important for a manager. A manager has to maintain a network of relationships outside the organization.

Managers have to collect, disseminate and transmit information and have three corresponding informational roles, namely monitor, disseminator and spokesperson. A manager is an important figure in *monitoring* what goes on in the organization, receiving information about both internal and external events and transmitting it to others. This process of transmission is the *dissemination* role, passing on information of both a factual and a value kind. A manager often has to give information concerning the organization to outsiders, taking on the role of *spokesperson* to both the general public and those in positions of influence.

As with so many writers about management, Mintzberg regards the most crucial part of managerial activity as that concerned with making decisions. The four roles that he places in this category are based on different classes of decision: entrepreneur, disturbance handler, resource allocator and negotiator. As *entrepreneurs*, managers make decisions about changing what is happening in an organization. They may have to both initiate change and take an active part in deciding exactly what is to be done. In principle, they are acting voluntarily. This is very different from their role as a *disturbance handler*, where managers have to make decisions which arise from events beyond their control and unpredicted. The ability to react to events as well as to plan activities is an important managerial skill in Mintzberg's eyes.

The *resource allocation* role of a manager is central to much organizational analysis. Clearly a manager has to make decisions about the allocation of money, people, equipment, time and so on. Mintzberg points out that in doing so a manager is actually scheduling time, programming work and authorizing actions. The *negotiation* role is put in the decisional category by Mintzberg because it is 'resource trading in real time'. A manager has to negotiate with others and in the process be able to make decisions about the commitment of organizational resources.

For Mintzberg these ten roles provide a more adequate description of what managers do than any of the various schools of management thought. In these roles it is information that is crucial; the manager is determining the priority of information. Through the interpersonal roles a manager acquires information, and through the decisional roles it is put into use.

The scope for each manager to choose a different blend of roles means that management is not reducible to a set of scientific statements and programmes. Management is essentially an art and it is necessary for managers to try and learn continuously about their own situations. Self-study is vital. At the moment there is no solid basis for teaching a theory of managing. According to Mintzberg, 'the management school has been more effective at training technocrats to deal with structured problems than managers to deal with unstructured ones'.

Mintzberg presents a way of understanding the design of organizations and suggests that there are seven types. As shown in the table, the first five types are differentiated according to which basic part of the organization forms the key to its operations. In the entrepreneurial organization it is the 'strategic apex' which is key. In a manufacturer, for example, this would be the president or chief executive, the board of directors, and their personal staff. In a machine organization, it is the 'technostructure' which is key: this includes those in planning, finance, training, operations research and work study, and production scheduling. The key part in a professional organization is the 'operating core', those at the working base of the organization. While in a manufacturer this would be the buyers, machine operators, salespeople and despatchers, in a professional organization it might be doctors and nurses (in a hospital) or teaching staff (in a college). The 'middle line' are key in the diversified organization, being the personnel who 'manage managers' in the hierarchy between the strategic apex and the operating core. In manufacturing these would include the heads of the production and sales functions and the managers and supervisors beneath them. In an innovative organization which Mintzberg calls an 'adhocracy', the 'support staff' are the key part. In a typical manufacturer they might be in public relations, industrial relations, pricing, payroll, even the cafeteria, as well as in research and development, but in an adhocracy the focus is upon the latter, the R & D. In the final two configurations, no part of the organization itself is key. Missionary organizations are pulled by ideology, and political organizations have no key feature.

Seven Organizational Types

Organizational configuration	Prime coordinating mechanism	Key part	Type of decentralization
Entrepreneurial	Direct supervision	Strategic apex	Vertical and horizontal centralization
Machine	Standardization of work processes	Technostructure	Limited horizontal decentralization
Professional	Standardization of skills	Operating core	Horizontal decentralization
Diversified	Standardization of outputs	Middle line	Limited vertical decentralization
Innovative	Mutual adjustment	Support staff	Selected decentralization
Missionary	Standardization of norms	Ideology	Decentralization
Political	None	None	Varies

Source: Mintzberg (1989).

In each of the first five types, its key part exerts a pull upon the organization. 'To the extent that conditions favour one over the others, the organization is drawn to structure itself as one of the configurations,' or designs. It is pulled towards one more than towards the others.

The first type, the *entrepreneurial organization,* in which the strongest pull is by the strategic apex towards centralization, is as simple as its name indicates. It has little or no technostructure, few support staff, minimal differentiation between departments and a small hierarchy. Coordination is by direct supervision, downwards from the strong apex where power is in the hands of the chief executive: so it does not need formal planning or training or similar procedures, and can be flexible and 'organic' (see also Burns, Chapter 2). The conditions favouring this form are those of the classic entrepreneurial owner-managed firm. A small organization is a simple yet dynamic environment which can be understood by one leading individual. Most organizations pass through this structure in their formative years, and some stay small enough to continue it. They could be as diverse as an automobile dealership, a retail store, a brand-new government department or a vigorous manufacturer on a small scale.

Some people enjoy working in such an organization because of the sense of mission it gives, and its flexibility. Others resent the domination from the top. They see it as paternalistic or autocratic, unfashionable in democratic times. The organization is also precarious: 'one heart attack can literally wipe out the organization's prime coordinating mechanism'.

The *machine organization* is far more secure (see Weber on bureaucracy, earlier in this chapter). It does not depend on a single person. The strongest pull on it is from its technostructure, the planners, financial controllers, production schedulers and their kind. They pull towards standardization. Once work has been divided into standard routine tasks, it can be controlled by them through formalized rules and regulations. Control is almost an obsession. It is second only to the entrepreneurial structure in centralization, but in it power is divided between the strategic apex and the technostructure. A post office, a steel manufacturer, a prison, a major airline or a vehicle assembler are all like this. They have the conditions favouring this design, mainly that they are older, larger organizations carrying out repetitive work in stable environments, probably themselves subject to control from a remote corporation head office or government.

Though efficient at repetitive work, this form of organization is riddled with conflict between top and bottom and between departments. To many of its personnel the work they do is meaningless. Its managers spend much of their energy just holding it together. It was fashionable at the height of the Industrial Revolution, but like the entrepreneurial structure it is no longer so.

The third kind of configuration or design, the *professional organization*, is pulled by its *operating core* towards professionalized autonomy. That is, it is dominated by highly trained professional specialists. These have to be employed because the work is too complex to be controlled and coordinated in any other way. So it is broken up into specialisms, and people are hired to do it who already have standardized skills. That means professionals already trained and indoctrinated who can be relied on to do what has to be done. This is the situation in universities, hospitals, schools, accountancy firms, social work agencies and some firms that employ highly skilled craftspeople (for example in fashion textiles designing). Since others without the training cannot interfere, the professionals are relatively independent. Their working autonomy is usually reinforced by a high demand for the service they give. Hence, whilst the machine organization is run by hierarchical authority, the professional organization emphasizes the power of expertise. While the machine organization sets its own standards, the bureaucratic administrative framework of a professional organization accepts standards set externally by professional bodies such as the medical and accounting institutions.

This design of organization is uniquely democratic, but it suffers from difficulties of coordination and jurisdiction. Who should teach the statistics course in the management degree – the staff of the mathematics department or the business department? And who can declare a professor incompetent, and what then can be done about it?

The *diversified organization* is most widely used by large private industrial corporations, but it can also be seen in those American universities that have several campuses, or in health administrations which control several hospitals, and generally in socialist economies where government ministries control numbers of enterprises. It piggybacks on the machine organization, for it is a headquarters controlling several divisions. These subsidiary machine organizations make a powerful *middle line*, in Mintzberg's terminology, the key part around which the organization functions. It is pulled towards Balkanization, for each division is relatively self-sufficient with its own marketing, purchasing and manufacturing (or equivalent) and so on, and each operates in its own market. Indeed, the diversified form is usually the result of a machine organization diversifying across more than one market, either into different products or into different geographical areas.

Though each division has a great deal of autonomy, headquarters decides how much capital each shall have and watches numerical performance indicators such as profits, sales and return on investment. This is where the problems arise. Headquarters may meddle too much in divisional decisions, and its concentration on numerical indicators may neglect other considerations such as product quality or environmental preservation. Mintzberg suspects that, though the diversified organization is a fashionable sign of the times, it may be the most vulnerable of the five designs to legal and social changes.

In contrast, a space agency, an avant-garde film company, a factory making complex prototypes or a petrochemicals company is likely to be designed as an *innovative organization* or *adhocracy*. These are young research-based organizations which need to innovate in rapidly changing conditions. The primary key part of an adhocracy is the *support staff* in research and development, but there may also be key operating core personnel, experts on whom innovation depends. Unlike the professional organization, the adhocracy is not seeking the repetitive use of professionally standardized skills. Instead, it groups its highly trained specialists in mixed project teams, hoping to generate new ideas. It is pulled towards coordination within and between teams by 'mutual adjustment' (see Thompson, Chapter 2), that is, by direct cooperation. Unified bureaucratic controls might get in the way. Of the five designs of organization, 'Adhocracy shows the least reverence for the classical principles of management' (for example as promulgated by Fayol, Chapter 4). It is uniquely both organic and decentralized.

There are two variants of adhocracy. An operating adhocracy works directly for clients, as in an advertising agency, whereas an administrative adhocracy serves itself, as did the National Aeronautics and Space Agency, NASA, in building up American space exploration.

Inevitably, adhocracy creates difficulties as well as innovations. People talk a lot, and this costs time. There is confusion over who is doing what. It is the most politicized design, breeding internal competition and conflict. But its strength in enabling flexibility of response means that new industries rely on this configuration. Mintzberg maintains that adhocracy is the structure of our present age, and he also confesses that this is the type of organization that he likes best.

The *missionary organization* does not have a key part, as such. Its key glue, which holds everything together, is the possession of an ideology, that is, a rich system of distinctive values and beliefs shared by all the members. It is rooted in a deep sense of mission, associated with charismatic leadership and developed through strongly held traditions which reinforce the identification of the individual with the organization. Coordination is through standardization of norms, reinforced by selection and indoctrination of members. In the West, we had thought this approach to be appropriate to religious institutions, but Japanese corporations have shown that it can be successfully applied in business settings. And not only in Japanese culture: many American firms have an overlay of the missionary approach – for example McDonald's or Hewlett-Packard – and build their effectiveness on an organizational ideology.

The final configuration is the *political organization*, which does not have overall coordinating mechanisms but is characterized by conflict. All organizations have a degree of conflict, where some 'political' activity takes place. This does not prejudice the organization's functioning and indeed has a positive role to play in stimulating change. But when the conflict is pervasive, the organization has become politicized. This form characterizes some large public sector institutions riven by conflicting approaches about both methods and objectives, and by private corporations after takeovers and mergers. If the conflict cannot be reduced, the organization will not survive – unless it is artificially protected by, for example, the government.

It is important for managers to understand the configuration of their particular organization in order to ensure that the various parts fit together and are consistent in what they do. But, Mintzberg warns, do not forget that there will always be contradictions among the forces in organizations. Managers should use these contradictions creatively, not ignore or try to suppress them. The process of strategy formulation must not be over-managed, only from the top down, or it will become rigid and sterile. Strategies can be emergent, rather than designed. They can take root in any part of an organization and then be successfully adopted by the top management.

BIBLIOGRAPHY

MINTZBERG, H., 'The Manager's Job: Folklore and Fact', *Harvard Business Review*, 1975, 49–1; reprinted in D. S. Pugh (ed.), *Organization Theory*, 5th edn, Penguin, 2007.
MINTZBERG, H., *The Structuring of Organizations*, Prentice-Hall, 1979.
MINTZBERG, H., *The Nature of Managerial Work*, Harper & Row, 1973; Prentice-Hall, 1980.
MINTZBERG, H., *Mintzberg on Management*, Free Press, 1989.
MINTZBERG, H., *Managers not MBAs*, FT Prentice Hall, 2004.

Charles Handy

Charles Handy is a British writer and broadcaster. Born in Ireland, he has been an oil company executive, a business economist and a professor at the London Business School. He was Warden of St George's House in Windsor Castle, which is a centre for discussion of issues of business ethics, on which topic he takes a Christian approach. He has served as Chairman of the Royal Society for the Encouragement of Arts, Manufacture and Commerce, and was the 1994 British Business Columnist of the year. His concern is with the changing nature of work and organization in modern economy and society.

Handy distinguishes four types of organizations, each symbolized by its characteristic Ancient Greek god or goddess. Each generates a distinctive organizational culture which pervades all its activities. The first type is the *club culture*, thought of as presided over by Zeus, who epitomizes the strong leader who has power and uses it. The visual image of this culture is a spider's web. Although there may be formal organizational departments and lines of authority, the only lines that matter are those, formal or informal, leading to the boss at the centre of the web. Most organizations begin in this culture, where the strength is in speed of decision. A limitation is that the quality of the decisions depends entirely on the calibre of the boss and the inner circle, since others can make little impact. You advance in this organization by learning to think and act as the boss would have done in your situation.

The second type of organization is the *role culture*, with its patron god Apollo, the god of order and rules. It is pictured as a Greek temple, where the pillars represent the functions and divisions of the organization. Within them it is assumed that people are rational, and that roles are defined, allocated and carried out according to systems of rules and procedures. It is the culture that Weber (see earlier in this chapter) called 'bureaucratic' and Burns (see Chapter 2) 'mechanistic', and many large organizations which value stability and predictability are of this type: government administration, insurance corporations, organizations with a long history of success with one product or service, for example. Its strength is shown when tomorrow can be expected to be like yesterday; conversely its weakness is its slowness to recognize the need for strategic change and its inability to adapt.

The third type is the *task culture* of Athena, goddess of knowledge. In this culture, management is regarded as a series of problems to be solved. First define the problem, then allocate resources for its solution, including people, machines and money. The picture of the organization is a net because it draws resources from all parts of the system. It is a network of loosely linked matrix structures in which task forces, working parties, ad hoc groups, and so on are brought together to achieve a particular goal. It is the culture that Burns (see Chapter 2) called 'organic' (or 'organismic'). It works well when flexibility is required because the organization's output is a series of solutions to particular problems; for example in consultancy companies, advertising agencies and R & D departments. But these cultures do not function well when repetition and predictability are required, or when low costs are a major factor in success.

The final type of organization is the *existential culture* presided over by Dionysus, god of wine and song. The key difference here is that, unlike the other types, where the individual is subordinate to the aims of the organization, in this type the organization exists to help in the achievement of the individual's aims. For example, groups of professionals such as doctors, lawyers or architects can come together to create an organization in order to share an office, a telephone or a secretary. In these organizations the individual professionals are supreme; they recognize no boss, although they may accept coordination from a committee of their peers. These organizations are so democratic that there are few sanctions available to administrators. Management, which is regarded as a chore, requires general consent, which leads to endless negotiation to obtain any coordinated effort.

There are no business or industrial organizations which operate completely with this last culture. But we are now witnessing an important change in the nature of organizations, in that they find it efficient to contract out more and more of their work to independent professionals. Organizations will therefore have to deal more and more with those who take a Dionysian view of the world.

This is only one of a number of changes that we are currently experiencing in regard to employment. They are not part of a predictable pattern, but are *discontinuous* changes in society. Such discontinuities happen from time to time in history. The change in the basis of economic activity from agriculture to industry was a previous example of this. The change now is from profitability based on machine power and brawn to profitability based on intelligence and professional skills. McKinsey, the management consultants, have estimated that, by the year 2000, 80 per cent of *all* jobs will require cerebral rather than manual skills, a complete reversal from 50 years earlier.

In this new situation, both the nature of work and the nature of organizations are changing. In general, people can no longer expect to work for the whole of their lives in one occupation, perhaps for one employer. Organizations can no longer afford the overheads of carrying large numbers of people who may only be wanted for part of the time. Instead, work must be reconceptualized in a much more flexible way as a 'portfolio of activities' based on professional knowledge and skill which an individual is able to offer to a number of organizations.

Handy uses the Irish national emblem, the shamrock, to characterize the ways in which people are linked to modern organizations. The *shamrock organization* has three parts to it: comparable to the three leaves which the clover-like shamrock has on each stem. Each part represents a different category of contribution to the organization made by separate groups of people who have differing expectations and who are managed and paid differently.

The first group is the *professional core* of qualified professionals, technicians and managers. They are people who are essential to the organization, owning the organizational knowledge which distinguishes it from its competitors. They are therefore hard to replace, and the organization pays them high salaries and offers fringe benefits. In return the organization wants commitment, hard work and long hours. They are managed in the task culture and are thus expected to be flexibly available to go anywhere at any time and do what is required. For this they are paid more and more. This means that they are expensive, and organizations look for ways to reduce their numbers. Downsizing has been characteristic of organizations in recent years, but output has gone up: half the number, paid twice as much, producing three times the output, appears to be the aim.

With a smaller core, more and more work is contracted out to specialists who can do it more efficiently and cheaply. So a *contractual fringe* has come into being and is taking a larger and larger proportion of the work. This is the second part of the shamrock. Manufacturing firms typically make fewer and fewer of the components of their products. They have become assemblers of parts manufactured by suppliers, hence the importance of Japanese just-in-time delivery systems. Organizations regularly contract out activities that were once regarded as a normal part of their work: advertising and market research, computing, catering, and so on. The contractual fringe is made up of individuals and organizations who are paid for the results achieved, that is, fees not wages, and this has great importance for the way in which they are managed. They are paid for output achieved, not for hours spent at work. But organizations are much more used to paying employees for time, and have to learn to manage the contractual relationship effectively across a very wide range of activities.

The third part of the organization is the *flexible labour force.* These are the part-time and temporary workers who are the fastest growing part of the employment market. As organizations wish both to increase their ability to respond to variations in demand and to improve profitability, they turn to this force to give them additional flexibility. Since people in this force are part-time or seasonal employees, there is a problem that employers may regard this part of the organization as merely casual labour, but if these workers are treated casually they will be casual in their attitudes to the organization and its outputs, which means that the standards aimed for will not be reached. They are managed in the Apollo role culture, and although they will never have the commitment of the core, they have to be treated fairly if they are to be adequate in their roles.

Along with the development of the shamrock organization has come another discontinuous change in the nature of authority in organizations, namely the emergence of the *federal organization.* This is more than just a decentralized organization, for the logic of that form implies that knowledge and power are at the top of the hierarchy and certain amounts of them are handed down to the component parts. In the federal organization the logic goes the other way, with the subsidiaries federating together to get benefits of scale, but where the drive and energy come mostly from the parts. The centre is small; it does not direct or control the activities of the parts, rather it advises and influences, only reserving to itself a few key decisions, for example capital allocations and appointment of top executives. Its vital task is to give a vision which shapes and gives a point to the work of all the parts. Handy compares this form of organization to a university or college, where the top management group can have only limited understanding about the large range of teaching and research activities being carried out.

For federalism to work well, two key principles must be understood and practised. The first is *subsidiarity:* the principle that the larger and higher body should not exercise functions which can be carried out efficiently by smaller and lesser bodies. For those at the centre, this is a much more difficult concept to put into practice than it appears, because a considerable amount of trust and confidence is required. The centre cannot be sure if the subsidiary organization can carry out the function efficiently before it has actually done so. But, in a Catch-22 situation, if it uses this lack of experience as an argument against allowing them to try, then subsidiarity will never occur.

The second principle refers to those in the subsidiaries: they must want to increase the range of activities in their roles. Handy uses the analogy of the *inverted doughnut* to focus on the changing nature of organizational roles. A doughnut (or bagel) has a hole in the middle; the inverted doughnut is filled in the middle but the surround is empty up to the round contours of the edge. The core represents that part of the job which is fully prescribed, often in a job description, which, if not done well, will be seen as a clear failure on the part of the job occupant. But there will also be discretionary opportunities in a job, which no one has specified but which, if carried out effectively, will be regarded as showing appropriate initiative. These can fill the space up to the outside rim of the doughnut, which represents the boundaries of the discretion allowed in the job.

Traditionally, jobs in organizations have had large cores and small areas of discretion, as in an Apollo role culture. This allows control of the processes and of the behaviour of the people. In federal organizations, there are much smaller cores, since the exercise of discretion by subsidiary staff is crucial for subsidiarity to occur. These are more likely to be the task cultures of Athena. Controls can only be exercised after the event through 'management by results', and mistakes will inevitably occur. Managements have to learn to forgive mistakes and not always punish them, because this is how learning takes place.

BIBLIOGRAPHY

HANDY, C., *The Gods of Management*, Souvenir Press, 1978; Pan Books, 1979.

HANDY, C., *The Age of Unreason*, Business Books, 1989.

HANDY, C., *Understanding Organizations*, 4th edn, Penguin, 1993.

HANDY, C., *Beyond Certainty*, Hutchinson, 1995.

HANDY, C., 'Trust and the Virtual Organization' in *Harvard Business Review* (May–June 1995), 40–50; reprinted in D. S. Pugh (ed.), *Organization Theory*, 5th edn, Penguin, 2007.

HANDY, C., *Myself and Other Matters*, Heinemann, 2006.

Christopher Bartlett and Sumantra Ghoshal

Christopher Bartlett and the late Sumantra Ghoshal (1948–2004) were business school academics who have studied the functioning of corporations which operate internationally. Bartlett is a professor at the Harvard Business School; Ghoshal was at the London Business School. Their research leads them to propose that a new type of organizational structure, with its concomitant distinctive managerial thinking, is required for success in the current global business environment.

Bartlett and Ghoshal maintain that the world's largest companies are in flux, as global pressures have forced them to rethink their traditional worldwide strategies. While some firms have prospered, most are struggling for survival. Even within particular industries big differences have been manifested in performance. For example, within the consumer electronics industry the Japanese Matsushita corporation has prospered, whereas the American General Electric was eventually forced to sell off its business in this sector. It is not just a matter of the Japanese being better at it than the Americans. In the soap and detergent market the American Proctor & Gamble was able to mount a major thrust into international markets, whereas the international efforts of Kao, the dominant Japanese competitor in this industry, have stalled.

The key is the organization's capability for effective international operations. This is a combination of its strategic posture, its organization structure and its attitude to learning and innovation. For each firm the particular characteristics of its organizational capability have been built up over previous decades in response to the problems faced. This administrative heritage is an organizational asset, but it has to be examined very carefully and questioned, since it is also a constraint in adapting to new global environmental demands.

In the 1980s three distinct types of cross-national firms, each with different capabilities, could be identified:

- multinational companies
- global companies
- international companies.

Multinational companies have developed a strategic posture and structure which allows them to be very sensitive to differences in national environments. Their key capability is *responsiveness*. They build a strong local presence by responding to local market opportunities and are prepared to vary their products and even their businesses as necessary in the different countries. Firms such as the Anglo-Dutch Unilever and the American ITT were pioneers in developing links to each host country's infrastructure and thus creating conglomerates. These are relatively decentralized confederations with distributed resources and responsibilities. The control exercised may be limited to little more than the supervision of financial results.

Global companies are those which are driven by the need for common global operations, and are thus much more centralized in their strategic and operational decisions. Their key capability is *efficiency*. They obtain cost advantages through building world-scale facilities to distribute standard products to markets everywhere. It is a form pioneered in the motor industry by Ford, and is the approach taken by many Japanese companies such as Matsushita and Toyota. The centre retains strong control in decision making, and foreign operations are seen as delivery mechanisms to global markets. Products and strategies are developed to exploit what is regarded as a worldwide unitary market.

International companies base their strategy primarily on transferring and adapting the parent company's knowledge and expertise to foreign markets. Their key capability is *transfer of learning*. The parent company retains considerable influence, but local units can adapt products and ideas coming from the centre. Firms such as the American IBM and the Swedish Ericsson run a 'coordinated federation' in which the subsidiaries have more autonomy than in the global company but less than in the multinational firm. Particular functions such as R & D product and market development and finance are kept close to the centre. So there is a degree of benefit in both responsiveness to local markets and integrated global development.

Within the last decade, because of the turbulence of the global environment, none of these three types of structure and its accompanying capability has been adequate for success. For example, customers are demanding differentiated products as provided by the multinational company, but with the same high quality and low costs as standard products provided by the global company. There are also frequent changes in economic, technological, political and social environments which require the firm to be readily responsive. But, in addition, the organization has to build in the capability to continue to be responsive to the inevitable changes that occur in tastes, technologies, exchange rates and so on.

A new form of organization has been emerging to cope with this complex and changing global situation. It does not demand responsiveness or efficiency or learning as the key capability, but requires all three to be achieved simultaneously. This is the *transnational* form of organization, in which managers accept that each of the three previous types is partially true and has its own merits, but none represents the whole truth. Bartlett and Ghoshal put forward the transnational organization concept as a managerial sophisticated ideal type towards which cross-national organizations will have to develop in order to obtain and retain global competitiveness.

In the transnational company there is developed an *integrated network* structure in which neither centralization nor decentralization is embraced as a principle, but selective decisions about location and authority have to be made. Certain activities may be best centralized within the home country (for example basic research, treasury function) but others are best concentrated in certain subsidiaries (for example component production in low-wage economies, technical development in countries with a technically sophisticated infrastructure) while yet others are decentralized to many national operations (for example differentiated product assembly, sales). So, for example, an American transnational may obtain the benefits of world-scale production for labour-intensive products by building in a low-wage economy like Mexico, while obtaining the benefits of producing technically sophisticated products in Germany, and assembling both in Britain for the European market. Thus there is a considerable degree of functional and national specialization, which requires the interdependencies to be well managed. Frequently these interdependencies are designed to build self-enforcing cooperation among different units, such as when the French subsidiary depends on Spain for one range of products, while the Spanish one depends on France for another.

The transnational organization requires a distinctively different approach from previous forms of international operations. Its management has the key task of developing a set of strategic capabilities and relevant organizational characteristics, as shown in the table.

To obtain global competitiveness with the transnational's dispersed and interdependent assets and resources requires balancing diverse capabilities and perspectives. As Crozier (see Chapter 5) and Hickson (see Chapter 1) have shown, the group that copes with the most critical strategic tasks of the organization gains power. So, for example, in Unilever (a multinational company), it was the geographic managers who became dominant, because their contribution was crucial to achieving the dispersed responsiveness required. But in Matsushita (a global company) it was the product division managers who dominated, since they were the key to the company's world-scale efficiency. In IBM (an international company) the strong technical and marketing groups retained their power through all reorganizations, since they were the basis of the company's strategy of building and transferring its core competencies for worldwide learning. The transnational company, however, must develop a multidimensional organization structure that legitimizes diversity and eliminates any bias that favours the management of any particular function, product or geographical area.

Similarly, the transnational needs to develop flexible coordination processes among the highly specialized and differentiated roles of its subsidiaries. It cannot rely on one preferred way of obtaining control. The preferred American way of a formalized control system (for example, as in ITT), the preferred Japanese way of a centralized decision-making structure (for example as in Kao), the preferred European way of a socialization process for instilling a common culture (for example as in Unilever) are all inadequate by themselves for the transnational. This requires a portfolio of highly flexible coordination processes calling on all these approaches. These are used in appropriate ways for different types of national subsidiaries.

Building and Managing the Transnational Company

Strategic capability	Organizational characteristics	Management tasks
Global competitiveness	Dispersed and interdependent assets and resources	Legitimizing diverse perspectives and capabilities
Multinational flexibility	Differentiated and specialized subsidiary roles	Developing multiple and flexible coordination processes
Worldwide learning	Joint development and worldwide sharing of knowledge	Building shared vision and individual commitment

Source: Bartlett and Ghoshal (1989).

One type of national subsidiary may act as a *strategic leader* in a particular product market. For example, the Phillips subsidiary in the UK is the lead company for the whole corporation in the teletext market. The dominant approach to coordination in this case is the process of socialization. Another type of subsidiary may act in a *contributor* role. This type has a good local resource capability but is operating in a market of limited strategic importance. An example is Ericsson's Australian subsidiary, which made important contributions to the development of its telephone-switching business, but whose home market is limited. It therefore has to be developed to contribute more widely to international operations. In this case direct headquarters coordination is appropriate. A further type of national subsidiary is the *implementer*, which carries out the corporation's operations in a market of limited potential. For example, Proctor & Gamble created teams to develop Euro brands which could be marketed on a coordinated European basis. This required its subsidiaries in various European countries to refrain from modifying the formula, changing the packaging or adjusting the advertising approach in order for the company to obtain efficiencies of scale. This implementer type of subsidiary is coordinated by formalized systems, which require the least corporate management time.

The internal differentiation both of subsidiary company roles and of types of coordination processes – which may change from issue to issue – can lead to severe conflict in a transnational. The need for worldwide sharing of knowledge can cause difficulties too. Therefore a final key task of the central management is the need to unify the organization through a shared corporate vision. This requires clarity, continuity and consistency of purpose. Transnational organizations have to work to establish and communicate these attributes if they are to form the basis for the generation of individual commitment. It requires, among other things, a sophisticated human resource management system, which pays particular attention to training and development and to career management in an international setting.

Bartlett and Ghoshal are very clear that the complex transnational structure is not just a more sophisticated matrix structure. It is much more than that, since a new management mindset is needed to understand the multidimensional nature of the tasks and to be prepared to interact openly and flexibly with others on them. As they put it: 'The task is not to build a sophisticated matrix structure, but to create a "matrix in the minds of managers".'

BIBLIOGRAPHY

BARTLETT, C. A. and GHOSHAL, S., 'Managing across Borders: New Organizational Responses', *Sloan Management Review*, (Fall 1987), 43–53; reprinted in D. S. Pugh (ed.), *Organization Theory*, 5th edn, Penguin, 2007.

BARTLETT, C. A., and GHOSHAL, S., *Managing Across Borders: The Transnational Solution*, Century Business, 1989; 2nd edn, Random House, 1998.

GHOSHAL, S., PIRAMAL, G. and BARTLETT, C. A., *Managing Radical Change: What Indian Companies Must Do to Become World-Class*, New Delhi: Penguin Books India, 2000.

Stewart Clegg

Stewart Clegg was born and educated in England, studying at the Universities of Aston and Bradford, but has spent most of his academic career at universities in Australia. He is currently Professor of Management at the University of Technology, Sydney, where he is also Director of the Research Centre for Innovative Collaborations, Alliances and Networks. His steady stream of research papers and books (several of the earlier ones in collaboration with David Dunkerley, now of the University of Glamorgan) have established him as a major contributor to what is referred to as 'post-modern' organization theory.

The key concern of Clegg in all of his writing is the exercise of power in organizations. He maintains that the use of power is central to the processes of organization and calls on the work of a very wide range of philosophers, political scientists, economists and sociologists to illuminate its workings. Starting from a neo-Marxist approach, Clegg distinguishes between two forms of the exercise of power: 'domination by coercion' and 'domination by hegemony'. Domination by coercion is the form of power that, say, an owner of a firm may exercise over an employee by saying: 'Either you will do what I say, or I will sack you.' It is based on coercion which in the capitalist economic system is legitimized by ownership of the means of production. Thus owners, or their representatives, the managers, have power *over* employees. This power is not limitless. It is subject to the laws of the state, the opposing power of trades unions and so on.

But people exercise power in more ways than by giving orders to those who wish to disobey them. Much of the time power does not have to be used in order to be felt; just the capacity for its use may be sufficient. Indeed the most powerful people are those who never need to give any orders, because their known potential for power ensures that what they want happens and what they oppose does not happen. This form of the exercise of power is referred to as domination by hegemony or 'soft' domination. It is the commonest way in which power is exercised.

With the development of large-scale, modern organizations domination by coercion of the owner-managers has become infeasible and domination by hegemonic power has largely replaced it. The authority may come from ownership, but it is the hierarchical structure and rules of correct procedure of bureaucratic organizations which ensures that directions from those at the top are carried out as Weber noted (see earlier in this chapter). The bureaucratic structure provides the ground rules for the exercise of power. In these organizations following a procedural rule demonstrates the same exercise of power as obeying an order.

From the power perspective organizational structures are not neutral systems of authority, rationally established to be efficient in achieving the organization's goals. Organizations do not have goals: only people have goals. Structures are 'sedimented' decision rules that is, rules that have been historically laid down to overcome opposition and resistance. They have been imposed by those exercising power, and are organized in such a way as to maintain that power. They establish that the powerful's goals are regarded as legitimate and equate to those of the organization. The goals of the unpowerful are regarded as illegitimate and are characterized as resistance which therefore needs to be overcome. A common conception is to regard the organization as a system and then, using an engineering analogy, to regard resistance in the system as bad.

Organizations develop a number of technical rules (for example work study, see Taylor in Chapter 4), social-regulative rules (for example incentive schemes, human relations policies, see Mayo in Chapter 6) and strategic rules (for example pursue vertical integration, engage in mass advertising), all of which provide a rational justification for the hegemonic soft domination of ownership in capitalism. Work study, in particular, performed the historical role of ushering in mass production with its deskilling of workers and their consequent disempowerment.

Power is inherent in these 'rules of the game'. The rules both enable and constrain action. They have to be interpreted and the discretion this inevitably affords gives opportunities for competition for power. In modern organizations with their large range of functional and professional specialists, hierarchical power by itself is inadequate to exercise all the control that is necessary. Other forms of control by non-owners develop, based on their strategic position in the organization (see Hickson earlier in this chapter). Accountants, marketers, IT specialists strive for power for their specialisms based on interpretations of the rules which are favourable to them. So organizations may be conceived of as arenas within which various sub-groups compete for resources and power (see Pettigrew, Chapter 7). But they are only legitimized to act within the rules laid down by the owners of the organization. It would not be regarded as legitimate, for example, for an IT specialist group to boycott a particular department or product as part of its campaign for more resources and power. This sets strict limits to the non-capitalists' exercise of power.

But at the present time such 'modernist' organizations with rigid bureaucracy, extreme differentiation of roles and strong hierarchical control are failing to achieve the capitalist goal of profit. Growth in productivity has slowed down because rationalization on Taylorist work-study principles is reaching its limits. With increasing globalization the relation between the head office centre and the far-flung operating subsidiaries cannot remain one of total hegemonic control. Other ways of exercising power have to be developed which are not stifled by hierarchy. This does not mean the abolition of hierarchy. There will always be a differential of knowledge, skill or capital by those contributing to the performance of any complex task which will lead to differences in power. But it would be a listening power, using the hierarchy to be receptive to the views of those lower down rather than to screen them out.

This new use of hierarchy is a key part of the postmodern organization. 'Where modernist organization is rigid, postmodern organization is flexible.' Modernist organizations create highly differentiated deskilled jobs, but jobs in postmodern organizations are de-differentiated and multi-skilled. Modernist organizations are procedurally tightly controlled even though as they increase in size, bureaucratic rigidities hamper their performance more and more. Postmodern organizational forms, on the other hand, emphasize flexibility through contracting out, alliances and networking.

The differences between modernist and postmodern organizations are summarized in the table below. It shows a number of distinctive dimensions along which organizations can differ thus demonstrating their progress towards postmodernity. Postmodern organizations are more democratic, people are more empowered, the skills required are more flexible. The rewards given for good performance are less targeted at individuals but are more collectivized, being aimed at group achievement. Leadership is based less on mistrust in subordinates leading to increasing control, and more on trust in them leading to greater autonomy. There is also a comparable change with regard to outputs. Where modernist organizations cater to mass forms of consumption, postmodern organizations provide for consumer niches.

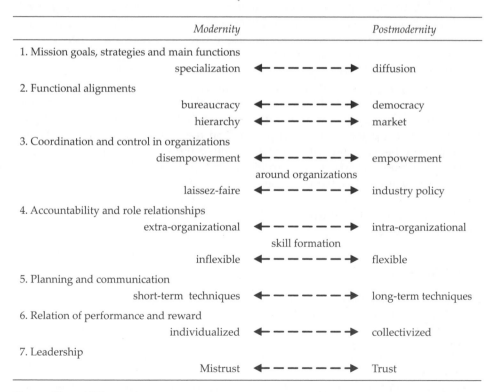

	Modernity	*Postmodernity*
1. Mission goals, strategies and main functions		
specialization	◄ ─ ─ ─ ─ ─ ►	diffusion
2. Functional alignments		
bureaucracy	◄ ─ ─ ─ ─ ─ ►	democracy
hierarchy	◄ ─ ─ ─ ─ ─ ►	market
3. Coordination and control in organizations		
disempowerment	◄ ─ ─ ─ ─ ─ ►	empowerment
around organizations		
laissez-faire	◄ ─ ─ ─ ─ ─ ►	industry policy
4. Accountability and role relationships		
extra-organizational	◄ ─ ─ ─ ─ ─ ►	intra-organizational
skill formation		
inflexible	◄ ─ ─ ─ ─ ─ ►	flexible
5. Planning and communication		
short-term techniques	◄ ─ ─ ─ ─ ─ ►	long-term techniques
6. Relation of performance and reward		
individualized	◄ ─ ─ ─ ─ ─ ►	collectivized
7. Leadership		
Mistrust	◄ ─ ─ ─ ─ ─ ►	Trust

Source: Clegg 1990.

While few enterprises can now be said to be postmodern already, Clegg sees signs of such organization in Asian industries, French bread production and Italian fashions. He argues that it is facile to say that the cultures of Japan, France and Italy are different so the distinctive organizations which occurred in those countries will not flourish in other cultures. Indeed the common characteristic which is found in those very different national settings is that organizational units are not bound together in a controlling bureaucracy but are linked in a functioning network.

Thus in Japan the basic economic unit is not the firm but the enterprise grouping that is, the interrelated network of firms to which each individual enterprise belongs. This may be within one industry where a large firm will have a series of long-term agreements with a number of smaller suppliers. Or it may be across industries where firms unrelated in production are interconnected financially by a bank or trading company. In both cases the network provides stability. In Korea, it is family ownership and management which provides the glue to keep the network, known as a *chaebol*, functioning (see Whitley, Chapter 2).

Networking is also the key to the operation of the French bread industry. France is distinctive in that the mass produced and packaged 'industrial bread', which is common in western countries, has only a very small proportion of the market there. This is because of the very large number of small local bakeries, each with its own shop, which provide *baguettes*, a much more popular fresh loaf. They have survived because they are all family enterprises linked together in a network, *Le Syndicat de la Boulangerie*, which has enabled them to maintain flour supplies even in difficult circumstances. Similarly Benetton, the Italian fashion wear company, is a network of networks. Its main production facility is supplemented by a network of suppliers, while all its sales outlets are franchised, forming a network of individually owned shops.

Networking is a postmodern form of organization because it is not a one-way ordering of domination and resistance between those who have power and those who do not. As Clegg sees it, moving away from his neo-Marxist roots, to regard power as the property of one group based on ownership rights is to 'reify' the phenomenon that is, to regard it as real in itself. But power can only be manifested in 'circuits of power' which flow from the interplay of reciprocal relationships. In the organizational network these circuits carry the episodes of continuing negotiation and renegotiation by the participating agents, which form the power relationship. These relationships can be those of domination and resistance, but they need not be so.

BIBLIOGRAPHY

CLEGG, S. R., *The Theory of Power and Organization*, Routledge and Kegan Paul, 1979.

CLEGG, S. R., *Frameworks of Power*, Sage, 1989.

CLEGG, S. R., *Modern Organizations: Organization Studies in the Postmodern World*, Sage, 1990.

CLEGG, S. R., and DUNKERLEY, D., *Organization, Class and Control*, Routledge and Kegan Paul, 1980.

CLEGG, S. R., KORNBERGER, M. and PITSIS, T., *Managing and Organizations*, Sage, 2005.

2   The Organization in its Environment

The beginning of administrative wisdom is the awareness that there is no one optimum type of management system.
TOM BURNS

The effective organization has integrating devices consistent with the diversity of its environment. The more diverse the environment and the more differentiated the organization, the more elaborate the integrating devices.
PAUL LAWRENCE and JAY LORSCH

Uncertainties pose major challenges to rationality.
JAMES D. THOMPSON

The key to organizational survival is the ability to acquire and maintain resources.
JEFFREY PFEFFER and GERALD R. SALANCIK

Efficient organizations establish mechanisms that complement their market strategy.
RAYMOND E. MILES and CHARLES C. SNOW

An ecology of organizations seeks to understand how social conditions affect the rates at which new organizations and new organizational forms arise, the rates at which organizations change forms, and the rates at which organizations and forms die out.
MICHAEL T. HANNAN and JOHN H. FREEMAN

Whether they like it or not the headquarters of multinationals are in the business of multicultural management.
GEERT HOFSTEDE

Differences in societal institutions encourage particular kinds of economic organization and discourage other ones.
RICHARD WHITLEY

All organizations are situated in an environment, be it business, governmental, educational or voluntary service. In this environment are other organizations and people with whom transactions have to take place. These will include suppliers, clients or customers, and competitors. In addition there will be more general aspects of the environment which will have important effects, such as legal, technological and ethical developments.

The writers in this section have been concerned to analyse how the need to function successfully in different environments has led organizations to adopt different structures and strategies. Tom Burns examines the effects of rapidly changing technological developments on the attempts of old-fashioned firms to adjust to new environments. Paul Lawrence and Jay Lorsch emphasize that it is the appropriateness of the organization's structure in relation to its environmental requirements which determines effectiveness.

James D. Thompson portrays organizations as open systems having to achieve their goals in the face of uncertainty in their environments. Jeffrey Pfeffer and Gerald Salancik argue for a 'resource dependence perspective' in which all organizational functioning is seen to result from the organization's interdependence with its environment. Raymond Miles and Charles Snow emphasize the strategic choices that managements have to make to adapt to the environmental pressures they face, while Michael Hannan and John Freeman take an ecological and evolutionary view of the chances of organizations surviving in their particular environments.

Geert Hofstede highlights national culture as it affects management values and processes. This environmental feature is particularly important in the ever more frequent international activities of organizations. Richard Whitley examines business structures in many countries, and relates them to the societal institutions in which they operate.

Tom Burns

Tom Burns (1913–2001) spent more than 30 years at the University of Edinburgh, retiring in 1981 as Professor of Sociology. His early interests were in urban sociology and he worked with the West Midland Group on Post-war Reconstruction and Planning. While at Edinburgh his particular concern was with studies of different types of organizations and their effects on communication patterns and on the activities of managers. He also explored the relevance of different forms of organization to changing conditions – especially to the impact of technical innovation.

In collaboration with a psychologist (G. M. Stalker), Burns studied the attempt to introduce electronics development work into traditional Scottish firms, with a view to their entering this modern and rapidly expanding industry as the markets for their own well-established products diminished. The difficulties which these firms faced in adjusting to the new situation of continuously changing technology and markets led him to describe two 'ideal types' of management organization which are the extreme points of a continuum along which most organizations can be placed.

The *mechanistic* type of organization is adapted to relatively stable conditions. In it the problems and tasks of management are broken down into specialisms within which each individual carries out their assigned, precisely defined task. There is a clear hierarchy of control, and the responsibility for overall knowledge and coordination rests exclusively at the top of the hierarchy. Vertical communication and interaction (that is, between superiors and subordinates) is emphasized, with an insistence on loyalty to the concern and obedience to superiors. This system corresponds quite closely to Weber's rational-legal bureaucracy (see Chapter 1).

The *organismic* (also called *organic*) type of organization is adapted to unstable conditions when new and unfamiliar problems continually arise which cannot be broken down and distributed among the existing specialist roles. There is therefore a continual adjustment and redefinition of individual tasks, with the contributive (rather then restrictive) nature of specialist knowledge emphasized. Interactions and communication (information and advice rather than orders) may occur at any level as required by the process, generating a much higher degree of commitment to the aims of the organization as a whole. In this system, organization charts laying down the exact functions and responsibilities of each individual are not found: indeed, their use may be explicitly rejected as hampering the efficient functioning of the organization.

The almost complete failure of the traditional Scottish firms to absorb electronics research and development engineers into their organizations leads Burns to doubt whether a mechanistic firm can consciously change to an organismic one. This is because individuals in a mechanistic organization are not only committed to the organization as a whole, but are also members of a group or department with a stable career structure and with sectional interests in conflict with those of other groups. Thus power struggles develop between established sections to obtain control of the new functions and resources. These divert the organization from purposive adaptation and allow out-of-date mechanistic structures to be perpetuated and 'pathological' systems to develop.

Pathological systems are attempts by mechanistic organizations to cope with new problems of change, innovation and uncertainty while sticking to their formal bureaucratic structure. Burns describes three of these typical reactions. In a mechanistic organization the normal procedure for dealing with a matter outside an individual's sphere of responsibility is to refer it to the appropriate specialist or, failing that, to a superior. In a rapidly changing situation the need for such consultations occurs frequently, and in many instances the superior has to refer the matter higher still. A heavy load of such decisions finds its way to the chief executive, and it soon becomes apparent that many decisions can be made only by going to the top. Thus there develops the *ambiguous figure system* of an official hierarchy and a non-officially-recognized system of pair relationships between the chief executive and some dozens of people at different positions in the management structure. The head of the concern is overloaded with work, while many senior managers whose status depends on the functioning of the formal system feel frustrated at being bypassed.

Some firms attempt to cope with the problems of communication by creating more branches in the bureaucratic hierarchy – for example contract managers or liaison officers. This leads to a system described as the *mechanistic jungle* in which a new job or even a whole new department may be created whose existence depends on the perpetuation of these difficulties. The third type of pathological response is the *super-personal* or *committee system*. The committee is the traditional way of dealing with temporary problems which cannot be solved within a single individual's role without upsetting the balance of power. But as a permanent device it is inefficient in that it has to compete with the loyalty demanded and career structure offered by the traditional departments. This system was tried only sporadically by the firms, since it was disliked as being typical of inefficient government administration; attempts to develop the committee as a super-person to fulfil a continuing function that no individual could achieve thus met with little success.

For a proper understanding of organizational functioning, Burns maintains, it is therefore always necessary to conceive of organizations as the simultaneous working of at least three social systems. The first of these is the formal authority system derived from the aims of the organization, its technology and its attempts to cope with its environment. This is the overt system in terms of which all discussion about decision making takes place. But organizations are also cooperative systems of people who have career aspirations and a career structure, and who compete for advancement. Thus decisions taken in the overt structure inevitably affect the differential career prospects of members, who will therefore evaluate them in terms of the career system as well as the formal system, and react accordingly. This leads to the third system of relationships in an organization – its political system. Every organization is the scene of 'political' activity in which individuals and departments compete and cooperate for power. Again all decisions in the overt system are evaluated for their relative impact on the power structure, as well as for their contribution to the achievement of the organization's goals.

It is naive to consider the organization as a unitary system equated with the formal system: to be successful, any change must be acceptable in terms of the career structure and the political structure as well. This is particularly so with modern technologically based organizations which contain qualified experts who have a career structure and a technical authority which goes far beyond the organization itself and its top management. Thus any attempt to change from a mechanistic to an organismic management structure has enormous implications for the career structure (which is much less dependent on the particular organization) and the power system (which is much more diffuse, deriving from technical knowledge as much as from formal position).

Concern with the interaction of these three social systems within the organization continues in Burns' study of the British Broadcasting Corporation. The BBC is a very segmented organization both horizontally where there are large numbers of departments (for example Drama, Outside Broadcasts, Finance) which appear to be competing as much as cooperating, and vertically, where in order to rise in the grading structure executives soon lose contact with the professional skills (for example journalism, engineering) which they are supposed to administer. In this situation the career and the political systems can become more important than the formal task system.

Burns charts the rise in power of the central management of the BBC in the 1970s at the expense of the creative and professional staff, which stems from the Corporation's financial pressures. He maintains that the Corporation can develop as a creative service dedicated to the public good only if it is freed from its financial client relationship with the government.

'A sense of the past and the very recent past is essential to anyone who is trying to perceive the here-and-now of industrial organization.' If the organizational structure is viewed as a result of a process of continuous development of the three social systems (of formal organization, career structure and political system) a study of this process will help organizations to avoid traps they would otherwise fall into. Adaptation to new and changing situations is not automatic. Indeed many factors militate against it. An important one is the existence of an organization structure appropriate to an earlier phase of development. Another is the multi-faceted nature of the commitments of organizational members: to their careers, their departments, their specialist sub-units. These are often stronger than their commitment to the organization as a whole.

BIBLIOGRAPHY

BURNS, T., 'Industry in a New Age', *New Society*, 31 January 1963, no. 18; reprinted in D. S. Pugh (ed.), *Organization Theory*, 5th edn, Penguin, 2007.

BURNS, T., 'On the Plurality of Social Systems' in J. R. Lawrence (ed.), *Operational Research and the Social Sciences*, Tavistock, 1966.

BURNS, T., *The BBC: Public Institution and Private World*, Macmillan, 1977.

BURNS, T. and STALKER, G. M., *The Management of Innovation*, 3rd edn, Oxford University Press, 1994.

Paul Lawrence and Jay Lorsch

Paul Lawrence and Jay Lorsch are professorial colleagues in Organizational Behavior at the Harvard Business School. Together with many collaborators (who include S. A. Allan, S. M. Davis, J. Kotter, H. Lane and J. J. Morse) they conducted a series of studies into the appropriate structure and functioning of organizations using what has become known as the 'organization and environment' approach, described in their seminal book of that title.

Lawrence and Lorsch begin their analysis with the question of why people seek to build organizations. Their answer is that organizations enable people to find better solutions to the environmental problems facing them. This immediately highlights three key elements in their approach to understanding organizational behaviour:

1. it is people who have purposes, not organizations;
2. people have to come together to coordinate their different activities into an organization structure;
3. the effectiveness of the organization is judged by the adequacy with which members' needs are satisfied through planned transactions with the environment.

It is in order to cope effectively with their external environments that organizations come to develop segmented units, each of which has as its major task the problem of dealing with some aspect of conditions outside the firm. For example, in a manufacturing firm with production, sales and design units, the production unit deals with production equipment sources, raw materials sources and labour markets; the sales unit faces problems with the market, the customers and competitors; the design unit has to cope with technological developments, government regulations and so on. This *differentiation* of function and task is accompanied by differences in cognitive and emotional orientation among the managers in different units; differences too, in the formal structure of different departments. For instance the development department may have a long-term horizon and a very informal structure, whereas production may be dealing with day-to-day problems in a rigidly formal system, with sales facing the medium-term effects of competitors' advertising with moderate formality.

In spite of this the organization is a system which has to be coordinated so that a state of collaboration exists in order to reap the benefits of effective transactions with the environment. This is the required *integration* and it, too, is affected by the nature of external conditions.

The basic necessity for *both* appropriate differentiation *and* adequate integration in order to perform effectively in the external environment is at the core of Lawrence and Lorsch's model of organizational functioning. The approach was developed in an important study which they carried out on ten firms in three different industries – plastics (six firms), food (two firms) and containers (two firms) – which constituted very different environments for the enterprises concerned.

The study recognized that all the firms involved segment their environment. Each of the ten was dealing with a market sub-environment (the task of the sales department), a techno-economic sub-environment (the task of the manufacturing unit) and a scientific sub-environment (the task of the R & D or design department). The greater the degree of uncertainty within each sub-environment and the greater the diversity between them, the greater was the need of the firms to *differentiate* between their sub-units of sales, production and research in order to be effective in each sub-environment. For example in the plastics industry, which was found to have great diversity (with the science sub-environment highly uncertain but the techno-economic one relatively stable), a considerable degree of differentiation within effective firms was found. In the container industry, on the other hand, all parts of the environment were relatively certain and so a much lower degree of differentiation was apparent.

But greater differentiation brings with it the potential for greater inter-departmental conflict as the specialist groups develop their own ways of dealing with the particular uncertainties of their own sub-environments. These differences are not just minor variations in outlook but may involve fundamental ways of thinking and behaving. In the plastics industry, a sales manager may be discussing a potential new product in terms of whether it will perform in the customers' machinery, whether they will pay the cost and whether it can be got on to the market in three months' time. A research scientist at the same meeting may be thinking about whether the molecular structure of the material could be changed without affecting its stability and whether doing this would open out a line of research for the next two years which would be more interesting than other projects. These two specialists not only think differently, they dress differently, have different habits of punctuality and so on. It therefore becomes crucial that a highly differentiated firm should have appropriate methods of *integration* and conflict resolution if it is to perform well in the environment.

The table on page 71 lists the integrative devices which were found to be operating in three high-performing organizations, one from each of the industries studied. The top row gives the rating for the degree of differentiation. It will be seen that the need to operate effectively in the plastics environment led the firm to develop a high degree of differentiation; the container firm had the lowest differentiation and the food firm was in between.

Comparison of Integrative Devices in Three High-Performing Organizations

	Plastics	Food	Container
Degree of differentiation	10.7	8.0	5.7
Major integrative devices	(1) Integrative department	(1) Individual integrators	(1) Direct managerial contact
	(2) Permanent cross-functional teams at three levels of management	(2) Temporary cross-functional teams	(3) Managerial hierarchy
	(3) Direct managerial contact	(3) Direct managerial contact	(3) Paper system
	(4) Managerial hierarchy	(4) Managerial hierarchy	
	(5) Paper system	(5) Paper system	

Source: Lawrence and Lorsch (1967).

Each of these firms used a different combination of devices for achieving integration. All of them used the traditional methods of paper systems, the formal managerial hierarchy and direct managerial contact between members of the different departments to some extent. For the container firm with the least differentiation these methods were sufficient, but in the food firm, which had a greater need for integration, temporary teams made up of specialists from the units involved were set up to deal with any particularly urgent issue. Managers within functional departments were also assigned integrating roles such as that of liaison officer. Clearly the effective food firm was devoting a larger amount of time and effort to integrating activity.

The plastics organization had in addition established a special department, one of whose primary activities was integration. It also had an elaborate set of permanent integrating teams, each made up of members from the various functional units and the integrating department. The purpose of these teams was to provide a formal setting in which inter-departmental conflicts (such as the one described above between the sales manager and the research scientist) could be resolved with the help of an integrator. The effective plastics firm needed to draw on the whole range of integrative devices because its necessary differentiation was so high.

It is the appropriateness of the three-way relationships (between the uncertainty and diversity of the environment, the degree of organizational differentiation, and the state of integration and conflict resolution achieved) which will lead to effective functioning. Inadequacy in any of these relationships was associated with lower performance. Thus, for example, the high performers in the plastics and food industry had *both* greater differentiation *and* greater integration than the low performers, since both were required. By contrast, in the low-performing container organization, there was no evidence that the integrating unit it possessed was serving a useful purpose given its low level of differentiation.

Effective conflict resolution, which is the behavioural basis of integration, was found to have a pattern in which inter-unit conflict was dealt with by managers working in a problem-solving mode to face the issues and work through them to the best overall solution – rather than smoothing over problems to avoid conflict or letting the party with the greater power force its solution on others. It was also found that in dealing with conflict effectively, the authority of the individuals primarily involved in achieving integration (whether superiors in the line hierarchy or persons appointed specifically to coordinating roles) needs to be based not just on their formal position, but largely on their knowledge of and competence regarding the issues, as perceived by all the groups involved, together with a balanced orientation between the parties. The power and influence to make decisions leading to the resolution of conflict must therefore be located where the knowledge to reach such decisions also exists.

By emphasizing that the appropriate organization structure will depend upon environmental demands the Lawrence and Lorsch framework takes a 'contingency' approach, rejecting the formulation that one particular structural form (for example bureaucracy, see Weber, Chapter 1) or one particular motivational approach (for example Theory Y, see McGregor, Chapter 6) is always best. Instead it is appropriateness which is the key.

In a further study Lorsch and Morse compared two manufacturing plants (one high-performing, one low-performing) with two research laboratories (similar high and low performers). The organization structures and processes of the high-performing manufacturer in a relatively certain environment included high formality, short time-horizons and highly directive management. The individuals working in this organization were found to have low cognitive complexity, low tolerance for ambiguity and dependency in authority relationships. The high-performing research laboratory in a relatively uncertain environment had low formality, long time-horizons and high participation. Its members had high cognitive complexity, high tolerance for ambiguity and independence in authority relationships. Yet both organizations were effective because they were appropriately organized with members appropriate for their environmental tasks. Indeed the less effective organization in each pair did not show most of the distinctive characteristics of structure and process to the same degree. On the other hand the characteristics of the members were as clearly differentiated as in the successful organizations. These less effective organizations, it seems, could obtain the appropriate people but not organize them in the appropriate way. But equally, in other cases, failure could be due to having inappropriate people even though they were appropriately organized.

In a later study of seven major US industries, including those of steel, agriculture, hospitals and telecommunication, Lawrence and Dyer developed the 'competitive principle'. This maintains that an industry needs to experience an appropriate degree of vigorous competition in its environment if it is to be economically strong. Either too little or too much competition will lead to inefficient and non-innovative performance. They argue for the setting up of a government agency to monitor the competitive pressures in each industry to determine whether they need to be increased or reduced.

The analysis of matrix organizations has been a particular concern of Davis and Lawrence. Matrix organization structures are those in which there is a multiple command system – many managers having two bosses. For example, finance managers would have a finance director to whom they would be responsible for professional standards and who would be concerned with their career development and promotion. In addition each would also report to a project director to whom they would be responsible for giving the appropriate cost accounting services needed for their current project, and who would therefore be in charge of the day-to-day work allocation. Clearly this form of structure violates Fayol's principle of 'unity of command' (see Chapter 4), its greater complexity being the preferred structure in only certain situations. These are:

1. when there are several highly salient sectors (products, markets, functions and so on) which are simultaneously necessary for goal achievement;
2. when the tasks are uncertain, complex and interdependent;
3. when there is a need to realize economies by using scarce resources effectively.

In these circumstances, there is a need for complex differentiation and integration via the matrix mode.

BIBLIOGRAPHY

CARTER, C. B. and LORSCH, J. W., *Back to the Drawing Board*, Harvard Business School Press, 2004.
DAVIS, S. M. and LAWRENCE, P. R., *Matrix*, Addison-Wesley, 1977.
LAWRENCE, P. R. and DYER, D., *Renewing American Industry*, Free Press, 1983.
LAWRENCE, P. R. and LORSCH, J. W., *Organization and Environment*, Harvard, 1967.
LORSCH, J. W. and MORSE, J. J., *Organizations and Their Members: A Contingency Approach*, Harper & Row, 1974.

James D. Thompson

After leaving the American armed forces subsequent to the Second World War, James Thompson (1920–1973) became a sociologist. Yet he made his contribution to the understanding of organizations through research in business schools. He was the founding editor of the world's leading research journal in organization theory, the *Administrative Science Quarterly*. He died prematurely only six years after the publication in 1967 of his classic book *Organizations in Action*. This book draws together a range of ideas which were developing at the time it was written, and which have continued to be at the centre of organization theory. It is a portrayal of complex organizations 'as open systems, hence indeterminate and faced with uncertainty, but at the same time as subject to criteria of rationality and hence needing determinateness and certainty'. It pictures organizations continually striving to act rationally in the face of technological and environmental uncertainties. Their basic problem is how to cope with these uncertainties.

In other words, organizations – or rather, their members – aspire to be reasoned and orderly despite circumstances and events which may prevent them from being so. These standards, or *norms of rationality* to which they aspire, demand of organizations both coordination within and adjustment without. The twin tasks of administration are to provide the needful coordination within the organization and the adjustment to circumstances outside it.

The first task therefore is to achieve the stable coordination of those basic work activities which Thompson calls the *technical core* of an organization. For example, in factory production work, supplies of components must be continuously in the right places at the right times if assembly is to proceed smoothly, just as in a college the teachers and students must be in the right rooms at the right times.

The second task of administration is to regulate transactions across the boundary of the organization; that is, its contacts with the world outside itself. This might be done by negotiating with outside interests for, say assured financial credit or raw materials, or by changing with the environment (as when a chain of toy stores changes what it sells in response to rising public standards of safety for children). Or it might be done by *buffering*. Buffering protects the technical core from the uncertainties of acquiring resources, or of disposing of outputs (for example by having a purchasing department to handle suppliers and a sales department to deal with customers). A public relations department can cope with challenges to the morality of what the organization is doing, as in the cases of nuclear power or cigarette manufacture. Such *boundary spanning units* are placed between the technical core and the outside world to buffer it from external shocks. Another possibility is to move the boundaries of the organization to encircle sources of uncertainty and bring them under control, for instance to ensure supplies by buying up a supplier firm.

Hence organizations come to be made up of a variety of different parts. These can be linked together in fundamentally different ways, so that internal interdependence may differ from one organization to the next, and within any one organization. Interdependence can be pooled, sequential or reciprocal. *Pooled interdependence* is where the work of each part of an organization is not directly connected to that of the others but is a 'discrete contribution to the whole'. Yet since each is supported by that whole organization, which in turn would be threatened by the failure of any of its parts, they have a pooled interdependence within it. Such is the situation in a university where the departments of biology, French language and management, for example, are not linked in any way other than by their common reliance upon the university as a whole.

In *sequential interdependence* one part cannot do its job until others have done theirs. Tasks have to be done in sequence, first this, then that. Such is the situation in a factory where one workshop must machine components to the right sizes before the next can put them through a hardening treatment, and so on through successive stages up to the final product.

In *reciprocal interdependence* each does something for the other. Unlike the one-way flow in sequential interdependence, the outputs of both become inputs for the other. That is the situation in an airline where the flight operations section constantly makes aircraft available to the maintenance engineers for servicing, and the engineers constantly turn out aircraft ready for the operations people to fly.

Reciprocal interdependence requires the closest coordination, sequential interdependence less, and pooled interdependence least. Whilst all organizations have a certain amount of pooled interdependence, and in some it may be the prevalent form, not all have sequential interdependence in addition to pooled, and fewer still have within them all three kinds of interdependence.

The various units are grouped in the hierarchy of an organization in such a way as to minimize the costs of coordinating what they do. The means of coordination differ. Reciprocally interdependent units have to coordinate what each does for the other by mutual adjustment; thus they are likely to be placed together in the hierarchy under common superiors who can ensure that they cooperate. If units are sequentially interdependent, then their work can be coordinated by *planning or scheduling,* the work of each being planned to dovetail in sequence with that of the next in line. In a factory, a prior department in the sequence has to turn out enough components so that the next department in the sequence is not left standing idle. If there is merely pooled interdependence, then some coordination within the whole can be achieved by *standardization* of the rules which link each part with the whole: in a university, for example, though the departments differ in their contributions to the whole, in principle they should all be dealt with in the same manner when it comes to examination procedures or budget allocations (which is not to say that they all get the same budget).

Organizations also differ in the activities undertaken by their technical core, using one or more of three technologies. A *long-linked technology*, as in manufacturing, performs a series of tasks in a set order, giving rise to the sequential interdependence of units referred to earlier. A *mediating technology* links other parties, as where banks mediate between lenders and borrowers or an employment agency mediates between prospective employers and employees. Thirdly, an *intensive technology* functions in response to feedback from the object worked upon, as where what is done and when it is done in a hospital depend upon the patient's condition, or at a construction site upon the condition of the ground.

The ways in which organizations attempt to encircle external sources of uncertainty by extending their boundaries are determined by these kinds of technology. Those with long-linked technologies tend to opt for a corresponding vertical integration, as when oil refiners own roadside service stations and automobile manufacturers own suppliers of components. Those with mediating technologies try to increase the populations they serve, so that airlines increase their route networks and banks put branches into new areas. Finally, organizations with intensive technology attempt to incorporate the object worked upon so as to control it better, for instance universities making their students also their members and therefore subject to their rules, or mental hospitals bringing patients inside for observation.

This extension of boundaries is not the only way of coping with environmentally derived uncertainty. As mentioned above, organizations can buffer their technical core by setting up boundary spanning units which allow the core to operate as if there were stability. By stockpiling supplies and outputs, for example, work can continue as if there were a steady stream of supplies and a steady demand by the market. Alternatively, fluctuations may be prevented, as when utilities offer cheap off-peak gas or electricity to smooth out demand, or may be anticipated, as when ice cream production is adjusted to seasonal changes. If buffering, smoothing and anticipating fail, organizations can resort to rationing. Thus the post office gives priority to first-class mail, a hospital may deal only with urgent cases and a manufacturer may limit the proportion of popular items taken by any one wholesaler.

The relation between technical core and boundary spanning activities gives rise to appropriate types of structure. Where technical core and boundary spanning activities can be isolated from one another, there is likely to be a layer of functionally specialized departments in the hierarchy (such as purchasing, sales and finance) which is comparatively remote from the core and under central control. Where core and boundary activities are more closely interdependent, there is more likely to be a divisionalized structure, decentralized into 'self-sufficient clusters' of units. Each cluster has only so much to deal with, for instance as in a divisionalized multinational firm which has one multi-department division covering Europe, another covering South East Asia and so on.

Norms of rationality (which Thompson repeatedly stresses are assumed in all that he has to say about organizations) require that organizations 'keep score' so that their performances can be assessed. The problem is how to do this. Where it is possible to trace clearly the consequences of what is done (that is, where there is a clear presumption that new equipment has reduced costs), then efficiency measures can be used. These assume understanding of cause and effect and known standards of performance, as is the case with many financial indicators in industry. However, if *intrinsic criteria* which indicate relatively directly the standard of work done are lacking, then *extrinsic criteria* have to be used. From these the quantity and quality of the work can be inferred but are not shown directly. Hence university research is measured by counting the money gained for it in competitive applications to funding institutions and by the number of resulting publications rather than by its results as such; similarly, mental hospitals emphasize discharge rates rather than the extent to which patients are cured.

Organizations are torn between the differing assessments made by a variety of assessors. The potential users of a public health service will look at it in one way; the government providing the money will regard it in another. Users are concerned with the treatment given; the government more with the cost of treatment. Shareholders stress dividends and profits; customers stress prices. Therefore each organization tries to do best on the criteria used by those on whom it is most dependent. Furthermore, it will try to score well on the most *visible criteria*. These are the most obvious to the most important assessors. Business firms are sensitive to the price of their stock on the stock exchange; schools announce the examination performances of top pupils, and so on. Less visible criteria may be neglected, even if they are intrinsically measures of more desirable objectives.

According to Thompson, the more sources of uncertainty there are, the more possibilities for gaining power (see also Crozier, Chapter 5), and the more likely that 'political' positions will be taken up. In general individuals higher in management have discretion in decision-making which is subject to their personal judgement, including their assessment of what will be acceptable to others. This political assessment would be crucial in deciding, for example, whether or not two departments could successfully be merged.

The making of decisions involves beliefs or assumptions as to what will happen if one course is taken rather than another, and preferences as to what is most desirable. There is less certainty about some beliefs and preferences than about others, as illustrated by Thompson's matrix.

The matrix shows four likely kinds of *decision-making strategies*. The two left-hand boxes represent situations where there is relative certainty about what is wanted. Those concerned are clear about what outcome they prefer. In the top left-hand box they are also certain of what the consequences of their decision may be. Such all-round certainty might occur if they were considering increasing existing production capacity in response to a steady rise in sales. Agreed on the need to expand and knowing the technology from past experience, management could confidently calculate likely costs and returns in a *computational manner*. However, the lower box represents a situation where cause and effect are less well known. Here the same management still wants to expand capacity, but to do so they may have to buy new machinery of an untried design. This decision is less susceptible to computation, more a *judgemental* matter of assessing the risk involved.

Preferences regarding
possible outcomes

	Certainty	*Uncertainty*
Certain	Computational strategy	Compromise strategy
Uncertain	Judgemental strategy	Inspirational strategy

Beliefs about cause/effect relations

In the two right-hand boxes, managers are not sure what they want and there may be divided opinions. Alternative outcomes may each be attractive, for instance increasing capacity either for mass production of low-quality products or for a smaller volume of higher-quality products. If the technology for both is well known and market forecasts are confident that either can be profitable, a *compromise strategy* results in some of each. However, if there is all-round uncertainty, as in the lower right-hand box, then an *inspirational strategy* is more likely. There are neither clear preferences for high-volume against low-volume production, nor is there confidence in what the consequences of new production machinery or of launching more goods on to the market will be. The strategy has to be an inspired leap in the dark.

In Thompson's view, the aim of management and administration when designing organizations and making decisions must be the effective alignment of organization structure, technology and environment. This central conception has been and continues to be at the heart of organization theory and is a constant stimulus to research. Again and again his analysis is returned to as a source of ideas, few of which have as yet been supplanted.

BIBLIOGRAPHY

THOMPSON, J. D., *Organizations in Action*, McGraw-Hill, 1967.

Jeffrey Pfeffer
and Gerald R. Salancik

Jeffrey Pfeffer is professor at the Stanford University Graduate School of Business, California. The late Gerald Salancik (1943–1996) was at the Graduate School of Administration, Carnegie-Mellon University, Pittsburgh. Pfeffer and Salancik contend that organizations should be understood in terms of their interdependence with their environments. They advocate a *resource dependence perspective.* For example, explaining discontent among the employees of a fast-food chain by poor human relations and poor pay is irrelevant if the organization can draw on a pool of easily recruited youthful labour; since its competitors can also draw on this pool, the organization is not going to incur the costs of better human relations and pay.

Organizations are not self-directed and autonomous. They need resources, including money, materials, personnel and information; to get these they must interact with others who control such resources. This involves them in a constant struggle for autonomy as they confront external constraints. They become 'quasi-markets' in which influence is bartered not only between internal sections, but between those sections or sub-units and external interests.

Interdependence with others lies in the availability of resources and the demand for them. It is of many kinds. For instance, there is the direct dependence of a seller organization upon its customers, and there is the indirect dependence of two seller organizations not in mutual contact upon each other, via a set of potential customers for whom they both compete.

Three conditions define how dependent an organization is. First is the importance of a resource to it. This is a combination of the magnitude of that resource (in other words, the proportion of inputs and outputs accounted for by the resource) and of its criticality, best revealed by how severe the consequences would be if it were not available. Second is how much discretion those who control a resource have over its allocation and use. If they have completely free control and can make rules about access, then an organization which needs the resource can be put in a highly dependent position. Third is how far those who control a resource have a monopoly of it. Can an organization which needs it find an alternative source or a substitute? Thus 'the potential for one organization's influencing another derives from its discretionary control over resources needed by that other, and the other's dependence on the resource and lack of countervailing resources or access to alternative sources'. Since the others on whom an organization depends may not be dependable, its effectiveness is indicated more by how well it balances these dependencies than by internal measures of efficiency of a financial or similar nature.

To Pfeffer and Salancik the possible strategies that an organization may adopt to balance its dependencies are of four kinds. It may:

1. adapt to or alter constraints;
2. alter its interdependencies by merger, diversification or growth;
3. negotiate its environment by interlocking directorships or joint ventures with other organizations or by other associations;
4. change the legality or legitimacy of its environment by political action.

There are numerous ways of carrying out the first kind of strategy – adapting to or altering external constraints. An organization can pay sequential attention (see March, Chapter 5) to the demands made upon it, attending first to one and then to another as each in turn becomes more pressing. For example, for a time customers may take priority, then attention may switch to financial economies required by owners or lenders. An organization can play one interest off against another (for example blaming different unions for current difficulties). It can influence the formulation of demands (for example by advertising); it can claim that it cannot comply because of, say, legal restrictions; it can minimize its dependence by creating stocks of materials or money; and so on.

Merging, diversifying or growing are each ways of pursuing the second kind of strategy – altering interdependent relationships. Mergers do this by bringing control of critical resources within one organization, stabilizing the exchanges of which they are part. They may be backwards, sideways or forwards, incorporating suppliers, competitors or purchasers. Diversification shifts and widens the inter-dependencies in which an organization is enmeshed, extricating it from over-dependence in any one field. Growth in size increases the power of an organization relative to others, and makes more people interested in its survival. Size has been found to improve stability more than profitability.

Third, negotiating the environment is a more common strategy than total absorption by merger. Interlocking directorships, whereby boards include members of the boards of other organizations, cartels to control supplies, trade agreements, memberships in trade associations, in coordinating industry councils and advisory bodies, joint ventures in which two or more organizations work together and the like are commonplace. Such links help to keep the participating organizations informed about what is happening outside themselves and to ensure mutual commitment. Normative expectations build up as to what each other will do, making each more sure of the other's reliability.

Fourth and finally if none of the other strategies is open to them, organizations resort to political action. They endeavour to obtain and sustain favourable taxation or tariffs or subsidies or licensing of themselves and their members (as where the practice of medicine or law, for example, is restricted to defined categories of qualified people), or they charge others with violating regulations (as when competitors are accused of prohibited monopolistic arrangements). There is constant political activity by organizations which give to political party funds, lobby the members of legislatures, and are represented on governmental and related agencies and councils. Indeed, if the level of state regulation is high, the decisions of lawmakers and government agencies become more important to an organization than those of its customers or clients.

How are the effects of the environment, with whose elements an organization is interdependent, transmitted to that organization? It is generally accepted that environments affect organizations, but how that happens is not made explicit. Pfeffer and Salancik suggest that one means is executive succession, that is, the removal of executives and their replacement by others. Through this the environment influences the political processes within organizations from which action emerges.

There are three causal steps in Pfeffer and Salancik's argument concerning executive succession. To begin with, changes in environmental uncertainty mould the pattern of power in an organization. This occurs as posited by the 'strategic contingencies theory of intraorganizational power' formulated by Hickson, Hinings and their colleagues (see under Pugh and the Aston Group, Chapter 1). According to this theory those sections or sub-units of an organization most able to cope with what is uncertain gain power. Thus a marketing department smoothing out erratic fluctuations in orders by shrewdly timed advertising, or a maintenance department keeping production flowing by skilled attention to breakdowns is likely to become powerful. This gain in power is subject to two conditions: the section must be non-substitutable (that is, no one else can do what they do) and central (that is, many others in the organization are affected by what they do, and the organization's main outputs would be damaged immediately if they ceased to do it).

The resulting distribution of power then affects the choice of top personnel. As Pfeffer and Salancik put it: 'We view administrative succession as a political process of contested capability, where the contest is resolved by sub-unit power.' There is a tendency to blame top management for difficulties – the counterpart to their own tendency to take credit for successes in a world over which they have limited control. Thus they tend to be removed if things go badly; who is removed and who replaces them follows the perceptions of the powerful concerning who can best cope with perceived uncertain dependencies.

The third step in the argument is that, once appointed, executives and administrators can and do influence the main directive decisions. Although their control over their world is limited, they do have sufficient authority to shape decisions. They take part in what Child has called 'strategic choice' (see under Pugh and the Aston Group, Chapter 1) which delineates the intended future course of their organization. They 'enact' an environment, acting according to how they perceive it and trying to change it to their organization's advantage. Further, changes in top personnel permit movement between organizations which can be a tacit means of coordination, the managers of one knowing the managers of another.

Top managements are especially concerned with scanning the environment to find out what is happening and what may happen, with loosening dependencies so that the organization does not become too dependent on one or a few others, and with managing conflicting external demands. It has been fashionable to forecast that the environment they face will become more and more dispersed and turbulent, but Pfeffer and Salancik do not agree. They foresee 'an increasingly interconnected environment in which power is increasingly concentrated'. Though they write in terms of the American variant of the capitalist system, their resource dependence perspective generalizes beyond that.

In later work, Charles O'Reilly (a colleague at Stanford) and Pfeffer argue that there is a common thread in the approach of many successful companies – they unlock the hidden value in all their employees. They do not expect to buy in their needs for personnel as they buy in their needs for other resources. Instead they operate a people-centred value system that establishes a sense of purpose among all employees. The senior managers put the emphasis on leading rather than just managing, so the employees are motivated to develop and achieve.

BIBLIOGRAPHY

O'REILLY, C. A. and PFEFFER, J., *Hidden Value: How great Companies Achieve Extraordinary Results with Ordinary People*, Harvard Business School Press, 2000.

PFEFFER, J. and SALANCIK, G. R., *The External Control of Organizations: A Resource Dependence Perspective*, Harper & Row, 1978.

Raymond E. Miles and Charles C. Snow

Raymond Miles and Charles Snow are both professors in American business schools. Miles is Emeritus Professor of Business Administration at the University of California, Berkeley. He has studied and advised a wide variety of organizations in the public and private sectors. Snow is Professor of Organizational Behavior at Pennsylvania State University.

Miles and Snow ask how and why organizations differ in strategy, in structure, in technology and in administration. Why do some offer a broad range of products or services and others a narrower range? Why are some structured around functional specialisms and others around product lines or services? Why are some more centralized, others more decentralized? For Miles and Snow the answers can be found with Thompson (see earlier in this chapter), in what he termed the alignment of organization with environment.

To align organization and environment successfully, management has to solve three problems, and solve them continuously. They are the entrepreneurial, engineering and administrative problems. The *entrepreneurial problem* is to choose a general market domain, or field of operation, in which the organization can be viable, to specify the precise target market and decide on the right products or services for it. Solving this problem, however, requires also solving the *engineering problem*, taking the word 'engineering' in a wide sense. Ways have to be found of making the products or offering the services. There must be appropriate technologies. Then the *administrative problem* is to organize and manage the work.

The aim should be an effective *adaptive cycle*. This means that the entrepreneurial, engineering and administrative problems are tackled in coherent, mutually complementary ways which enable the organization as a whole to survive.

In studies of a variety of kinds of organization Miles and Snow find four types of *adaptation strategies*, pursued by organizations, which they name Defenders, Prospectors, Analysers and Reactors. Defenders and Prospectors are at opposite ends of the continuum of possible strategies. Analysers are somewhere in between, with some of the features of both. Each of these three types has its own typical solutions to the entrepreneurial, engineering and administrative problems. Reactors are different again. They seem unable consistently to pursue any of the other three types of strategy, reacting to events in an inconsistent way.

The first type, the *Defenders*, chooses to solve the entrepreneurial problem by aiming at a narrow and stable domain. They set themselves to sustain a prominent position in a narrow market segment, competing on either or both of quality and price to keep a particular clientele satisfied. They grow cautiously, step by step, by deeper penetration of this limited market. They reap the benefits of familiarity with it and with what they are doing, but tend to miss new developments because their managerial personnel has a restricted range of external contacts. There is a risk of their being caught by a major market shift to which they cannot adapt quickly enough.

Defenders are inclined to concentrate mostly on their engineering problem. Solving it is the key to their success. They succeed by being cost-efficient in doing what they know how to do well. They concentrate on improving quality control, production scheduling, materials handling and inventory control, distribution and the like. They buffer their core technology from external disturbance, as Thompson would put it, by carrying stocks of supplies and of products so that, though there may be ups and downs in stocks, the production work itself can proceed steadily. Buffering may be helped through vertical integration with other organizations (that is, by mutual ownership or contracts which ensure supplies and orders). However, while a Defender may work efficiently, here again there is a risk. It may be a long time before the investment in technology pays off.

Defender-type strategies lead to a typical administrative solution. Efficient supplying of a limited clientele requires relatively centralized control. Instructions flow down from the top, and reports and explanations flow upwards, via a 'long-looped vertical information system'. There is a central array of specialist departments, such as accounting, sales and personnel, administering a range of formalized documented procedures, such as budget returns, work schedules and stock listings. Together with the chief executive, the crucial finance and production functions dominate the centralized system. As always there are risks. While the system is orderly, novel opportunities may pass it by.

A Defender strategy has been pursued successfully by a food company in North California described by Miles and Snow. It has stayed within a speciality market for dried fruits and fruit juices. Beginning just by growing these, it met competition by extending into processing the fruit for consumption. This work has been mechanized, costs of growing fruit have been held down, and a small team specializes in improving quality. Control is centralized on the president and the heads of field operations, sales and finance, and higher than average wages ensure a stable labour force. The firm has a long-term coherence of entrepreneurial, engineering and administrative solutions.

The second type, *Prospectors*, the opposite of the Defenders, aims to find and exploit new opportunities. They stress 'doing the right things' rather than 'doing things right' as Defenders do. They may value a reputation for innovation more than they value profitability. Solving the entrepreneurial problem this way requires keeping in touch with trends and events across a wide field of view. A variety of individuals and sections in the organization bring in news of current happenings, not necessarily only the more obvious ones such as the market research or research and development departments. Growth comes from new products or services and from new markets, rather than from deeper penetration of the same market, as with a Defender. It is likely to occur in spurts, as opportunities are successfully taken up, rather than gradually. The gain to Prospectors from being open to fresh possibilities has to be balanced against the risks: that they may not be fully efficient in any one activity, and may over-extend themselves by taking on too much without sufficient recompense.

Their enterprising approach to the entrepreneurial problem requires a flexible solution to the engineering problem, so they use a variety of technologies. They do many things at once and can switch between them. Each line of work can be built up or discontinued fairly readily. There has to be trial and error work on prototypes. The gain is a flexible workforce; the cost is the difficulties of coordinating such a diversity of differing activity.

These solutions to the entrepreneurial and engineering problems are accompanied by a typical solution to the administrative problem. In the case of a Prospector, the administrative problem is how to facilitate all this activity, rather than how to control it. How can resources be deployed effectively without impeding the work by imposing inappropriately rigid central control? The answer is to plan broadly but not in detail. Skilled personnel can be relied on to know their jobs without detailed overseeing from the top. Small groups are gathered in project teams or task forces to work on new initiatives, and these, together with easy lateral contact between departments, create 'short horizontal feedback loops'. In other words, lines of communication are comparatively short. People can communicate quickly with anyone they need to contact without having to go to the top first. The structure is comparatively decentralized, and the marketing and the research and development functions are more influential than in a Defender. The advantage of this administrative solution overall is that it can respond rapidly to change, but inevitably there are risks. Some attempts to launch new products or services will be wasteful failures, costly both in capital and in the time of highly paid personnel.

Miles and Snow exemplify the Prospector strategy by relating the success of an electronics corporation. This huge enterprise, with 30,000 employees, makes and sells an extensive range of equipment, including small computers, calculators, electric meters and electrical testing equipment. Its entrepreneurial strategy is to keep one step ahead. There are frequent launches of new products with novelty value which fetch high prices. By the time prices fall, either the firm can manufacture cheaply just as its competitors have learned to, or another new launch is ready. Teams of scientists and engineers work on new possibilities, backed by the powerful marketing function whenever a new product is ready. The tendency is to create relatively autonomous divisions in each new product area. The company has a widely active and decentralized entrepreneurial, engineering and administrative pattern, quite different from the focused centralized Defender pattern.

Analysers attempt to achieve some of the strengths of both Defenders and Prospectors. They try to balance the minimizing of risk and the maximizing of profits. Their solution to the entrepreneurial problem is a mixture of stable and changing products and markets. Their stable activities generate earnings sufficient to enable them to move into innovative areas already opened up by Prospectors who have taken the early risks. The Analyser is a follower of change, not an initiator.

Since Analysers have something both of the Defender and of the Prospector entrepreneurial solutions, they are likely to have something of both engineering solutions. They are likely to have a dual technical core. That is, some of the work will be stable and routinized, while some will be shifting as new products are accepted and put into production quickly without the prolonged experimentation that a Prospector has to do. This combined solution to the engineering problem demands a corresponding dual administrative solution. There is both detailed control of stable lines and broad planning of innovations. Both production and marketing are influential, but so too, uniquely, are the personnel in applied research, since they are critical to getting new products into production. There are both central functional specialisms and also autonomous self-contained product groups.

Among examples of Analysers, Miles and Snow cite a medium-sized American general hospital. After many years of stability as a Defender, it underwent a series of changes. These were intended to enable it to offer new services already offered by more innovative hospitals while still sustaining its traditional, relatively conventional, patient care. This change in solution to its entrepreneurial problem required it to move towards Prospector-type engineering and administrative solutions. While retaining existing medical technology, it acquired modern diagnostic equipment and the technical and medical staff to go with it. Administratively, its previous unitary structure was broken down into three semi-autonomous divisions, one of which contained all the new diagnostic services and clinics. It succeeded in following others into this kind of work, and in attracting a fresh range of lower-income patients, while keeping its established higher-income clientele.

Defenders, Prospectors and Analysers have viable strategies, but *Reactors* do not. They are an unstable form. They fail to achieve or hold to an appropriate defending, prospecting or analysing strategy. As a result, they are liable merely to react to change and to do so in ways that are both inconsistent and inappropriate, so they perform poorly. This makes them hesitant over what to do next. There are many possible reasons for this condition. Miles and Snow give examples of three. Perhaps the strategy is not articulated, so that managers are not fully aware of it, as sometimes happens when a strategy pursued successfully by a firm's founder dies with him and leaves the managers in disarray, not knowing what to do without him. Perhaps, even though there is a recognized strategy, the technology and the structure do not fit, as when a publishing firm aspired to an Analyser strategy but could not separate its stable lines of work which needed careful central control from its changing lines which needed scope for trial and error. Possibly, both strategy and structure persist inappositely, as when a foods firm clung on to its long-established Defender strategy and structure even though declining profitability in a changing market pointed to the need for change.

Miles and Snow look beyond this typology of strategies to conjecture over signs of the future emergence of yet another type. This they call the *Market-Matrix* form of organization. It would 'pursue mixed strategies with mixed structures'. Some have moved towards it, from among recent kinds of organizations, such as conglomerates, multinational corporations, aerospace firms and certain educational institutions. They have matrix sections where lines of authority deliberately intersect or double up (for example where a department head also has responsibility for a major innovative project). A further step is then to expect such a project manager to bargain internally, market-fashion, for resources and for skilled personnel, the personnel having to be 'purchased' from existing departments. So a new form may be arising which is fitted to complex tasks.

Miles and Snow intend their typology to help managers determine what kind of strategy to pursue. They present a diagnostic checklist of questions on an organization's present and potential strategies to use for this purpose. Their later work emphasises that the major task facing large organizations is that of maintaining the capacity for innovation. They advocate alliances of collaborative business networks, which would enable the smaller participating units to be entrepreneurial.

BIBLIOGRAPHY

MILES, R. E., MILES, G. and SNOW, C. C., *Collaborative Entrepreneurship*, Stanford University Press, 2005.

MILES, R. E. and SNOW, C. C., *Organizational Strategy, Structure and Process*, 2nd edn, Stanford University Press, 2003.

MILES, R. E. and SNOW, C. C., 'Fit, Failure and the Hall of Fame', *California Management Review*, 26 (1984), 10–28; reprinted in D. S. Pugh (ed.), *Organization Theory*, 5th edn, Penguin, 2007.

MILES, R. E. and SNOW, C. C., *Fit, Failure and the Hall of Fame*, Free Press, 1994.

Michael T. Hannan and John H. Freeman

Michael Hannan and John Freeman are both American social scientists: Hannan at Stanford University, California and Freeman at the University of California at Berkeley. Freeman is a former editor of the journal, *Administrative Science Quarterly*.

It has been the shared aim of Hannan and Freeman to lift the view taken of organizations to a wider perspective. They have done this by looking at organizations much as a bioecologist or naturalist looks at animal life. They see populations of organizations surviving or thriving or declining in particular environments, just as populations of, say, rabbits survive or thrive in a particular ecological situation but die out in another. Just as the understanding of wildlife has been enhanced by the study of ecology, so can the understanding of organizations be enhanced. The wider ecological perspective goes beyond the problems each organization alone has in coping with the environment to see an organization as one of a population which coexists with or competes with other populations of organizations. The environment of each consists mainly of other organizations, so the existence of each is bound up with that of its own kind and of other kinds. Hence the *population ecology of organizations*.

Societies engage in many kinds of activities, and there are many different kinds of services and manufacturing organizations to do these activities. Why so many, and why does the number of different kinds rise and fall? This question is the same as 'Why are there so many species of animals?' and, for both organizations and animals, population ecology explains the replacement of outmoded forms by new forms.

Indeed, the ability of a whole society to keep up with change depends upon the development of new forms of organization. If a society contains many differing forms of organization, there is a good chance that one or more of these may fit some new circumstances which arise, and these new circumstances can then be taken advantage of quickly. If there are comparatively few forms of organization in a society, it has to adapt to change by modifying one or more of these or by creating a new form, and this takes longer. So a society that already has, among its hospitals, some which specialize in advanced surgery can readily add on heart transplant techniques; if it has only a uniform range of general hospitals dealing with the most common and cheaply treated ailments it has more difficulty in doing so.

This view assumes that populations of organizations evolve much as populations of biological species evolve. Those that fit their situation survive and thrive and those that do not die out. This is a 'Darwinian evolutionary position'. It argues that change takes place more by the growth of new forms of organization than by the intended reform of existing ones. Many theorists have pointed out that change in an organization is largely uncontrolled. Though its management may well believe that they are making changes according to plan, what happens is more haphazard than that. Differing views, unreliable information and unforeseen eventualities make it uncertain whether they will get what they want, even if they know what they want (March, Chapter 5; Thompson, earlier in this chapter). Therefore a Darwinian explanation that some forms fit the situation and prosper while others fail to fit and so decline is more tenable than supposing managements succeed in deliberately redesigning existing organizations to bring them up to date. Burns (earlier in this chapter) describes an example of this. Several well-established firms in Britain were unable to change sufficiently to move into the new field of electronics, though offered every encouragement to do so. Their form of organization was too fixed.

The evolution of populations of organizations is not necessarily a steady process. It is more likely that there are periods of rapid change as new forms are tried out, interspersed with comparative stability, during which existing forms persist. This would match contemporary views of biological evolution which regard it as 'punctuated equilibria' – long periods of comparatively balanced stability broken by shorter spasms of change. American labour unions did not grow steadily in number: there were spurts of activity at the end of the nineteenth century, again after the First World War, and again in the 1930s, when many new unions were founded. In between these peaks relatively few new ones appeared.

Hannan and Freeman concentrate on the density within each population (that is, the number of organizations of a particular form). The density of a population is determined by the number of organizations that come and go. In other words, it is determined by how many are newly founded or come in from elsewhere, and by how many cease to exist or leave to do something different.

There are limits to density. Each *niche* in an environment can support a population density up to the limit of the *carrying capacity* of that niche. When the resources of a niche are exhausted, density can rise no further. That is, when competition for money and supplies and customers, or whatever else is needed, reaches an unsustainable level, some organizations will be squeezed out. This is analogous to what happens to wildlife when numbers become too great. Those who study wildlife regard a niche for insects or animals as 'the set of environmental conditions within which a population can grow or at least sustain its numbers'. In the niches inhabited by organizations, too, there is only room for so many.

Given these assumptions about organizations, Hannan and Freeman consider first how fast new organizations in a population are founded (the rate of founding), and then how fast they die out (the rate of disbanding).

Consider *founding*. The fact that there are a growing number of a particular form of organization relative to the capacity of an environmental niche does not necessarily stop new entrants. Indeed Hannan and Freeman contend that at first the rate of founding increases as density increases. The more there are, the more new ones attempt to get in. This is because a high density means more of that form of organizations are around, so people become accustomed to them. Their existence is less likely to be questioned. They acquire greater legitimacy, as labour unions did after precarious early years when their right to exist was challenged. Further, the rate of new foundings may increase as total numbers grow also because there are more and more people who have experience of the way to set up such an organization. The know-how is available. But there comes that level at which the niche can take no more, the level at which some are being squeezed out, and then launching new ones is no longer attractive. Then the rate of founding falls. So Hannan and Freeman argue that, as the total number of organizations of a given form grows, first there are more new entrants and then there are fewer, because 'density increases legitimacy at a decreasing rate' but 'increases competition at an increasing rate'. If foundings are plotted against density, there should be an inverted U-shape.

This is shown in the US in populations of organizations as different as labour unions, newspapers and semiconductor electronics firms. The history of unions and newspapers shows the patterns of first a rise and then a fall in foundings, while total numbers (density) increase, the pattern originating far back in the nineteenth century. Electronics is a much more recent and volatile population of the mid-twentieth century. Here density increased rapidly as firms rushed to join this new industry, and so competition forced down the rate of entry to the industry much more quickly than was the case with the unions and newspapers.

Disbanding, or 'mortality', is held to be the other way around. As the total number of organizations in a population grows, there are first fewer disbandings and then more. Of course, the number of disbandings, the fatalities in a population through closures or withdrawals from their field, may actually start quite high for the same reason that foundings start low, because legitimacy and know-how are hard to get when few of a kind exist. But the rate of disbandings soon drops as survival becomes easier, and so there are fewer and fewer disbandings, and more and more survivors. Once again, however, when density reaches a level where the niche can support no more, the trend changes. It swings round from a falling rate of disbandings to an increased rate. Competition forces organizations out, and the number of disbanding begins to rise and may go on rising as long as density goes on rising.

Plotting disbandings against density should produce a U-shaped curve. So indeed it did for the unions, newspapers and electronics populations. The rate of disbanding dropped sharply for all three as their total numbers increased, and then rose again under the pressure of competition. But the force of competitive pressure appeared to differ. It seemed weaker for newspapers, stronger for electronics firms and strongest for unions, which squeezed each other out more and more once the critical density of union population was reached. The existence of a large number of craft unions, with members from the same occupations in many industries, seemed detrimental, especially to industrial unions with members from many occupations in a single industry, for as the density of craft unions rose, so too did the disbanding of industrial unions.

Disbandings are also influenced by age and size of organization. Hannan and Freeman do not agree with assertions that modern organizations are (or should be) in a state of constant flux and innovation. As they see it, organizations persist because of their reliability in outputs of goods and services and their accountability for the use of resources, each of which increases with institutionalization and stability. So the stability of age improves the chances of survival, despite the inertia that ageing can bring. There are fewer disbandings in populations of older organizations. Older unions and older firms are less likely to close down or merge than are younger ones.

Growth, too, improves the chances. Although bigger organizations similarly may have greater structural inertia, they have the resources to withstand shocks from their environments. 'Small organizations are more likely than large ones to attempt change, but are more likely to disappear in the process.'

Within populations, sub-populations are found to respond differently to different environmental niche conditions. Thus among both restaurants and semiconductor firms, generalists (with a relatively wide range of services or products) are found to do better under variable conditions. Specialists (with a narrower range) do better in stable cyclical conditions, called 'coarse-grained environments' (where there are known long-term business cycles). In further work Hannan and his colleague Glenn Carroll show that these characteristics also apply to other niches. These include the American brewing and banking industries and the population of newspapers in both Argentina and Ireland.

As applied to organizations by Hannan and Freeman, population ecology theory questions the usefulness of the efforts commonly made to reform existing organizations as managements attempt to keep up with change. It implies that populations of organizations change more effectively by selection and replacement than by adaptation. To effect change, start a new organization.

Here population ecology theory becomes practical, for potentially it can show whether 'the dice are loaded for or against a particular way of doing business'. There is no best form of organization, but many forms for many niches.

BIBLIOGRAPHY

HANNAN, M. T. and CARROLL, G. R., *Dynamics of Organizational Populations*, Oxford University Press, 1992.

HANNAN, M. T. and FREEMAN, J., 'The Population Ecology of Organizations', *American Journal of Sociology*, 82 (1977), 929–964. Reprinted in D. S. Pugh (ed.) *Organization Theory*, 5th edn, Penguin, 2007.

HANNAN, M. T., and FREEMAN, J., *Organizational Ecology*, Harvard University Press, 1989.

Geert Hofstede

Geert Hofstede is a social psychologist who, until his retirement, was Professor of Organizational Anthropology and International Management at the University of Maastricht, the Netherlands, and Director of the Institute for Research on Inter-Cultural Cooperation there. In the early 1970s he and his colleagues carried out a major systematic study of work-related attitudes based on two questionnaire surveys, which produced a total of over 116,000 questionnaires from over 70 countries around the world, making it by far the largest organizationally based study ever to have been carried out.

Those respondents whose replies were used by Hofstede for research purposes were all sales and service employers of subsidiaries of IBM, a US-based multinational corporation which operates in most countries in the world. Within the sales and service function all types of employees were surveyed – sales clerks, professional engineers, top managers, and so on – using the language of each country. A total of 20 different language versions of the questionnaire had to be made. The IBM employees represented well-matched subsets from each country: same company, job and education but different nationalities. National cultural differences found within the company, therefore, are likely to be a conservative estimate of those existing within the countries at large. The survey was repeated after four years with stable results, underlining the persistent cultural nature of the differences found.

Hofstede identifies four basic dimensions of the differences between national cultures based on the 40 larger subsidiaries on which the first analyses were made. Each of the national cultures can be positioned from high to low on each of the four scales, and thus has a distinctive cultural profile. The four dimensions are:

1. power distance
2. uncertainty avoidance
3. individualism
4. masculinity.

The *power distance dimension* is concerned with how close or how distant subordinates feel from their superiors. This is not physical distance, but how big the personal gap is felt to be. In a high power distance culture (for example France, India) being a boss means exerting power and keeping that gap open. Inequality is accepted: 'a place for everyone and everyone in their place'. So employees are frequently reluctant to express disagreement with their bosses and prefer to work for managers who take the decisions – and the responsibility – and then simply tell them what to do.

In a low power distance culture (for example Austria, Israel) superiors and subordinates consider each other to be colleagues, and both believe that inequalities in society should be minimized. So those in power should try to look less powerful than they are. Employees are seldom afraid to disagree and expect to be consulted before decisions are made.

The *uncertainty avoidance dimension* is the ease with which the culture copes with novelty. In strong uncertainty avoidance cultures (for example Japan, Greece) people feel the need for clarity and order. They feel threatened by uncertain situations, and higher anxiety and stress are experienced. This is combated by hard work, career stability and intolerance of deviancy. Thus employees believe that company rules should not be broken – even when to do so is shown to be in the company's best interest – and look forward to continue working with the firm until they retire.

In a weak uncertainty avoidance culture (for example Denmark, Hong Kong) the uncertainty inherent in life is more easily accepted and each day is taken as it comes. A very pragmatic view is taken about keeping or changing those rules which are in existence, and employees expect to be working for the firm for much shorter periods.

The *individualism dimension* focuses on the degree to which the culture encourages individual as opposed to collectivist, group-centred concerns. In an individualist culture (for example USA, Britain) the emphasis is on personal initiative and achievement, and everyone has the right to a private life and opinion. By contrast, a collectivist culture (for example Iran, Peru) is characterized by a tighter social framework, where people are members of extended families or clans which protect them in exchange for loyalty. Careers are pursued to increase standing in the family by being able to help other members of it. The emphasis is on belonging and the aim is to be a good member, whereas in the individualist culture the ideal is to be a good leader.

The *masculinity dimension* highlights masculine cultures (for example Australia, Italy) where performance is what counts; money and material standards are important, ambition is the driving force. Big and fast are beautiful; machismo is sexy. In contrast, in feminine cultures (for example the Netherlands, Sweden) it is the quality of life that matters: people and the environment are important, service provides the motivation, small is beautiful and unisex is attractive. The expected relationship of men to women differs considerably along this dimension. In masculine cultures the sex roles are clearly differentiated: men should be assertive, dominating; women should be caring, nurturing. In feminine cultures the sex roles are more flexible, and there is a belief in equality between the sexes. It is not unmasculine for a man to take a caring role, for example.

Equipped with measurements which locate the 40 cultures along the four dimensions, Hofstede then offers a set of cultural maps of the world. Two points should be remembered in interpreting the results. The first is that countries spread along the whole of each of the four dimensions, not only at the extremes. So cultures are not only masculine like Italy or feminine like Sweden; there are also many countries in between: Belgium exactly in the centre, Britain on the masculine side, France on the feminine one.

The second point to remember is that the position of a culture along a dimension is based on the averages for all the respondents in that particular country. Characterizing a national work culture does not mean that every person in the nation has all the characteristics ascribed to that culture – there are bound to be many individual variations. There are, for example, many Japanese who are risk-takers and many from Hong Kong who avoid uncertainty; many Indians with low power distance values and many Israelis with high power-distance attitudes. What these scales are doing is describing the common values of the central core of the culture which come about through the 'collective mental programming' of a number of people (a tribe, a nation or a national minority) who are conditioned by the same life experience and the same education. Although this will not make everybody the same, a country's nationals do share a cultural character, which is, indeed, more clearly visible to foreigners than to themselves.

The table on page 95 gives a classification of the nations grouped by cultural similarity according to the statistical technique of cluster analysis. They fall into eight areas. Since a culture's work-related values are so distinctive and different, it is to be expected that its organizational processes and behaviour would be so too. So Hofstede argues very strongly that we should not expect the same conceptions and prescriptions about management to be appropriate for all culture areas.

Some years later, Hofstede joined Michael Bond, a Canadian social psychologist working in Hong Kong, in research which added a fifth dimension to the previous four. Bond, realizing that most questionnaires have questions devised by Westerners, as did Hofstede's IBM surveys, investigated what would happen if the questions were developed by Asians. He asked Chinese social scientists in Hong Kong and Taiwan to define some Chinese cultural values. From these a questionnaire was made up in Chinese and then translated into English and other languages – the other way round from the usual practice. The questionnaire was given to matched sets of students in different countries, East and West.

The most compelling finding was that three of the dimensions obtained were compatible with those found previously. Power-distance, individualism and masculinity again differentiated among the national groups. The most distinctive finding was that a new dimension replaced Hofstede's, possibly Western-biased, uncertainty-avoidance. It distinguishes cultures in which persistence, thrift and a firm status order in society, plus a keen sense of shame, are much more important than are respect for tradition, saving face socially, personal steadiness and mutual honouring of favours and gifts. In so far as what is most important is more forward-looking, Bond called this Eastern-oriented characteristic 'Confucian dynamism'. Hofstede subsequently preferred to call it 'long-term versus short-term orientation'.

Remarkably, all the most vigorous Asian economies – Japan, Taiwan, South Korea, Hong Kong, Singapore and China itself – were high in Confucian dynamism, that is, had a long-term orientation. Could this element in the cultures of their peoples partly explain their economic success, much as the so-called Protestant work ethic of earlier centuries in the West has been held to partly explain the Industrial Revolution (see Weber, Chapter 1)?

Country Clusters and their Characteristics

I: More developed Latin *high power distance* *high uncertainty avoidance* *medium to high individualism* *medium masculinity*	II: Less developed Latin: *high power distance* *high uncertainty avoidance* *low individualism* *whole range on masculinity*	
BELGIUM FRANCE ARGENTINA BRAZIL SPAIN (ITALY)	COLOMBIA MEXICO VENEZUELA CHILE PERU PORTUGAL	
III: More developed Asian medium power distance high uncertainty-avoidance medium individualism high masculinity	*IV: Less developed Asian* high power distance low to medium uncertainty avoidance low individualism medium masculinity	*V: Near Eastern* high power distance high uncertainty avoidance low individualism medium masculinity
JAPAN	PAKISTAN TAIWAN THAILAND HONG KONG INDIA PHILIPPINES SINGAPORE	GREECE IRAN TURKEY (YUGOSLAVIA)

VI: Germanic
low power distance
medium to high
    uncertainty avoidance
medium individualism
medium to high
    masculinity
	VII: Anglo
	low to medium power
	    distance
	low to medium uncertainty
	    avoidance
	high individualism
	high masculinity
		VIII: Nordic
		low power distance
		low to medium uncertainty
		    avoidance
		medium to high
		    individualism
		low masculinity

AUSTRIA ISRAEL GERMANY SWITZERLAND	AUSTRALIA CANADA BRITAIN IRELAND NEW ZEALAND USA (SOUTH AFRICA)	DENMARK FINLAND NETHERLANDS NORWAY SWEDEN

Source: Hofstede (1980).

Hofstede illustrates the difficulties of applying management practices insensitively in very different cultures by what befell an American idea when attempts were made to introduce it elsewhere. 'Management by Objectives' (MbO) started in the USA (see Drucker, Chapter 4) and has had most success there, particularly in situations where the manager's results can be objectively measured. Why is this so? MbO requires that:

1. subordinates are sufficiently independent to negotiate meaningfully with the boss (that is, low power distance);
2. both are willing to take some risks – the boss in delegating power, the subordinate in accepting responsibility (that is, low uncertainty-avoidance);
3. the subordinate is personally willing to have a go and make a mark (that is, high individualism);
4. both regard performance and results achieved as important (that is, high masculinity).

This is the Anglo work-culture pattern, as the table shows.

But how would MbO work out in other culture areas? For example, the Germanic culture area has low power distance which fits, as do the results orientation of high masculinity. However, the Germanic group is high on uncertainty avoidance which would work against the risk-taking and ambiguity involved in the Anglo process. But the idea of replacing the arbitrary authority of the boss with the impersonal authority of mutually agreed objectives fits well in this culture. This is, indeed, the way MbO has developed in Germany, emphasizing the need to develop procedures of a more participative kind. The German name for MbO is 'Management by Joint Goal Setting', and elaborate formal systems have been developed. There is also great stress on team objectives (as opposed to the individual emphasis in the Anglo culture) and this fits in with the lower individualism of this culture area.

The more developed Latin group, as represented by France, has high power distance and high uncertainty avoidance, completely the opposite of the Anglo group, so MbO is bound to encounter difficulties there. It did gain some popularity in France for a time, but it was not sustained. The problem was that, in a high power distance culture, attempting to replace the personal authority of the boss with self-monitored objectives is bound to generate anxiety. The boss does not delegate easily and will not hesitate to short-circuit intermediate hierarchical levels if necessary – and subordinates will expect this to happen and to be told what to do. And in a high uncertainty-avoidance culture, anxiety will be alleviated by sticking to the old ways.

Cultural differences, then, have an important impact on the way organizations function, and manufacturing cars or treating the sick will call for different structures and processes in France or Japan or Britain. So it is important even for international organizations to have a dominant national culture to fall back on (as with the American or Japanese multinationals). Organizations without a home culture, in which the key decision makers can come from any country (for example UNESCO, the EU Commission), find it very difficult to function effectively because of this lack.

It is less of a problem for the political part of such organizations, since negotiation between representatives is their task. But for the administrative apparatus, where the members represent not their countries but the organizations as a whole, it is crippling – and most such cultureless organizations are inefficient and wasteful.

BIBLIOGRAPHY

HOFSTEDE, G., *Culture's Consequences*, Sage Publications, 1980; 2nd edn, 2001.
HOFSTEDE, G., 'Motivation, Leadership and Organization: Do American Theories Apply Abroad?, *Organizational Dynamics* (Summer, 1980), 42–63; reprinted in D. S. Pugh (ed.), *Organization Theory*, 5th edn, Penguin, 2007.
HOFSTEDE, G., *Cultures and Organizations: Software of the Mind*, McGraw-Hill, 1991.

Richard Whitley

For many years, Richard Whitley has been Professor of Organizational Sociology at the Manchester Business School, England. His first research work was on the sociology of how the natural and social sciences are organized and controlled. His current extensive work examines business structures in many countries, and relates them to the societal institutions in which they operate.

Whitley argues that despite globalization, divergent forms of capitalistic enterprises are persisting, arising as they do from differing national social and economic systems. The prevailing institutions in each society shape how capital and skills are owned and used; shape therefore the kind of capitalism that results. So globalization is not obliterating national differences. The idea that a single form of capitalism will override all others is rejected and a comparison made of the various kinds of firms and business systems that have arisen in different countries using what he terms the 'comparative business systems' approach.

A 'business system' is the aggregate of the relationships between all those institutions involved in business transactions. These include: providers and users of capital, customers and suppliers, competitors, firms in different sectors, and employers and employees. How all these do, or do not, interact makes up the system. Thus, owner control can be direct as in owner-managed firms, or be delegated by shareholders to managers. Between customer and supplier firms there can be one-off market bargains, or more cooperative arrangements with mutual obligations to buy and supply over an indefinite period. Competitors may be adversarial or collaborative in, say, negotiations with unions. Firms in different industries make differing kinds of alliances. Between employers and employees there can be out-and-out conflicts, or forms of cooperation (as in German employee representation) or interdependence in which each relies on the other (as with long-term core workers in Japan). The resultant varying patterns of control and coordination typify different business systems.

Whitley identifies six such business systems, each in the institutional setting that fosters it. They are: fragmented, coordinated industrial districts, compartmentalized, state organized, collaborative and highly coordinated.

In a *fragmented* system small owner-managed firms compete in adversarial mode, making short-term contracts with both suppliers and customers. Commitment to these suppliers and contractors, and to employees, is low. Hong Kong exemplified this when small Chinese-owned firms moved rapidly from making plastic flowers to toys to property development as markets changed. Such a system develops in low trust cultures where confidence in other firms or sources of funds or public regulation is lacking, and the state is, at best, neutral.

Small owner-managed firms also feature in *coordinated industrial districts* but there is greater employer–employee commitment, and firms are often linked in production chains where part-finished goods are passed on to another with mutual confidence. This kind of localized business system is exemplified in various European regions, such as in the industrial districts of northern Italy. It develops where local governments, local banks and local unions work with craftsmen entrepreneurs to moderate competition and promote a quality reputation.

A *compartmentalized* business system is composed of much larger units with diversified activities over different production chains and markets. Collaboration between these firms is minimal, as is employer–employee commitment. Owner control is not managerial but financial, at arm's length. Firms are islands of controlled activity amid market disorder. The state arranges the minimum regulation needed by fluid impersonal financial and labour markets. In such a relatively impoverished institutional infrastructure, relationships are typically adversarial. A prime example is the United States.

This is in sharp contrast to *state organized* business systems. Although in these there is a similar domination by widespread large firms, the firms are usually directly personally controlled by families or partners, who are supported by the state with cheap credit and probably a protected domestic market. With firms dependent on state agencies and officials, the state can closely guide economic development. This institutional context and form of business system is the basis for the growth of the *chaebol* business form of South Korea.

Where large firms have more alliances and other forms of cooperation, usually within a market sector rather than across sectors, *collaborative* business systems arise. There is greater employer–employee interdependence, and reliance on trained and trusted skilled workers. The state provides a supportive institutional framework and usually protective market regulation for this kind of system which is typical for countries on the European continent.

In *highly coordinated* business systems, the activities of firms are coordinated by state involvement as well as by inter-firm alliances. In addition, financial institutions such as banks, which provide most of the capital, are effectively locked in to firms by their investments and so play a part in major decisions. The links of both with the state give rise to a 'corporatist' form of mutual coordination, which includes strong unions that join in regulating labour markets to encourage employer investment in employee skills. There is paternalism as well as contractual authority. This kind of business system developed in post-Second World War Japan.

Having described the six kinds of business systems that are likely in different institutional settings, the part played by the state (or not played, as the case may be) being especially significant, Whitley identifies the kinds of firms that are likely in such settings. He names five types, the opportunistic, the artisanal, the isolated hierarchy, the cooperative hierarchy and the allied hierarchy. There is no one-to-one correspondence between business system and type of firm, but certain business systems are most likely to give rise to particular types of firm. The business system broadly indicates what type of firm to expect, even though many actual firms may not accord exactly with the characteristic type.

In a highly adversarial environment, where the state stands back, where market regulation is minimal and unions are weak, and there is little trust in formal institutions, the first type of firm, the *opportunistic*, is likely. Their owners of such firms take advantage of the unfettered situation to seize any business opportunity that may increase their personal wealth. The Chinese family businesses which have flourished in Asia in fragmented business systems outside Communist China are characteristic.

A more supportive environment is more likely to give rise to *artisanal* firms. In this relatively trusting environment the state, nationally or locally, fosters inter-firm cooperation in financing and marketing, with public systems of worker training and some domestic market protection. This kind of situation found in Denmark and also in the coordinated industrial districts of Italy has resulted in firms where highly skilled artisans turn out high quality and innovative products.

An adversarial, rather than supportive environment, is not necessarily inhabited only by opportunistic firms. If there is confidence in financial institutions and the legal framework, then *isolated hierarchy* firms are more likely. Owner control is merely financial and aims at short-term returns, and manager–worker relationships are impersonally market-based. This sort of firm is commonplace in the compartmentalized business systems of the Anglo-Saxon economies.

Cooperative hierarchy firms are characteristic where the state itself supports inter-firm relationships. It may protectively regulate markets, and back financial credit. The firms that develop share their risks by collaborating with banks and competitor firms, improve employee skills, and aim for stable growth rather than immediate profitability. These are the firms of collaborative business systems, as in some European nations such as Germany.

Finally, *allied hierarchy* firms develop where institutions encourage links between them. Allied through industry associations, cartels, mutual shareholdings and state coordination of investment in new technology, in protected markets, such firms are even more interdependent than are cooperative hierarchy firms. Unions are enterprise-based rather than representative of occupations across firms, so that management can deploy employees flexibly. Such firms are typical of the highly coordinated business systems in Japan.

Whitley has used the comparative business systems approach to analyse in detail the institutional settings of a number of regions such as Asia and eastern Europe and to explore the concomitant business systems they engender. For example, in examining East Asia he compares South Korea and Taiwan.

Just as there are many varieties of Western capitalism, so there are varieties of Asian capitalism. The identifying feature of the South Korean business system is the *chaebol*, as mentioned earlier. The names of leading *chaebol* such as Daewoo, Hyundai and Samsung are familiar worldwide. They are large, widely diversified corporations, which have grown rapidly to dominate Korean business and exports. They are mostly family owned and personally controlled, senior positions being held by family members or trusted personal associates. It is said that for three decades the founder of Samsung was present at every interviewing of candidates for jobs, many thousands of interviews all told. This demonstrates, in an extreme way, the patriarchal, not to say authoritarian, control from the top. Relationships between *chaebol* are competitive, and they dominate their relatively small supplier and customer firms. In the Korean business system, employer–employee relations lack trust and commitment, at least compared to what they can be like in another Asian country, Japan.

By comparison, while the Taiwanese business system also has large dominant corporations, they are not the same in either ownership or activity. They are state owned, and concentrated in the basic industries of power, petroleum, mining, chemicals, steel and engineering, banks and insurance. There is thus state ownership of capital intensive industry and financial institutions. Beyond that there are the comparatively small family owned and run firms typical of Chinese business in the many countries outside mainland China where they flourish – 'opportunistic firms' as Whitley calls them. Among these, inter-firm business links usually rest on personal relationships with other family members, school fellows and the like.

So the South Korean and Taiwanese systems are very similar in this prevalence of the patrimonial family, and low trust outside its networks, but where they differ most obviously is in the role of the state. The South Korean state has protected the *chaebol* and acquiesced in their domination of the smaller firms, whereas the state in Taiwan directly owns the large corporations but then leaves greater freedom in the rest of the economy.

These characteristics of the two national systems are not accidental. They are due to past and present *institutional features* in the two societies. In both pre-industrial Korea and pre-industrial China, then including Taiwan, the position of the family and its head was paramount. The consonant patriarchal and authoritarian rule through the centuries was reinforced by long periods of Japanese colonial rule, ending with the Second World War. Hence the similarly assertive governance of both countries, and the state control of organized labour, together with the family ownership of business.

However, at the end of the 1950s war South Korea lost such industry as there was to Communist North Korea. The military-backed regime in the South, fearful of the Communist North, supported the family controlled *chaebol* as the means to fast industrialization. What happened in Taiwan, however, was different. The Kuomintang party rulers of China, finally defeated by Communist armies in 1948, fled to the island. They became a superimposed outsider military regime which kept direct control of the principal industries for fear of armed attack from without or within, and was relatively aloof from native Taiwanese business.

Thus both the divergences and similarities between South Korea and Taiwan can be explained in terms of institutional histories. Their business systems continue to be distinctive despite the increased volume of their international trade and foreign investment.

South Korea and Taiwan are just two examples of differences in business systems around the globe which challenge the facile view of globalization. Whitley is sceptical about the impact of globalization on business systems. He rejects the view that a new global economy based on global capital markets and transnational firms is transcending national economies and national firms, and leading to greater uniformity in business systems in firms and in management everywhere. He points out that international trade (and competition) has not increased in the way it is widely supposed to have done. Although its volume has increased absolutely, it has not increased as a proportion of total economic activity as measured by GDP, gross domestic product. Most Western economies are no more dependent on external trade now than they were a century ago. The same is true for FDI, foreign direct investment. For most richer countries this is no greater a proportion of total investment than it was then, and remains relatively small, even though it too has increased in absolute terms. And like investors who hold mainly domestic securities, most firms most of the time, even when they do go outside their own national boundaries, prefer to operate close to home, no further than neighbouring countries.

Nor are all businesses readily homing in on a uniform best practice. When attempts are made to imitate what is seen as best practice in foreign competitors, this usually has to be modified considerably to fit into the domestic situation, which therefore remains distinctive. Multinational corporations (MNCs) could be the main agencies of converging change, but even their impact is limited. They are often holding companies controlling subsidiaries by financial targets as much as or more than by direct management. Differing local practices therefore continue within them. In the reverse direction, these local ways rarely get transferred back to the MNC home corporation to erode its distinctiveness, because they do not fit. National business systems are fundamental in this, and affect the outcome. For example, the chance that Japanese firms can install their management practices in their subsidiaries in the compartmentalized and weakly coordinated business system in Britain is much higher than any chance British firms might have of transferring their practices into the highly coordinated Japanese system.

Even in the European Union, where there are considerable attempts to establish supra-national regulations of, say, competition and employment, these have not yet resulted in distinctive transnational European firms different from nationally based ones. An exception to this general argument that Whitley recognizes is where investment in a newly industrializing country, such as those in South East Asia or Africa, is predominantly from a former colonial power. This does take with it the business system and management typical of that power, which are already familiar to the erstwhile colony.

But basically there is a marked tenacity of national institutional arrangements and national business systems. Though firms do alter when they go international, these are unlikely to be radical changes. Even if adaptations do occur, they will be different in different institutional settings. Hence 'globalization has been less significant in its scale and consequences than some enthusiasts have claimed'. Since societies are significantly different, so then are their capitalist operations, and so will they continue to be.

BIBLIOGRAPHY

WHITLEY, R., *Business Systems in East Asia: Firms, Markets and Societies*, Sage, 1992.
WHITLEY, R., *Divergent Capitalisms: The Social Structuring and Change of Business Systems*, Oxford University Press, 1999.

3 The Functioning of Organizations

The cooperative system is incessantly dynamic, a process of continual readjustment to physical, biological and social environments as a whole.
CHESTER I. BARNARD

People move in the course of their daily work from a role in one system to a different role in another system; it is essential that this be recognized and that behaviour appropriate to the role be adopted if trouble is to be avoided.
WILFRED BROWN

I hope not for greater efficiency in our problem-solving but for better understanding of our problem setting.
SIR GEOFFREY VICKERS

If modification of the organization is involved, an understanding of the structure and dynamics of the thing acted upon is essential so that the chain reaction of change in one part coursing through other parts can be calculated.
E. WIGHT BAKKE

Most organizations most of the time cannot rely on their participants to carry out their assignments voluntarily.
AMITAI ETZIONI

By beginning from, and attempting to make sense of, the definition of the situation held by the actors, the Action perspective provides a means of understanding the range of reactions to apparently 'identical' social situations.
DAVID SILVERMAN

Is it surprising that prisons resemble factories, schools, barracks, hospitals, which all resemble prisons?
MICHEL FOUCAULT

Work expands to fill the time available for its completion.
C. NORTHCOTE PARKINSON

In a hierarchy every employee tends to rise to his level of incompetence.
LAURENCE J. PETER

Accepting the likelihood of a number of different types of organizations, as writers on structure suggest, is it feasible to think of analysing their activities? Is it possible to break down into categories what an organization does? Several theoretical schemes have been proposed for this purpose applicable both to industrial enterprises and, more generally, to all organizations. Their originators take the view that some common classification is essential to bring order to the thoughts of those who try to understand organizations.

Attempts to develop such unified analyses of organizational functioning, using differing but widely applicable concepts, have been offered by both managers and academics. Three top managers, Chester I. Barnard, Wilfred Brown and Sir Geoffrey Vickers, have put forward analyses based on their long experience of and personal insight into working at the top of organizations. E. Wight Bakke, Amitai Etzioni and David Silverman are three academics who propose broad conceptualizations of different facets of organizational activity based on sociological research. Michel Foucault explores the methods by which those at the top of organizations, and of society, maintain their control.

In the sub-section on Organizational Practices, C. Northcote Parkinson and Lawrence J. Peter amusingly but insightfully highlight certain practices of which organizations must be aware if they are to function efficiently.

Chester I. Barnard

Chester I. Barnard (1886–1961) was for many years President of the New Jersey Bell Telephone Company. On two occasions he was seconded for duty as State Director of the New Jersey Relief Administration, a government organization that allowed him many opportunities for contrasting the functioning of an established organization with one created ad hoc under conditions of stress. During the Second World War he developed and managed the United Service Organizations, Inc. As a practising top manager he had a continuing interest in describing organizational activities and the social and personal relationships between the people involved. This culminated in his classic book *The Functions of the Executive*, first published in 1938. His selected papers have also been published under the title *Organization and Management*.

Barnard begins his analysis from the premise that individuals must cooperate. This is because human beings have only a limited power of choice. They are confined partly by the situations in which they act, and partly by the biological restrictions of their nature. The most effective way of overcoming these limitations is cooperative social action. This requires that people adopt a group or non-personal purpose and take into consideration the processes of interaction. The persistence of cooperation depends on its effectiveness in accomplishing the cooperative purpose and also on its efficiency in satisfying the individual's motives.

A formal organization for Barnard is a 'system of consciously coordinated activities or forces of two or more persons'. This definition, and the analysis based on it, can be applied to all forms of organization: the state, the church, the factory, the family. An organization comes into being when '(i) there are persons able to communicate with each other (ii) who are willing to contribute action (iii) to accomplish a common purpose'. Willingness to *contribute action* in this context means the surrender of the control of personal conduct in order to achieve coordination. Clearly the commitment of particular persons to do this will vary from maximum willingness through a neutral point to opposition or hatred. Indeed Barnard maintains that, in modern society, the commitment of the majority of possible contributors to any given organization will lie on the negative side. Equally important, the commitment of any individual will fluctuate, and thus the total willingness of all contributors to cooperate in any formal system is unstable – a fact which is evident from the history of all such organizations. Willingness to cooperate is the result of the satisfactions or dissatisfactions obtained, and every organization depends upon the essentially subjective assessment of these made by its members.

All organizations have a *purpose*, but this does not produce cooperative activity unless it is accepted by members. A purpose thus has both a cooperative and a subjective aspect. The subjective aspect is not what the purpose means to the individual, but rather what the individual thinks it means to the organization as a whole. Thus workers will carry out a disagreeable job if they can accept it as relevant to the aims of the whole organization and their part in it.

The essential basis for cooperative action is a cooperative purpose which is believed by the contributors to be that of the organization. 'The inculcation of belief in the real existence of a common purpose is an essential executive function.' The continuance of an organization depends on its ability to carry out its purpose, but there is the paradox that it destroys itself by accomplishing its objectives, as is shown by the large number of successful organizations which disappear through failure to update their objectives. To continue, organizations require the repeated adoption of new purposes. This process is often concealed by stating a generalized purpose which appears not to change; for example giving a service, making motor cars. But the real purpose is not 'service' as an abstraction, but specific acts of service; not making motor cars in general, but making specific motor cars from day to day.

The other essential for a formal organization is *communication*, linking the common purpose with those willing to cooperate in achieving it. Communication is necessary to translate purpose into action. The methods of communication are firstly language – oral and written – and, secondly, 'observational feeling'. This is the ability to understand, without words, not merely the situation but also the intention. It results from special experience and training as well as continuity in association, which leads the members of an organization to develop common perceptions and reactions to particular situations.

Large organizations are made up of numbers of basic units. These units are small – from two to 15 persons – and are restricted in their growth by the limitations of intercommunication. The size of a unit depends on the complexity of its purpose and the technological conditions for action, the difficulty of the communication process, the extent to which communication is necessary, and the complexity of the personal relationships involved. These last increase with great rapidity as the number of persons in the unit group increases. Moreover, groups are related to each other. As the number of possible groups increases, the complexity of group relationships increases exponentially.

Interactions between persons which are based on personal rather than joint or common purposes will, because of their repetitive character, become systematic and organized. This will become the informal organization, which will have an important effect on the thought and action of members. Barnard envisages a continual interaction between formal and informal organization. To be effective, an informal organization – particularly if it is of any size – must give rise to a formal organization, which makes explicit many of its attitudes and institutions. Once established, formal organizations must create informal organizations if they are to operate effectively both as a means of communication and cohesion and as a way of protecting the integrity of the individual against domination by the formal organization. This last function may seem to operate against the aims of the formal organization, but is in fact vital to it. For it is by giving individuals a sphere where they are able to exercise personal choice and not have decisions dominated by the impersonal objectives of the formal organization that the personalities of individuals are safeguarded and their continuing effective contribution to the formal organization made more likely.

On the basis of his analysis of organizational functioning, Barnard describes the functions of the executive. The members of the executive organization are contributors to two units in a complex organization – a basic working unit and an executive unit. Thus a foreman is regarded as a member of a shop group as well as of the department management group; an army captain is a member of the company and of the 'regimental organization'. Under such conditions a single action is an activity inherent to two different unit organizations. It is this simultaneous contribution which makes the complex organization into an organic whole.

It is important to recognize that not all work carried out by the executive is executive work. Executive work is 'the specialized work of maintaining the organization in operation' and consists of three tasks:

1. the maintenance of organizational communication;
2. the securing of essential services from individuals;
3. the formulation of purpose and objectives.

The task of *communication* has two phases: the first is the definition of organizational positions – the 'scheme of organization'. This requires organization charts, specification of duties and the like, representing a coordination of the work to be done. But the scheme of organization is of little value without the personnel to fill positions. The second phase of the task of communication is the recruiting of contributors who have the appropriate qualifications. But both phases are dependent on each other. 'Men are neither good nor bad but only good or bad in this or that position.' Thus often the scheme of organization has to be changed to take account of the staff available.

The informal executive organization has the function of expanding the means of communication and thus reducing the need for formal decisions. The issuing of formal decisions, except for routine matters and for emergencies, is unnecessary with a good informal organization. In this situation, a formal order is the recognition that agreement has been obtained on a decision by informal means. It is part of the art of leadership to eschew conflict in formal order-giving by issuing only those formal orders which are acceptable. Disagreements must be dealt with by informal means.

The task of *securing the essential services* from individuals has two main divisions: bringing persons into cooperative relationship with the organization, and eliciting the services of such people. Both are achieved by sustaining morale, and by maintaining schemes of incentives, deterrents, supervision and control, and education and training.

The third executive task is the *formulation of the purposes* of the organization. The critical aspect here is 'the assignment of responsibility – the delegation of objective authority'. Responsibility for abstract long-term decisions on purpose lies with the executive organization, but responsibility for action remains at the base. The definition of purpose in particular situations is a widely distributed function; hence there is a need to indoctrinate those at lower levels with general purposes and major decisions if the organization is to be a cohesive organic whole.

As a practising manager in industry and in public service, Barnard combined a thorough knowledge of the workings of organizations with a wide reading of sociology. As a result his work has had a great impact on the thinking both of managers and of academics.

BIBLIOGRAPHY

BARNARD, C. I., *The Functions of the Executive*, Harvard University Press, 1938.
BARNARD, C. I., *Organization and Management*, Harvard University Press, 1948.

Wilfred Brown

For over 20 years Wilfred (later Lord) Brown (1908–1985) was Chairman of the Glacier Metal Company and also Managing Director for most of that time. He later became a government minister and entered the House of Lords. The Glacier Metal Company, which manufactured bearings, was the subject of an important set of studies of management processes conducted by Elliott Jaques and the Tavistock Institute (see Chapter 1). Wilfred Brown thus had both long experience as a practising manager and a longstanding acquaintance with social research. His ideas are derived from his own experience and he does not claim that they are necessarily appropriate outside the engineering industry. Nonetheless, he argues that: 'The absence of a language, concepts and a general theory of administration is a serious impediment to the efficiency of industry.' He himself aims at clarifying what he believes happens in organizations.

Brown breaks away from the kind of analysis initiated by Fayol (see Chapter 4) which describes management as a mixture of elements such as forecasting, planning and organizing. Brown is less concerned with the nature of a manager's activities as such than with the social organization or set of social systems through which the manager works. His fundamental tenet is that a conscious recognition of these social systems will promote good management.

Brown proceeds to distinguish three social systems whose structures, taken together, comprise the organization of a company: the Executive System, the Representative System and the Legislative System.

The *Executive System* is the structure of roles more commonly referred to as the organization chart or hierarchy (including operators, clerks and so on, as well as managers or executives). It exists irrespective of people. Individuals may come and go, but the role does not disappear. New roles can be added to the system before any thought is given to who should fill them. The work content of roles can increase or decrease in importance without the persons in the roles changing their personal capacity to do the work. Because this social structure exists as an entity in itself, it can be consciously thought about and altered.

Brown contends 'that there seems to be quite a considerable tendency to construe all problems in industry in terms of the personal behaviour of people, and to exclude the notion that we can design trouble into, or out of, an executive system'. Thus people blame difficulties on the personalities of others or their own personality, seldom stopping to think whether the difficulty actually results from the design of the social system of which their own roles form a part.

Brown suggests that wherever there is an Executive System there will be within it, or alongside it, a *Representative System* to convey the views and feelings of subordinates to superiors. There may be no explicit recognition of this role structure, but it exists nonetheless. For example, a managing director who introduces changes will be faced with ad hoc deputations: groups with grievances to air will send forward spokespersons. Individuals in these representative roles are not necessarily stating their own views, of course, and cannot be held responsible by their managers as would be the case if they were acting in their executive roles. In Glacier Metal, representatives are formally elected by all levels of employees.

Brown's concept of the *Legislative System* differs from his concepts of Executive and Representative Systems. Each of the latter is a separate series of interrelated roles occupied by people, but the Legislative System is the interaction of four related role systems. These are the shareholders and directors, the customers, the Representative System and the Executive System. Each of these four role systems has very considerable power vis-à-vis a company. The power of each circumscribes what the company may do and their interaction legislates, in effect, for what is done.

Thus chief executives who feel that action is required which exceeds their authority may refer the matter to the board or to a shareholders meeting, or they may test customer reaction through the sales organization. In effect, these then interact with the Executive and Representative Systems. Glacier Metal has established councils for the purpose of legislating on general principles; for example, stating the obligations of employees on hours of work. Councils are composed of representatives and management members, but do not have executive authority. Through them the Representative and Executive Systems are brought into contact, and discussions are conducted with the reactions of the board, shareholders and customers in mind.

In the course of his discussion of the Executive System, Brown makes an analysis of the *operational work* and *specialist work* of businesses which is in contrast, say, to Bakke's analysis of activities (see later in this chapter). In Brown's view, all businesses carry out three functions – development, production and sales – which at Glacier Metal are called 'operational work'. But he also holds that all work activity implies (1) a staffing of activity, (2) a technique of activity and (3) a chosen quantified and timed deployment of activity on a particular operational task. Hence each of the three categories of operational activity – development, management and sales – may be thought of as having three possible dimensions of specialist work: a personnel aspect (organizational and personnel), a technical aspect (concerned with production techniques), and a programming aspect (balancing, timing and quantification of operations). Specialists arise in all these aspects. There may be personnel officers, engineers, production controllers, chemists and many more. Glacier has organized these specialists in divisions corresponding to Brown's analysis – a personnel division, a technical division and a programming division – whose specialist work supports the three operational work functions. Specialists are attached to the various levels of operational (or line) managers.

In *Piecework Abandoned*, Brown is concerned with methods of payment rather than with organization, but his conclusions stem from the same mode of thinking as is found in *Exploration in Management*. Under payment by results, manager–worker relationships are different from those under time rates; that is, the actual organization is different. He takes the view that a 'full managerial role' should include knowing subordinates, assessing their performance, being responsible for it and deciding whether or not they are capable of the roles required. In this case a full manager–subordinate relationship exists in which subordinates are assessed on their whole behaviour and are aware of their accountability to their manager. Wage incentive systems lay across this relationship a bargaining relationship in which the worker becomes a sub-contractor and the foreman abdicates the full managerial role. Thus the organization is changed. Employees are not held to account for loss of output because as sub-contractors they are paying for it themselves. They cease to hold fully responsible roles in the organization and regard lost time as their own affair. Using the same argument, Brown also attacks time-clocks which have the same effects on the role structure and behaviour as does piecework. Both wage incentives and clocking-on have been abandoned at Glacier's factories.

Brown's originality as a writer on management is in his use of the concepts of 'structure' and 'role'. His insistence on detached analysis using these concepts leads him to conclude that: 'Effective organization is a function of the work to be done and the resources and techniques available to do it.'

BIBLIOGRAPHY

BROWN, W., *Exploration in Management*, Heinemann Educational Books, 1960.
BROWN, W., *Piecework Abandoned*, Heinemann Educational Books, 1962.
BROWN, W. and JAQUES, E., *Glacier Project Papers*, Heinemann Educational Books, 1965.

Sir Geoffrey Vickers

Sir Geoffrey Vickers (1894–1982) served in the First World War and was awarded the Victoria Cross for bravery. He worked as a solicitor and then took charge of British economic intelligence during the Second World War. He was knighted in 1946 and subsequently became a member of the National Coal Board in charge of manpower, education, health and welfare. It was in the last 20 years or so of his life that he developed, systematized and recorded his ideas about institutions, organizations and policy making. At his death in his 88th year, he was visiting Professor of Systems at the University of Lancaster and still engaged on fresh work.

The processes of policy making, decision making and control are at the centre of Vickers' analysis. All of these processes take place within an organized setting – a group, an organization, an institution or a society. They are the key to understanding how organizations actually work.

Much of Vickers's extensive writing derives from his principal concern with the idea of *regulation*. Regulation is essentially the process of ensuring that any system follows the path that has been set for it. It is a concept that derives from information theory, systems theory, cybernetics and the control of machines. Vickers used ideas deriving primarily from technological contexts as a basis for developing a whole range of analytical concepts about policy making and management.

If one is to ensure that an organization is to carry out the functions and activities specified by its controllers, a number of activities have to happen, which taken together, constitute the regulation of a system. First, it is necessary for the controllers (the managers) to establish what the state of the system is, to find out what is happening. For Vickers this involves making what he calls *reality judgements* – establishing the facts. But facts do not have an independent meaning; their significance has to be judged. This involves the second part of the process of regulation, namely making a *value judgement*. This can only be done by comparing the actual state of an organization with a standard which acts as a norm. The third part of the process involves devising the means to reduce any disparity between the norm and actuality. Taken together, these three elements make up the regulative process of information, valuation and action.

It may initially sound as though regulation is a mechanical process, but this would be far from the truth. While the basic ideas come from machine systems, Vickers is very clear that adaptations and additions are necessary when it comes to the management of organizations and other human systems. The making of judgements is a uniquely human function which he describes as an art (see *The Art of Judgement*). Central to making judgements is the process of *appreciation* because judgements involve the selection of information, the application of values and the choice of action. None of these processes is self-evident or straightforward. Any manager facing a situation has to make an appreciation of it. This is true not just of arriving at standards, but also of collecting information. Appreciation involves the manager in making choices and selections; deciding what indicators to use to describe the state of the organization; choosing what standards to set and what courses of action to follow. Appreciation requires the specifically human capacity of a readiness to see and value objects and situations in one way rather than another.

There is a very important relationship between regulation and appreciation. To regulate (control), the regulator (manager) has to deal with a series of variables, elements of a situation which establish how well a system (organization) is performing. But a manager can deal with only a limited number of such variables. Which variables are chosen for the purpose of regulation is a function of the manager's appreciative system. Like Herbert Simon (see Chapter 5) on whose work he draws, Vickers points out that there are cognitive limits to what an individual can handle – the amount that can usefully be watched and regulated. Managers are also limited by their interests in selecting which variables to attend to. Thus both cognition and personal interests are key elements in a manager's appreciative system.

Appreciation has a major role to play in organizational and institutional management because it steers the judgements that controllers make by setting the system. Because it is through their appreciative systems that managers make both their reality and value judgements, such a system sets the limits to what are to be regarded as choices and what as constraining. This steering function establishes what is enabling, what is limiting and what is crucial. The basic policy choice in any organization is what to regard as regulatable; this choice then lays down what the key relations and central norms of the system are to be.

Having established the central analytical constructs of regulation and appreciation and their relationship to one another, much of Vickers' work is then concerned with integrating a psychologically based approach to control, emphasizing individual characteristics, with further analysis which places the controller in a collective setting. Managers have to operate with and through others; the process of regulation is not machine-like for human systems. This means that choice and action have to be organized and operated on a collective basis. For this to happen, there has to be a set of shared understandings, an agreed set of norms.

Through their organizational positions and appreciative systems, managers have a key role in both building up the general appreciative setting of the organization through which its members establish common ways of operating, and also in setting up communication systems to deal with disparities that arise. It is a central issue for any manager to have to cope with the fact that shared norms, shared understandings and shared communication cannot be taken for granted. Indeed, Vickers suggests that control and regulation in organizations and institutions are becoming more problematic precisely because of the difficulty of maintaining agreement. This is because, on the one hand, there is a continuing escalation of expectations; organizations reflecting this attempt to regulate more and more relations. On the other hand, the capacity of individuals for accepting regulation is steadily being eroded, with the evaporation of loyalty to organizations and the growing emphasis on *individual* self-realization (of which Vickers is highly critical). Together these produce a paradox for the contemporary manager who has to deal with employees and clients who are at one and the same time highly *dependent* and very *alienated*.

Attempting to deal with this paradox brings the wheel full circle, back to the importance of the appreciative system. This is because it is the manager's appreciative system which determines how issues will be seen and defined and what action will be taken. The manager is involved in making choices which are problematic because they are multi-valued. Choices are not simple and straightforward; they require the assessment of a number of dimensions which can be valued in a variety of ways. To regulate this involves the ability to predict possible outcomes and to learn about the relationship between action and outcomes.

The ability to deal with the paradox and so to regulate an organizational and institutional system is limited by the nature of what is changing. The rate and predictability of regulatable change sets limits to what is regulatable. To regulate an organization, the variables which the appreciative system regards as key in evaluating performance have to be predicted over time. Indeed, such variables need to be predicted over a time period at least as long as the time needed to make an effective response. Part of the reason for the breakdown of confidence in institutions derives from the fact that rates of change are high, shared understandings of what they mean and why they occur are difficult to establish, and the prediction of future action is extremely problematic.

In the end, it is the manager with an individual appreciative system operating in a particular setting who carries out control and regulation. The manager helps to set, and is affected by, what are regarded as standards of success, what scope of discretion is allowed and what is the extent of power. Crucial to the operation is what is regarded as possible. It is necessary for those responsible for control constantly to examine how they appreciate the world, rigorously to test the limits of their logic and skill, and always to be open to new ideas. Learning is control because of the role of appreciation in regulation.

BIBLIOGRAPHY

VICKERS, Sir G., *The Art of Judgement*, Chapman & Hall, 1965.
VICKERS, Sir G., *Towards a Sociology of Management*, Chapman & Hall, 1967.
VICKERS, Sir G., *Value Systems and Social Process*, Tavistock Publications, 1968.
VICKERS, Sir G., *Making Institutions Work*, Associated Business Programmes, 1973.

E. Wight Bakke

E. Wight Bakke (1903–1971) was a professor at the Labor and Management Center of Yale University for many years. He largely concerned himself with the general problem of the integration of people into organizations, but before his work developed in this direction he was interested in unemployment. In 1931 he investigated the plight of the unemployed worker in Britain.

Bakke's work on organization theory is focused on the problem of developing concepts – and meaningful words to denote them – with which to define and analyse organizations and their activities. Some order must be brought into the miscellany of findings from research and from the lessons of experience. His aim is to create theoretical means of analysis which can be applied not only to economic organizations, but to schools, churches and so forth. He is thus confronted with the task of reducing the seemingly endless diversity of forms of human social organization to some kind of common elements.

Bakke begins by thinking of a social organization as a continuing system of differentiated and coordinated human activities which welds together resources into a whole that then develops a character all its own. Of itself, this definition is perhaps no more than a truism, but by thinking in these terms Bakke makes the task of analysis a little clearer. If indeed it is useful to conceptualize a social organization as a system of activities, then a classification of activities is needed. If in addition it is useful to see those activities as operating on resources, then a classification of resources is a necessary complement.

The basic *resources* essential to the operation of an organization are held to fall under one of six headings. These are human, material (raw materials and equipment), financial, natural (natural resources not processed by human activity) and ideational (the ideas used by the organization and the language in which these are communicated). There is also the organization's operational field: for a company its sales market, for a trade union the labour market. Bakke's intention is that these categories, not unfamiliar for the most part, should be so defined as to be appropriate to the resources employed by any kind of 'specific purpose' social organization, be it economic, military, religious or any other. Similarly, he contends that all the *activities* of such organizations can be fitted into one or other of five categories: perpetuation, workflow, control, identification and homeostasis.

It is axiomatic that, if an organization is to continue in being, resources of the kinds listed above must be available to it. Activities which ensure this availability are called *perpetuation activities*. In industry, for example, the buying department discovers sources of supply of raw materials and endeavours to sustain the required supply. Perpetuation of personnel is achieved by appointing new people and instructing them in their duties, an activity which may be specialized in a personnel department. A meeting to consider a share issue may be classified as a finance-perpetuating activity.

Workflow activities comprise all that is done to create and distribute the output of an organization, whether that output is a product or a service. A wide range of activities can be classified in this way. For example, a production activity in an organization might be a telephone exchange operator making connections for long-distance calls, or an assembly worker sealing tops on car batteries, or an army crew driving a tank on manoeuvres. On the distribution side are sales activities, and so on.

Bakke groups under *control activities* all activities designed to coordinate and unify. He breaks these down into four sub-categories:

1. directive activities, being those which initiate action, such as determining what shall be done and to what standard, and giving instruction – for example, a foreman allocating jobs;
2. motivation activities, rewarding or penalizing behaviour – for example an office supervisor recommending a salary increase for a clerk, or a foreman recommending discharge of a worker;
3. evaluation activities – for example reviewing and appraising people's performance or comparing alternative courses of action;
4. communication activities – providing people with the premises and data they need.

If the character of an organization – or 'charter' as it may be called – is to be reflected in a commonly held image of the organization in the minds of its members and of outsiders, activities must be carried out which define this charter and symbolize it. These are *identification activities*. Instances are an article in the company magazine stressing the unique qualities of the service the company has always given, or an address by the chief executive on the history and traditions of the undertaking.

Bakke argues that the four types of activities outlined above must be so arranged and regulated that they maintain the organization in existence in a state enabling it competently to perform its function. In short, there must be what he calls *homeostatic activities* which preserve the organization in 'dynamic equilibrium'. These activities are of four kinds: the fusion process, the problem-solving process, the leadership process and the legitimization process.

The concept fundamental to Bakke's *fusion process theory* is that both individuals and organizations are entities striving for self-realization. In this, he and Argyris (see Chapter 7) think on much the same lines. An organization attempts to shape in its own image all the individuals who join it, while individuals who join an organization likewise try to express their own personalities by shaping the organization accordingly. Each experiences some change, but there may be times when the organization and its members are mutually opposed. Hence the need for fusion process activities to reconcile, harmonize or fuse organization, groups and individuals. (W.H. Whyte, Chapter 8, pillories some of these activities.) In the same way, an organization has to be more or less integrated with a diversity of other organizations outside itself; the process of accommodating divergent interests can again be thought of as fusion. Bakke himself has given particular attention to this idea of fusion processes, looking on it as a single frame of reference with which to simplify thinking about the array of human problems encountered in organizations, both in research and in daily experience.

The continual solving of non-routine problems in an organization is termed the *problem-solving process*. Bakke sets out what he believes to be a logical sequence of steps normally taken in problem solving. He also distinguishes a *leadership process* which provides imagination and initiative. Finally, there is the *legitimization process*, activities to justify and get accepted the end of the organization and what it does to pursue them. Thus a company secretary registering articles of association is performing a legitimization activity, for these articles state what the company has a legal right to do. Similarly, managers frequently persuade other people (and each other) that the organization's products are beneficial to those who use them, and that the organization is a good thing for all involved in it and for society. Ultimately, an organization cannot survive without acceptance of its legitimacy.

The idea of homeostatic activities is intended to apply to a very wide variety of organizations, but taking work organizations in particular, it appears to have much in common with what is usually meant by the words 'management' or 'administration'.

The point of constructing a theoretical framework, in the way Bakke does, is to clarify thinking. Does it help to make sense of what before seemed too complicated? Does it make like and unlike comparable, when before they seemed to defy comparison? Bakke is less concerned with management as such; the test of his contribution is whether, after any initial feelings of strangeness have been overcome, managers and researchers find that the use of his concepts helps them in their understanding.

BIBLIOGRAPHY

WIGHT BAKKE, E., *The Unemployed Worker*, Yale University Press, 1933.
WIGHT BAKKE, E., *Bonds of Organization*, Harper, 1950; 2nd edn, Archon Books, 1966.
WIGHT BAKKE, E., 'Concept of the Social Organization', in M. Haire (ed.), *Modern Organization Theory*, Chapman & Hall, 1959.

Amitai Etzioni

Amitai Etzioni is a sociologist who is the Founder and Director of the Institute of Communitarian Policy Studies at George Washington University, Washington, DC, USA. He is currently working in the area of social diversity and social conflict. Earlier, his concerns with fundamental sociological problems led him to examine organizations as promising research sites for their solution.

In his work he starts from the problem of social order, asking the question, why do organizations or other social entities keep going? This is the problem of social control which has intrigued social philosophers since Plato and which was put in its most pristine form by Hobbes. It is similar to the concern of Weber (see Chapter 1); for Etzioni, too, the question to be answered is 'why do people in organizations conform to the orders given to them and follow the standards of behaviour laid down for them?' This problem occurs in all social organizations, from the family to the nation-state, but Etzioni sees it as being particularly crucial in formal organizations. This is because organizations are designed as instruments. When one is formed, whether it be in government, business, education or recreation, it has a specific reason for existing, a goal or purpose; natural social systems such as the family or a community are much more diverse in what they do and it is difficult to think of them as having goals. But because organizations have this characteristic of attempting to reach a goal, it becomes important to measure how well they are doing. The result is an emphasis on performance.

Organizations continuously review their performance and will change their practices in the light of this. Organizations therefore face special problems of controlling the behaviour of their members: they must make sure that behaviour is in line with the requirements of performance.

Etzioni starts from the proposition that organizations, like other social units, require compliance from their members. Because of their intensive concern with performance (and also, in the modern world, their size), organizations cannot rely on members' total commitment to the aims of the organization to guarantee compliance. Also they cannot rely on an informal control system based on one individual influencing another such as occurs in the family. Organizations have formal systems for controlling what goes on in them; they have rewards and penalties of a clear and specific kind to ensure compliance from their members.

Compliance in any organization is two sided. On the one hand it consists of the control structures that are employed: the organizational power and authority structure which attempts to ensure that obedience is secured. This Etzioni calls the 'structural aspect' since it is concerned with the formal organizational system and the kind of power that the organization uses to enforce compliance. As organizations cannot rely implicitly on their members to carry out orders perfectly, it is necessary to have a hierarchy of authority, to have supervisors: it is necessary to have job descriptions and specified procedures for doing things; it is necessary to have a division of labour. All of these are attempts to make the organization less dependent on the whims of individuals by controlling behaviour. The organization exercises its power by these bureaucratic means.

The second aspect of compliance is based on the extent to which members of the organization are committed to its aims and purposes. This is the 'motivational aspect' and is expressed in the kind of involvement that the individual member has with the organization. The more intensely members are involved with the organization, the more likely they are to work towards the realization of its goals. Etzioni argues that the more employees are committed, the fewer formal control mechanisms are needed. These two aspects of compliance are then used to produce a typology of organizations.

Etzioni outlines three kinds of power according to which organizations can be classified. The classification is based on the different means used to ensure that members comply. He distinguishes between coercive power, remunerative or utilitarian power, and normative or identitive power. These are based on physical, material and symbolic means respectively.

Coercive power rests essentially on the (possible) application of physical force to make sure that members of an organization comply with orders. Thus, to inflict physical pain or to cause death for non-compliance involves the use of this kind of power. Examples of organizations using physical means to different degrees are concentration camps and custodial mental hospitals.

Remunerative or *utilitarian power* rests on the manipulation of material resources. The organizational member's compliance is enforced because the organization controls materials, such as money, which the member desires. Thus, a system of reward based on wages and salaries constitutes this kind of power. Business organizations are typically based on remunerative control.

Normative or *identitive power* comes from the manipulation and allocation of symbols. Examples of pure symbols are love, affection and prestige which can be used to extract compliance from others. Etzioni suggests that alternative (and perhaps more eloquent) names would be 'persuasive' or 'suggestive power'. He sees this kind of power most often found in religious organizations, universities and voluntary associations.

These ideas are useful for making broad comparative analyses of organizations based on predominant characteristics. But not all organizations with the same general objectives have similar control structures. Etzioni suggests that labour unions can be based on any of the three: 'underworld' unions controlled by mobsters rely on coercion; 'business' unions offering members wage increases and better working conditions are essentially remunerative; and 'political' unions, centred on ideologies, rely on normative power. Most organizations attempt to employ all three kinds of power, but will usually emphasize one kind and rely less on the other two. Often different means of control are emphasized for different participants in the organization. Members at the bottom are often more likely to be subject to coercive measures, whereas higher participants are more likely to be subject to normative power.

As with power, Etzioni suggests three kinds of involvement. His classification is based on a dimension of low to high involvement, the types labelled as alienative, calculative and moral. In essence, involvement in an organization can run from intensive negative feelings to highly positive feelings, with mildly negative and mildly positive in between.

Alienative involvement is the intensely negative end and denotes dissociation from the organization by the member. Convicts and prisoners of war are usually alienated from the organizations of which they are members. With *calculative involvements*, the member's relationship with the organization has little intensity and can thus be either positive or negative in a mild way. This is typical of business relationships. Finally, *moral involvement* denotes a positive and favourable view of the organization which is very intense. It is found in the highly committed church member, the loyal party member and so on.

When examined together, the three kinds of power and the three kinds of involvement generate nine types of compliance relationships in an organization: Etzioni argues that a particular kind of power and a particular kind of involvement usually occur together; thus the most common forms of compliance found in organizations are 1, 5 and 9. Coercive power produces alienative involvement, and vice versa; remunerative power and calculative involvement will be found together; similarly normative power and moral involvement are congruent with one another.

	Kinds of involvement		
Kinds of power	*Alienative*	*Calculative*	*Moral*
Coercive	1	2	3
Remunerative	4	5	6
Normative	7	8	9

Organizations which represent these three empirically dominant types are a prison (with an emphasis on custody rather than rehabilitation), a factory and a church, respectively. The other six possibilities are incongruent in the sense that the power system does not fit the involvement of members. The result will be strain and a shift in one of the bases of compliance. Etzioni suggests that organizations which have congruent compliance structures will be more effective than those which suffer the strain and tension of incongruent systems. This means that business organizations function more effectively when they use remuneration rather than coercion or symbols as their basis of control. They need a system which is subject to ease of measurement and which can be clearly related to performance. Coercion (such as threats of dismissal) and normative control (such as appeals to loyalty) can only be used secondarily.

However, it should always be remembered that there are many outside factors which affect the kind of control structure that an organization can use. In the kinds of societies which produce many complex organizations, the state monopolizes the use of force; indeed, we find that it is state-run institutions, such as prisons, which use coercive power. Other organizations, including business, are not allowed to. Similarly, general market conditions (such as the extent of competition or the presence of a labour pool) will affect the extent to which the utilitarian control used by a business firm will veer towards the coercive or normative end of the spectrum. Also, the beliefs that the participants bring to the organizations of which they are members, together with their personality makeups, will affect the degree to which they recognize particular kinds of control as legitimate. Etzioni points out the differences in response between the US of today and of two generations ago that would result from the same exercise in coercive power – for example, a teacher slapping a pupil. Changing belief systems mean that organizations have to change their compliance structures.

Overall, Etzioni is interested in laying the base for a wide-scale comparative analysis of organizations. As such he produces a conceptual framework which is applicable to all organizations and which emphasizes similarities and differences between them in different institutional areas.

BIBLIOGRAPHY

ETZIONI, A., *A Comparative Analysis of Complex Organizations*, Free Press, 1961.

ETZONI, A., *Modern Organizations*, Prentice-Hall, 1964.

ETZIONI, A., 'Organizational Control Structure', in J. G. March (ed.), *Handbook of Organizations*, Rand McNally, 1965.

ETZONI, A., *Rights and The Common Good: The Communitarian Perspective*, New York: St. Martin's Press, 1995.

David Silverman

David Silverman is Emeritus Professor of Sociology at Goldsmiths' College, University of London. After studying at the London School of Economics, he spent a period in the US before taking up his present post. Working within the discipline of sociology, Silverman's interest has been to develop a sociological critique of organization theory. Much of his research work has been carried out in public sector organizations, including local government administration and the British National Health Service. In particular, he has studied selection processes, administrative occupations and professional–client relationships.

Silverman's main contribution has been the introduction of an 'action-oriented' perspective to organization theory. He has argued that an alternative is needed to what he regards as the dominant perspective in the study of organizations, namely systems theory. The alternative is to view organizations as the product of the actions and interactions of motivated people pursuing purposes of their own. For Silverman most organizational analysis is based on a mistaken set of assumptions, the basic mistake being to conceptualize organizations as systems which can be described and understood without reference to the motivations and interpretations of the people in them. Most organization theory mistakenly involves *reification*; that is, attributing thought and action to social constructs.

According to Silverman, organizational analysis started as a separate area of study by trying to offer answers to questions posed by those who control the operation of organizations, namely the managers. This has led to a consistent bias (through which the analysis of organizations is presented in a dehumanized, neutral way) in which only the concerns of managers are dealt with. It is Silverman's purpose to expose such biases which are apparent in all established approaches, and to set up a more satisfactory theory.

By contrast, Silverman distinguishes three characteristics of a formal organization. The first is that it arises at a discernible point in time and is easier than most sets of social relationships to perceive as an artefact. The second is that relationships are not taken so much for granted by those organizational members who seek to coordinate and control. The third characteristic is that planned changes in social relations and the rules of the game are open to discussion. Thus this definition looks at organizations from the point of view of the social relationships within them and how organizational actors (that is, the members) interpret and understand those relationships. Silverman's criticisms of organization theory are based on this view.

The dominant theoretical view of organizations analyses them as systems and is concerned with general patterns and points of similarity between all organizations, rather than with individual action. A systems view regards organizations as a set of interdependent parts with needs for survival. In adapting to these needs, organizations are seen as behaving and taking action. Organizations have to transform a variety of inputs (people, money materials) into outputs; the process of regulation through which this occurs has been a predominant area of study. But systems theorists fail to consider that it is the *members* of organizations – interpreting what they understand as the environment, imparting meanings and common definitions – who do the regulating and adapting.

Because, like so much organizational analysis, systems theory starts from the viewpoint of the executive, it confuses the actions of managers with the behaviour of the organization. In carrying out this abstraction, systems theory directs attention away from purposive human action. Such an approach sees structures as *transcendental*, that is, with a logic of their own and analysable independently of human actions, perceptions and meanings. Silverman sees structures as *immanent*, that is, continuously constructed and reconstructed out of the meanings that actors take from them and give to them. These differences in approach are at the heart of conceptualizing organizations. Given these theoretical structures, the same problems are to be found in the two main variants of systems theory: *functionalism* which is derived from sociology, and *socio-technical systems theory* which is interdisciplinary in character. Both are concerned with the consequences rather than the causes of behaviour. Both rest on a biological analogy which is unsatisfactory for the description and explanation of human events. Both stress processes of adaptation and states of equilibrium, and cannot adequately deal with change and conflict. Both involve reification rather than dealing with the sources of orientations of organizational members.

However, within these rather severe limitations, Silverman does see some limited steps forward in the socio-technical systems perspective. The idea of behaviour and motivations as an outcome of technology has involved some writers in dealing with conflicts of interests and strategies. Seeing organizations as interrelations of technology, environment, sentiments and structures, with no one factor dominant, means stressing the absence of any one most efficient form of organization. But in the end any form of systems approach is unable to explain why particular organizations occur; it can only describe patterns of adaptation and their consequences in its own terms.

Silverman also sees problems with the other main approach that he identifies, *organizational psychology*. Admittedly, the issue of reification does not arise and there is a concern with people. But as with systems theory, the emphasis is still on needs, almost as if people were systems. Individuals are conceptualized as having needs to fulfil (for example physiological, social, self-actualizing) which form a hierarchy and are often in conflict with organizational goals. Silverman suggests that there are major problems in validating the existence of such needs and that it is not clear whether they would explain behaviour anyway. Also, writers using this approach are far too concerned with general patterns of need and behaviour rather than with individual action which, for Silverman, should be at the heart of organizational analysis.

To deal with all such problems inherent in established ways of theorizing about organizations there is only one solution – the adoption of an *action frame of reference*. The essential element in this approach is to view organizations as the outcome of the interaction of motivated people who are attempting to resolve their own problems and pursue their own ends. The environment is conceptualized as a source of meaning for organizational members, being made up of other actors who are defining situations in ways which allow actors inside organizations to defend their own actions and make sense of the actions of others. Some are given significance, others are not. Actions have no meaning other than those given to them by actors.

This method of analysis and theoretical approach is illustrated and developed in the work that Silverman has carried out with Jill Jones (now of the University of Westminster) on staff-selection interviews in public sector organizations. In empirical terms the emphasis on action, social construction of reality and the development of shared orientations leads to an emphasis on the study of language. It is through language that actions, perceptions and meanings of organizational rules, for example, are established and continuously reaffirmed.

Selection is thus not an objective process of getting the right candidate for the job, but a case of making sense of what goes on in a socially organized setting. In an interview situation, the actors may start with conflicting views of reality or the facts. An outcome has to be managed through verbal exchanges to arrive at an acceptable 'account' of the character of the interviewee and the process of selection. In doing this the actors usually confirm the existing structures of power and authority, shared meanings and rules of operation. The selection process is important in confirming the actors' understanding of what happens and why in the particular organizations of which they are members.

In further studies Silverman compared the specialist-patient interaction in private and National Health Service clinics. In NHS clinics the patient is allocated to a team of doctors and could well see different ones in successive consultations. The relationship is inevitably largely seen as impersonal. Private patients, by contrast, can organize their relationship to obtain a personalized service since they are perceived by the doctors as being entitled to act like the clients of any fee-paying service. They participate more in the consultation, including asking questions about the experience and competence of the practitioner. They are entitled to evaluate and comment on the service and they may shop around.

What happens in organizations, then, is a continuous product of motivated human action. For Silverman this is merely emphasizing a general principle of all social life. Because of this it is difficult to distinguish organizations as entities from other types of social structures – and not worth it. The study of organizations should not be seen as an end in itself, but as a setting within which general social processes can be studied from a clear *sociological* perspective. By doing this it is possible to ensure that analysts do not impose their own or management's view of what the issues and problems are.

BIBLIOGRAPHY

SILVERMAN, D., *The Theory of Organizations*, Heinemann, 1970.
SILVERMAN, D., 'Going Private', *Sociology*, 18 (1984), 191–204.
SILVERMAN, D., *Communication and Medical Practice*, Sage, 1987.
SILVERMAN, D. and JONES, J., *Organizational Work: The Language of Grading: The Grading of Language*, Collier Macmillan, 1976.

Michel Foucault

Michel Foucault (1926–1984) was a French philosopher and cultural historian, although his iconoclastic approach makes him reject as inadequate any categorization of his work using such pre-existing concepts. After qualifying in philosophy and subsequently in abnormal psychology, he held positions in a number of universities in France and abroad. In 1970 he was appointed to the prestigious Collège de France where, for the first time, he was able to determine the precise title he wished to take. He chose the distinctive one of 'Professor of the History of Systems of Thought'. He remained in this post until his death.

During his career Foucault published extensively, having to his credit a series of weighty volumes, numerous articles and lectures, as well as reports of interviews. His work, with its highly nuanced use of the French language, is difficult to understand, particularly in English. He writes in the profuse style of French philosophers to elaborate and complicate the ideas he presents, and as he develops his thought his analyses and arguments are not consistent from one volume to the next. In spite of this (from the Anglo-Saxon viewpoint) or because of this (as the French tradition would have it) his writings in this genre of 'literary philosophy' have led him to be widely considered as one of the leading cultural commentators who feature prominently in intellectual life in France.

Foucault's work deals with historical topics, although to emphasize that his concerns are very different from those of traditional historians he does not use the term 'history' to describe his work. His first major impact was his writing on the way in which the conceptualization and treatment of insanity has changed over the past four hundred years. He details the changes from the seventeenth to the twentieth centuries in the notions of what constitutes madness and how it should be treated. These analyses are characterised as 'archaeological investigations' to indicate that they refer to the all the philosophical, social and economic changes that have contributed to society's characterization of the insane. The English title of his major work on this topic, *Madness and Civilization*, illustrates the wide range of factors on which he draws.

His basic argument uses historical sources to show that madness is not an objective scientific condition which some people have while others do not. Its characterization is a result of society's philosophies and practices which change over the course of time. Until the eighteenth century philosophical revolution known as 'the Enlightenment', madness was not sharply distinguished from reason. It was associated with knowledge of sacred mysteries and could provide insights into the human experience. In Shakespeare's plays, for example, this is illustrated by the character of the Fool or the Jester with his wise idiocy.

In the Enlightenment the distinction between reason and unreason (madness) became much sharper. People with reason worked, and thus achieved salvation. Those who did not work – the destitute, the idle (that is, unemployed), the beggars, the criminals, as well as the insane – were now regarded as scandalous and shameful by society and were excluded. The establishment of a physical separation was assisted because the dying out of leprosy across Europe meant that empty former leper colonies became asylums where they could all be incarcerated.

The harsh discipline of the asylum came later to be regarded as a form of ill-treatment and the insane were physically less restrained. They were then subject to the attentions of psychiatrists and the medical approach of attempting a cure was established. But, Foucault maintains, they were even less free, since now their minds were being pressured. Madness was a social failure and the doctor's exercise of absolute authority was a reflection of the stratification of the wider bourgeois society in which the mad were at the bottom of the social scale.

At each stage in history, it was not the objective nature of madness but the complex systems of moral discourse and social practice which determined how all the actors both the mad and the sane participated in the endeavour. These are the 'systems of thought' that Foucault is concerned with, as in the title of his Professorship. In later work on the history of sexuality, he uses a similar range of historical, cultural and ethical influences to analyse the processes by which individuals in modern Western society come to experience their sexuality.

The Foucault project which has had the biggest impact on organization theory is his analysis of power and authority in the organization. The organizations which he considers are those where the exercise of power in their everyday working is very visible; for example prisons, armies, hospitals, schools. In these organizations the warders, the officers, the doctors and the schoolmasters legitimately exercise considerable powers of discipline and control over the other members. His major work *Discipline and Punish: The birth of the prison* is an historical examination of the treatment of prisoners in the French penal system. Once again, to emphasize his particular approach he does not use the word 'history' but uses the term 'genealogy' to identify his analytical concerns. Genealogy is a 'form of history which can account for the constitution of knowledges, discourses and domains of objects'. It draws on historical, literary, medical, religious and philosophical bodies of knowledge to establish the distinctive 'discourse' on discipline and punishment which is the basis of power in the organization.

It is the discourse or frame of reference of those involved which determines the way they think and act, and therefore how the organization and those in it function. The nature of the discourse explains the way in which organizations emerge, develop and sustain themselves. In his *genealogical* investigations Foucault examines all the many factors which affect that discourse, coming to feel that the earlier *archaeological* investigations were too limited in focussing on the structural influences of social hierarchies.

Discourse, as Foucault formulates it, may be considered as 'the rules of the game' for those in the organization. It is the way of thought that they take for granted. It shows not just in what they say, but also in the arrangements and technological devices which are used for control.

Here Foucault takes up the notion of the 'panopticon' as designed by the early nineteenth-century British philosopher Jeremy Bentham. Bentham developed a theoretical design for a prison building which allowed the warder to continually survey many prisoners each in their own cell, while not being seen themself. Thus the prisoners could not know whether they were being watched or not (hence 'panopticon', that is, all-seeing machine). The aim, in addition to being a cost-effective, low-staffed prison, was to instil correct behaviour into the prisoners. Since they cannot know if they are being watched, they have to act properly all the time and so they internalize the rules. In Foucault's terms, the physical setting is thus part of the discourse.

In organizational life what is considered as true are not objective 'facts' but what is part of the discourse. For example, it may have been established that managerial work is worth more and should be paid more than physical work and this is accepted without question. But only certain facts are regarded as knowledge whereas other facts are omitted. In a discussion about the closure of a plant, for example, the profitable operation of the company will be taken to be part of the discourse. But the consequent economic and psychological disruption to redundant long-serving workers may not be included in the discourse, being deemed irrelevant to the company's performance. Prohibitions on discourse by the powerful serve to order and control it against the resistances of the rest.

Surveillance and discipline are also crucial parts of the discourse by which the powerful establish their 'truth' in organizations. Writing in the 1970s Foucault presciently focuses on surveillance as the key control process of the powerful, even before modern technological developments such as CCTV, e-mail trails and large-scale computer databases vastly increased the reach of this process. So, 'Is it surprising that prisons resemble factories, schools, barracks, hospitals, which all resemble prisons?'

The aim of the discourse is thus to establish what is taken to be 'normal' by all the participants. But Foucault does not regard this argument as meaning that the powerful in organizations can simply impose their domination on the powerless. Power is relational. The discourse is a 'battlefield' in which the powerful fight for their conceptions of truth and the powerless have ways of resisting. It may be established that joining trades unions or going on strike are also normal parts of the discourse. The fact that 'resistance to change' (that is, resistance to management's proposals for change) is endemic in organizations is indicative that lower levels are part of the discourse. For the powerful, of course, such resistance is itself a justification of the need for surveillance and discipline.

So the basic question that Foucauldian analysts ask is: 'What is the discourse and how is it being formed?' Barbara Townley has applied this approach to human resource management. An employment contract must leave much of the relationship between the organization and the individual undetermined. It can specify the system of remuneration to be paid, but can be only very general about the commitment and effort required from an employee. How then is the discourse governing these to be established? Managements acquire knowledge about employees by the application of personality and aptitude tests, grading systems, incentive schemes, developmental appraisals or training programmes. The results of these procedures do not constitute 'objective facts' which are value neutral. What they do is give more information about the employee and thus increase the opportunities for classification, evaluation and control by top management while at the same time establishing in the discourse that this is a normal acceptable way to proceed.

Similarly, the establishment of bureaucracies (see Weber, Chapter 1) or the introduction of scientific management (see Taylor, Chapter 4) are not only, or primarily, for efficiency as their proponents argue. Their aim is to obtain knowledge to enable the organizationally powerful to establish the discourse which normalizes their control. Alfred P. Sloan's concept of 'coordinated decentralization' (see Chapter 4) or Drucker's 'management by objectives' (see Chapter 4) are ways of establishing a discourse in which managers accept self-control by internalizing the aims of the top management. Foucault coined the term 'governmentality' to mean the strategies both of the organizational governance of those at the top and the self-governance of those below. The aims of modern accounting and IT systems are, likewise, to establish 'governmentality' by obtaining knowledge to make the managers in the organization more open to both higher control and self-control.

Foucauldian analysis by emphasizing the subjective, contested nature of knowledge in the establishment of discourse provides another way of looking at the functioning of organizations.

BIBLIOGRAPHY

FOUCAULT, M., *Madness and Civilization: A History of Insanity in the Age of Reason*, Tavistock, 1977.
FOUCAULT, M., *Discipline and Punish: the Birth of the Prison*, Allen Lane, 1977.
FOUCAULT, M., *The History of Sexuality*, Vols 1, 2 and 3, Penguin Books, 1990.
RABINOW, P. (Ed.), *The Foucault Reader*, Penguin Books, 1991.
TOWNLEY, B., 'Beyond Good and Evil: Depth and Division in the Management of Human Resources', in A. McKinley and K. Starkey (eds), *Foucault, Management and Organization Theory*, Sage 1998.

Organizational Practices

Organizational Patterns

C. Northcote Parkinson

C. Northcote Parkinson (1909–1993) was, as he himself put it, 'an Englishman with a distinguished academic career who has been writing scholarly books since 1934'. He taught at the Universities of Malaya, Liverpool and Illinois, but for most of his life devoted himself to full-time writing.

Parkinson confronts the manifest fact that there is little or no relationship between the work to be done in an organization and the size of staff doing it. The growth of administrative hierarchies may be independent of the work itself. To explain this phenomenon he propounds Parkinson's Law: 'Work expands to fill the time available for its completion.'

As a graphic analogy with the world of administration, he cites the case of the elderly lady with nothing else to do who spends an entire day sending a postcard to her niece, ending 'prostrate after a day of doubt, anxiety and toil'. This is because, having nothing else to do, she elevates each single activity, such as finding a pen and a stamp and getting to the post box, into a major effort which demands much time and energy. In the same way an administrative task in an organization can either be regarded as incidental and done in a few minutes, or it can be elevated to a series of component tasks, each of which makes demands so great that in total they fill the working day.

Small wonder, then, that administrative officials find themselves overworked. What they will do about it is foretold by the motivational axiom, 'an official wants to multiply subordinates, not rivals'. Hence rather than share the work with colleague B, overworked official A appoints subordinates C and D. By appointing two, A preserves the position of being the only official comprehending the entire range of work. When C inevitably complains of overwork, A preserves equity by allowing C to have subordinates E and F and also by allowing D to appoint G and H. With this staff, A's own promotion is now virtually certain. Moreover, by this stage a second axiom has taken effect: 'officials make work for each other'. For seven are now doing what one did before, but the routing of drafts, minutes and incoming documents between them ensures that all are working hard and that A is working harder than ever.

Parkinson cites impressive evidence of this process. British Royal Navy estimates disclose that over the first half of the twentieth century, while the numbers of ships and of officers and men declined, the numbers of Admiralty and dockyard officials increased rapidly. Indeed, the men of Whitehall increased by nearly 80 per cent; it may be concluded that this would have occurred had there been no seamen at all. Similarly in the Colonial Office; in 1947 and again in 1954 the figures for staff had risen substantially even though during and after the war the size of the Empire had shrunk markedly.

Once constituted, administrative hierarchies are bestrewn with committees, councils and boards through which the weightier matters of finance must pass. Now since a million is real only to a millionaire, these committees and the like are necessarily made up of persons accustomed to think in tens or hundreds, perhaps in thousands, but never more than this. The result is a typical pattern of committee work which may be stated as the 'Law of Triviality'. It means that 'the time spent on any item of the agenda will be in inverse proportion to the sum involved'.

Thus a contract for a £10 million atomic reactor will be passed with a murmur of agreement, after formal reference to the engineers' and the geophysicists' reports and to plans in appendices. In such cases the Law of Triviality is supplemented by technical factors, since half the committee, including the chairperson, do not know what a reactor is and half the rest do not know what it is for. Rather than face these difficulties of explanation, any member who does know will decide that, despite any misgivings about the whole thing, it is better to say nothing. However, when the agenda reaches the question of a roof for the bicycle shed, here is both a topic and a sum of money which everyone understands. Now all can show they are pulling their weight and make up for their silence over the reactor. Discussion will go on for at least 45 minutes, and a saving of some £100 may be satisfactorily achieved.

Of course, such a committee will have passed the size of approximately 21 members, which Parkinson's 'Coefficient of Inefficiency' (a formula is given) predicts as critical. Where such a number is reached, conversations occur at both ends of the table, so that to be heard one has to rise. Once standing, the member cannot help but make a speech, if only from force of habit. At this point the efficient working of a committee becomes impossible.

This might have happened in any case from self-induced 'injelitis' – the disease of induced inferiority. From an examination of moribund institutions, it has been ascertained that the source of infection comes from the arrival in an organization's hierarchy of an individual combining both incompetence and jealousy. At a certain concentration these qualities react to induce 'injelitance'; soon the head of the organization, who is second rate, sees to it that the next level subordinates are all third rate, and they see to it that their subordinates are fourth rate, and so on. The organization accepts its mediocrity and ceases to attempt to match better organizations. After all, since little is done mistakes are rare, and since aims are low, success is complete.

The characteristics of organizations can be assessed even more easily than this, simply by their physical accoutrements. Publishers, for example, or again research establishments, frequently flourish in shabby and makeshift quarters. Lively and productive as these may be, who is not impressed by the contrasting institution with an imposing and symmetrical façade, within which shining floors glide to a receptionist murmuring with carmine lips into an ice-blue receiver?

However, it is now known that a perfection of planned layout is achieved only by institutions on the point of collapse. During exciting discovery or progress, there is no time to plan the perfect headquarters. This comes afterwards – and too late. Thus by the time the Palace of Nations at Geneva was opened in 1937, the League had practically ceased to exist. The British Empire expanded whilst the Colonial Office was in haphazard accommodation, and contracted after it moved into purpose-built premises in 1875. The conduct of the Second World War was planned in crowded and untidy premises in Washington, the elaborate layout of the Pentagon at Arlington, Virginia being constructed later.

In public affairs there is a propensity for expenditure on elaborate and inappropriate constructions such as those mentioned, as indeed there is for any other kind of expenditure. In fact, all forms of administration are prone to expenditure. This is due to the effects of Parkinson's Second Law: 'Expenditure rises to meet income.' The widely understood domestic phenomenon which unfailingly appears after each increase in household income is equally prevalent in administration – with the important difference in government administration that expenditure rises towards a ceiling that is not there. Were revenue to be reduced there would actually be an improvement in services. The paradox of administration is that if there were fewer officials, each would have less to do and therefore more time to think about what is being done.

Turning to the business corporation, Parkinson's historical eye provides a lively view of tycoons and their giant creations. His whimsical and colourful résumés of how the world's biggest businesses came to be what they are do not overlook their degrading and polluting consequences. At the same time, Parkinson's serious conclusion from his stories of multinational corporations and their most famous or infamous bosses is that their control requires a more international form of government, not a futile attempt to return to nationalistic control. Thus the growth of the multinationals could unintentionally lead to a global political gain, for 'Set quite apart from the bloodstained arena of nationalism is the new world of big business, a world where the jealousies of the nation-states are actually forgotten.'

BIBLIOGRAPHY

PARKINSON, C. N., *Parkinson's Law and Other Studies in Administration*, Murray, 1958; Penguin, 1965.
PARKINSON, C. N., *The Law and the Profits*, Murray, 1960; Penguin, 1965.
PARKINSON, C. N., *Big Business*, Weidenfeld & Nicolson, 1974.
PARKINSON, C. N., *The Rise of Big Business*, Weidenfeld & Nicolson, 1977.

Laurence J. Peter

Laurence J. Peter (1919–1990) was born in Canada and studied education at Washington State University. He was Professor of Education at the University of Southern California, where his work concerned emotionally disturbed and retarded children. He has been a school psychologist, prison instructor, counsellor and consultant. His co-author Raymond Hull (1919–1985) was born in England, then moved to Canada. He wrote many plays for television and stage and also articles for leading periodicals. He also developed Peter's principle into a book, Peter himself having reached a level in the University hierarchy where he was unable to do anything about it.

This latter fact can be understood by 'hierarchiologists' (those who study hierarchies) from the *Peter Principle*. Derived from the analysis of the hundreds of cases of incompetence in organizations which can be seen anywhere, the Principle states: 'In a hierarchy every employee tends to rise to his level of incompetence.' This applies to all organizations.

The Principle assumes a constant quest for high performance. Hence people competent at their jobs are promoted so that they may do still better. Competence in each new position qualifies for promotion to the next, until people arrive at jobs beyond their abilities; they then no longer perform in a way that gains further promotion. This is the individual's level of incompetence. Given two conditions – enough ranks in the hierarchy to provide promotions and enough time to move through them – all employees rise to and remain at their level of incompetence. This can be stated as *Peter's Corollary*: 'In time, every post tends to be occupied by an employee who is incompetent to carry out its duties.' Every employee ultimately achieves *Peter's Plateau* at which his *Promotion Quotient* is zero.

How then is any work ever accomplished? Work is done by those who have not yet reached their level of incompetence. There can be occasional instances of 'summit competence' where competent company chairmen or victorious field marshals have not yet had time to reach their level of incompetence. Frequently such persons side-step into another field whose hierarchy enables them to attain a level of incompetence not available to them before. In general, classical pyramidal structures divided horizontally by a class barrier are more efficient than classless or egalitarian hierarchies. Beneath the class barrier many employees remain, unable to rise high enough to reach their level of incompetence. They spend their whole careers on tasks they can do well. Above the class barrier the pyramid apex narrows rapidly thus holding below their incompetence level many who joined because of opportunities of starting at this high point in the hierarchy. Aptitude tests for promotion candidates do not in fact foster efficiency the main difference being that tested people reach their levels of incompetence sooner.

There are two main methods of accelerating promotion to the incompetence level, namely *pull* and *push*. 'Pull' is defined as 'an employee's relationship – by blood, marriage or acquaintance – with a person higher in the hierarchy'. 'Push' is usually shown by an abnormal interest in training and general self-improvement. The question is which of these two methods is more effective? The force of push is overestimated, for it is normally overcome by the downward pressure of the seniority factor. Pull, of course, is comparatively unaffected by this, which yields the dictum 'never push when you can pull'.

Non-hierarchiologists are sometimes deceived by apparent exceptions to the Peter Principle. Being kicked upstairs or sideways to a job with a longer title in a remote building is mistakenly thought to contravene the Principle. But the Principle applies only to genuine promotion *from* a level of competence, whereas both the above cases are pseudo-promotions between levels of incompetence.

Another error is in the notion of what is success. It is said that 'nothing succeeds like success'. In fact, hierarchiology shows that nothing fails like success. What is called 'success' the hierarchiologist recognizes as *final placement*. The so-called success ailments such as ulcers, colitis, insomnia, dermatitis and sexual impotence constitute the *final placement syndrome*, typical of those working beyond their level of competence.

Obviously the longer a hierarchy has been established the less useful work will be done, and eventually no useful work may be done at all (as in the injelitis coma discussed by Parkinson, earlier in this chapter). Parkinson's theory holds that as work expands to fill available time, so more subordinate officials are appointed whose arrival necessarily expands the work further, and so on; hence, hierarchical expansion. But the Peter Principle shows that the expansion is due to a genuine striving for efficiency. Those who have reached their levels of incompetence seek desperately some means of overcoming their inadequacy and as a last resort appoint more staff to see if this will help. This is the reason why there is no direct relationship between the size of the staff and the amount of useful work done.

BIBLIOGRAPHY

PETER, L. J. and HULL, R., *The Peter Principle*, William Morrow, 1969.

4   The Management of Organizations

To manage is to forecast and plan, to organize, to command, to coordinate and to control.
HENRI FAYOL

I am convinced that a logical scheme of organization, a structure based on principles, which take priority over personalities, is in the long run better both for the morale of an undertaking as a whole and for the happiness of individuals, than the attempt to build one's organization around individuals.
LYNDALL F. URWICK

Scientific management will mean, for the employers and the workmen who adopt it, the elimination of almost all causes for dispute and disagreement between them.
FREDERICK W. TAYLOR

It [modern management] was to ensure that as a craft declined the worker would sink to the level of general and undifferentiated labour power, adaptable to a large range of simple tasks, while as science grew, it would be concentrated in the hands of management.
HARRY BRAVERMAN

How can we avoid the two extremes: too great bossism in giving orders, and practically no orders given? ... My solution is to depersonalize the giving of orders, to unite all concerned in a study of the situation, to discover the law of the situation and obey that.
MARY PARKER FOLLETT

The needs of large-scale organizations have to be satisfied by common people achieving uncommon performance.
PETER F. DRUCKER

An organization does not make decisions; its function is to provide a framework, based on established criteria, within which decisions can be fashioned in an orderly manner.
ALFRED P. SLOAN

Excellent companies were, above all, 'brilliant on the basics'.
THOMAS J. PETERS and ROBERT H. WATERMAN

A 'Z' company can balance social relationships with productivity because the two relate closely anyway: a society and an economy represent two facets of one nation.
WILLIAM OUCHI

The degree to which the opportunity to use power effectively is granted or withheld from individuals is one operative difference between those companies which stagnate and those which innovate.
ROSABETH MOSS KANTER

An organization ... quite literally does impose the environment that imposes on it.
KARL E. WEICK

Organizations with different structures, functioning in different environments, have to be managed. As long as there is management there will be the problem of how to manage better. In one sense, attempts at answers to the problem will be as numerous as there are managers, for each will bring an individual approach to the task. Nonetheless, at any one time there is enough in common for there to be broad similarities in what is thought and what is taught on this issue. The writers in this section have each sought to improve the understanding of administration and its practice. They have looked for the ingredients of a better management.

Henri Fayol puts forward a classic analysis of the management task, based on his long practical experience of doing the job and the personal insights he gained. Lyndall Urwick and Edward Brech have over many years collated and expounded general principles of administration, aiming at a unified body of knowledge. Frederick Taylor's name is synonymous with the term 'scientific management'. His extremely influential ideas made him a controversial figure in his own day and have remained a subject for much argument. Harry Braverman mounts a critique, from a Marxist perspective, of the degradation which Taylor's ideas bring to modern work.

Mary Parker Follett's emphasis is on the 'law of the situation' which presents its own solutions if people will only look beyond the interplay of personalities. Peter Drucker emphasizes the necessity of 'management by objectives' if high performance is to be achieved.

Alfred P. Sloan, drawing on his experience as the head of one of the largest corporations in the world, is concerned with establishing the management framework within which objectives are established and decisions made. Thomas Peters and Robert Waterman, in an influential analysis, report a set of eight attributes which characterize excellent firms and propose that they should be widely adopted. William Ouchi asks what management lessons the West can learn from Japanese companies and suggests adaptations which can be beneficially applied. Rosabeth

Moss Kanter proposes ways in which organizations should be managed to draw more fully on the total human resources within them. Karl E. Weick points to the way in which each individual's subjective attempts to make sense of the organization must be understood and taken into account in the management process.

Henri Fayol

Henri Fayol (1841–1925) was a mining engineer by training. A Frenchman, he spent his working life with the French mining and metallurgical combine Commentry-Fourchamboult-Decazeville, first as an engineer but from his early thirties onwards in general management. From 1888 to 1918 he was Managing Director.

Fayol is among those who have achieved fame for ideas made known very late in life. He was in his seventies before he published them in a form which came to be widely read. He had written technical articles on mining engineering and a few preliminary papers on administration, but it was in 1916 that the *Bulletin de la Société de l'Industrie Minérale* printed Fayol's *Administration Industrielle et Générale – Prévoyance, Organisation, Commandement, Coordination, Contrôle.* He is also among those whose reputation rests on a single short publication still frequently reprinted as a book; his other writings are little known.

The English version appears as *General and Industrial Management*, translated by Constance Storrs and first issued in 1949. There has been some debate over this rendering of the title of the work, and in particular of expressing the French word *'administration'* by the term 'management'. It is argued that this could imply that Fayol is concerned only with industrial management, whereas his own preface claims that: 'Management plays a very important part in the government of undertakings; of all undertakings, large or small, industrial, commercial, political, religious or any other.' Indeed, in his last years he studied the problems of State public services and lectured at the École Supérieure de la Guerre. So it can be accepted that his intention was to initiate a theoretical analysis appropriate to a wide range of organizations.

Fayol suggests that all activities to which industrial undertakings give rise can be divided into the following groups:

1. technical activities (production, manufacture, adaptation)
2. commercial activities (buying, selling, exchange)
3. financial activities (search for and optimum use of capital)
4. security activities (protection of property and persons)
5. accounting activities (stocktaking, balance sheet, costs, statistics)
6. managerial activities (planning, organization, command, coordination, control).

Be the undertaking simple or complex, big or small, these six groups of activities or essential functions are always present.

Most of these six groups of activities will be present in most jobs but in varying measure, with the managerial element in particular being greatest in senior jobs and least or absent in direct production or lower clerical tasks. Managerial activities are specially emphasized as being universal to organizations. But it is a commonplace to ask: What is management? Is it anything that can be identified and stand on its own, or is it a word, a label, that has no substance?

Fayol's answer was unique at the time. The core of his contribution is his definition of management as comprising five elements:

1. to forecast and plan (in the French, *prévoyance*) – 'examining the future and drawing up the plan of action';
2. to organize – 'building up the structure, material and human, of the undertaking';
3. to command – 'maintaining activity among the personnel';
4. to coordinate – 'binding together, unifying and harmonizing all activity and effort';
5. to control – 'seeing that everything occurs in conformity with established rule and expressed command'.

For Fayol, managing means looking ahead, which makes the process of *forecasting and planning* a central business activity. Management must 'assess the future and make provision for it'. To function adequately a business organization needs a plan which has the characteristics of 'unity, continuity, flexibility and precision'. The problems of planning which management must overcome are:

- making sure that the objectives of each part of the organization are securely welded together (unity);
- using both short- and long-term forecasting (continuity);
- being able to adapt the plan in the light of changing circumstances (flexibility);
- attempting accurately to predict courses of action (precision).

The essence of planning is to allow the optimum use of resources. Interestingly, Fayol in 1916 argued the necessity of a national plan for France, to be produced by the government.

To *organize* is 'building up the structure, material and human, of the undertaking'. The task of management is to build up an organization which will allow the basic activities to be carried out in an optimal manner. Central to this is a structure in which plans are efficiently prepared and carried out. There must be unity of command and direction, clear definition of responsibilities and precise decision making backed up by an efficient system for selecting and training managers.

Fayol's third element comes logically after the first two. An organization must start with a plan, a definition of its goals. It must then initiate an organization structure appropriate to the achievement of those goals. Third, the organization must be put in motion, which is *command*, maintaining activity among the personnel. Through an ability to command, the manager obtains the best possible performance from subordinates. This must be done through example, knowledge of the business, knowledge of the subordinates, continuous contact with staff, and by maintaining a broad view of the directing function. In this way the manager maintains a high level of activity by instilling a sense of mission.

Command refers to the relationship between a manager and the subordinates in the area of the immediate task. But organizations have a variety of tasks to perform, so *coordination* is necessary 'binding together, unifying and harmonizing all activity and effort'. Essentially this is making sure that one department's efforts are coincident with the efforts of other departments; also keeping all activities in perspective with regard to the overall aims of the organization. This can only be attained by a constant circulation of information and regular meetings of management.

Finally, there is *control*, logically the final element which checks that the other four are in fact performing properly: 'seeing that everything occurs in conformity with established rule and expressed command.' To be effective, control must operate quickly and there must be a system of sanctions. The best way to ensure this is to separate all functions concerned with inspection from the operation departments whose work they inspect. Fayol believed in independent, impartial staff departments.

Fayol uses this classification to divide up his chapters on how to administer or manage. It is probable that when he wrote of '*une doctrine administrative*' he had in mind not only the above theory, but the addition of experience to theoretical analysis to form a doctrine of good management. He summarizes the lessons of his own experience in a number of General Principles of Management. These are his own rules; he does not assume that they are necessarily of universal application nor that they have any great permanence. Nonetheless, most have become part of managerial know-how and many are regarded as fundamental tenets. Fayol outlines the following 14 principles:

1. Division of work: specialization allows the individual to build up expertise and thereby be more productive.
2. Authority: the right to issue commands, together with the equivalent responsibility for its exercise.
3. Discipline: this is two-sided, for employees only obey orders if management play their part by providing good leadership.
4. Unity of command: in contrast to F. W. Taylor's functional authority (see later in this chapter), Fayol was quite clear that each worker should have only one boss with no other conflicting lines of command. On this issue history has favoured Fayol, for most managers adhere to his principle.
5. Unity of direction: people engaged in the same kinds of activities must have the same objectives in a single plan.
6. Subordination of individual interest to general interest: management must see that the goals of the firm are always paramount.

7. Remuneration: payment is an important motivator although, by analysing a number of different possibilities, Fayol points out that there is no such thing as a perfect system.
8. Centralization or decentralization: again this is a matter of degree depending on the condition of the business and the quality of its personnel.
9. Scalar chain: a hierarchy is necessary for unity of direction but lateral communication is also fundamental as long as superiors know that such communication is taking place.
10. Order: both material order and social order are necessary. The former minimizes lost time and unproductive handling of materials. The latter is achieved through organization and selection.
11. Equity: in running a business, a 'combination of kindliness and justice' is needed in treating employees if equity is to be achieved.
12. Stability of tenure: this is essential due to the time and expense involved in training good management. Fayol believes that successful businesses tend to have more stable managerial personnel.
13. Initiative: allowing all personnel to show their initiative in some way is a source of strength for the organization even though it may well involve a sacrifice of 'personal vanity' on the part of many managers.
14. *Esprit de corps*: management must foster the morale of its employees. To quote Fayol, 'real talent is needed to coordinate effort, encourage keenness, use each person's abilities and reward each one's merit without arousing possible jealousies and disturbing harmonious relations'.

Fayol's pride of place in this field is due not so much to his principles of how to manage, enduring though these are, as to his definition of what management is. He is the earliest known proponent of a theoretical analysis of managerial activities – an analysis which has withstood almost a century of critical discussion. There can have been few writers since who have not been influenced by it; indeed, his five elements have provided a system of concepts by which managers may clarify their thinking about what it is they have to do.

BIBLIOGRAPHY

FAYOL, H., *General and Industrial Management*, Pitman, 1949. Translated by Constance Storrs from the original *Administration Industrielle et Générale*, 1916.

Lyndall F. Urwick
and Edward F. L. Brech

Lyndall F. Urwick (1891–1983) had experience of both industry and the army, and was director of the International Management Institute in Geneva. He founded and until 1951 was head of Urwick, Orr and Partners, the first British firm of management consultants. Subsequently he devoted himself to lecturing and writing about management.

Edward F. L. Brech (1909–2006) was a consultant colleague of Urwick's and co-author with him of the trilogy compiled and published as *The Making of Scientific Management*. He was director of the Construction Industry Training Board, and in later life took on the task of researching and writing a history of the development of British management in the late nineteenth and twentieth centuries. At the age of 85 he was awarded a PhD for a thesis on the concept and gestation of a professional body for British management in the first half of the twentieth century. He was in the Guinness Book of Records as the then oldest British recipient of a PhD. At the age of 96 he was awarded a higher doctorate (DLitt) for his historical research, and at his death in his 98th year was engaged on further historical work.

Both Urwick and Brech approach the subject of management in a manner similar to that of Fayol (see previous section). In Urwick's prolific output of books and booklets, Fayol's theoretical analysis and principles of application reappear continually. Indeed, the place of Urwick and Brech in the history of management is due less to innovations that either may have made in contemporary thinking, than to their gathering together of current ideas and the thoughts of pioneers such as Fayol, Taylor (see next section) and Follett (see later in this chapter), and expounding them. Both have striven to gain recognition for a broad range of principles of administration and for developing a body of professional administrative knowledge.

Much of what Urwick has said and written on general management has been arranged under Fayol's headings of forecasting, planning, organization, coordination, command and control. In discussing these elements, Urwick has over the years drawn together a number of principles of good organization, founded on his conviction that a logical structure is better for efficiency and morale than one allowed to develop around personalities. For example, the *Principle of Specialization* states that as far as possible each individual should perform a single function only. This implies an increasingly specialized division of activities in industry, giving rise to three kinds of formal relations: Line, Functional (where a department is responsible for a specialized function such as Personnel or Accounts) and Staff. Urwick strongly advocates the use of staff subordinates to help with the detailed work of coordination. These subordinates have staff relationships with other subordinates, in which they act not on their own authority but only on behalf of their chief.

Despite the complexity of highly specialized organizations, the *Principle of Authority* should be observed. There should be a clear line of authority, known and recognized, from the top to each individual. The duties, authority and responsibility of each position, and its relationships with other positions, should be defined in writing and made known to everyone concerned – the *Principle of Definition*. Moreover, in defining positions the *Principle of Correspondence* – authority being commensurate with responsibility – should be applied. The *Span of Control* of any manager should not exceed five, or at most six, subordinates whose work interlocks. This is because the manager has to supervise not merely individual subordinates, but the numerous interrelationships between them. Thus the maximum feasible span of control determines how far specialization can extend by the addition of subordinates and may set a limit to delegation. Nevertheless, Urwick is of the opinion that managers overwhelmed with detail must blame their own failure to delegate.

But Urwick deals with far more than the structure of organization. He has a great deal to say on leadership, for instance. A leader should remember that there are four functions to the role. These are: (i) embodying and representing the organization; (ii)initiating thought and action; (iii) administering routine; and (iv) interpreting to others the purpose and meaning of what is done. In addition, Urwick describes what makes a good plan for a business. He criticizes those who spend months choosing the right machine but imagine they have a flair for choosing the right subordinate in an interview lasting a few minutes. He argues that superiors must take absolute responsibility for what their subordinates do. Indeed, there can be few topics in administration on which Urwick has not something to say.

Edward Brech emphasizes management as a social process. He provides many examples of organization charts and job descriptions of managers' authority and responsibilities. But he warns against considering these as 'the structure', when what is required is an agreed interpretation of the relationships. These cannot be presented in a chart alone, but require management. This is on the one hand a task of judgement and decision, and on the other the motivating of people to cooperative participation in carrying out the decisions reached. It is characteristic that he prefers to drop the word 'command' from among the elements of management, using instead the term 'motivation'.

Brech takes up and re-states most of Urwick's views, but in a way which brings them into line with current practice and attitudes. He does not always agree with Urwick. For example, in his opinion, a span of control need not necessarily be five or six; it will vary with the capacity of the manager concerned and the task in hand. Some managers may find four subordinates too many; others may be able to carry eight or nine. Brech gives greater stress to management's responsibility for the personal and social satisfactions of its employees. Moreover, he believes that the morale of an organization is, in the end, largely a reflection of the outlook of its chief executive.

Between them, Urwick and Brech have surveyed the field of management so widely that nothing as succinct as this summary can do them justice. This, in fact, is the measure of their contribution.

BIBLIOGRAPHY

BRECH, E. F. L., *Management: Its Nature and Significance*, Pitman, 1948.
BRECH, E. F. L., *Organization: The Framework of Management*, 2nd edn, Longmans, 1965.
BRECH, E. F. L., (ed.), *The Principles and Practice of Management*, 3rd edn, Longmans, 1975.
BRECH, E. F. L., *A History of Management*, vols. 1–5, Institute of Management, 2006.
URWICK, L. F., *The Elements of Administration*, Pitman, 1947.
URWICK, L. F. and BRECH E. F. L., *The Making of Scientific Management*, 3 vols, Pitman, 1945–50.

Frederick W. Taylor

Frederick Winslow Taylor (1856–1917) was an engineer by training. He joined the Midvale Steel Works as a labourer and rose rapidly to be foreman and later Chief Engineer. He was afterwards employed at the Bethlehem Steel Works, then became a consultant and devoted his time to the propagation of his ideas.

He first published his views on management in a paper entitled 'A Piece Rate System', read to the American Society of Mechanical Engineers in 1895. These views were expanded into a book *Shop Management* (1903) and further developed in *Principles of Scientific Management* (1911). As a result of labour troubles caused by the attempt to apply his principles in a government arsenal, a House of Representatives' Special Committee was set up in 1911 to investigate Taylor's system of shop management. (A full description of events at the arsenal is given in Aitken's case study.) In 1947, *Shop Management*, the *Principles* and Taylor's Testimony to the Special Committee were collected together and published under the title of *Scientific Management*.

Taylor was the founder of the movement known as 'scientific management'. 'The principal object of management,' he states, 'should be to secure the maximum prosperity for the employer, coupled with the maximum prosperity of each employee.' For the employer, 'maximum prosperity' means not just large profits in the short term, but the development of all aspects of the enterprise to a state of permanent prosperity. For employees 'maximum prosperity' means not just immediate higher wages, but personal development so that they may perform efficiently in the highest grade of work for which their natural abilities fit them. The mutual interdependence of management and workers, and the necessity of their working together towards the common aim of increased prosperity for all, seemed completely self-evident to Taylor. He was thus driven to ask: why is there so much antagonism and inefficiency?

He suggests three causes: first, the fallacious belief of the workers that any increase in output will inevitably result in unemployment; second, defective systems of management which make it necessary for workers to restrict output in order to protect their interests ('systematic soldiering'); third, inefficient rule-of-thumb, effort-wasting methods of work. Taylor conceived it to be the aim of scientific management to overcome these obstacles. This could be achieved by a systematic study of work to discover the most efficient methods of performing the job, and then a systematic study of management leading to the most efficient methods of controlling the workers. This would bring a great increase in efficiency and with it prosperity to the benefit of all, since a highly efficient prosperous business would be in a much better position to ensure the continuing well-paid employment of its workers. As Taylor put it: 'What the workmen want from their employers beyond anything else is high wages and what employers want from their workmen most of all is low labour cost of manufacture ... the existence or absence of these two elements forms the best index to either good or bad management.'

To achieve this Taylor lays down four 'great underlying principles of management':

1. THE DEVELOPMENT OF A TRUE SCIENCE OF WORK

He points out that we do not really know what constitutes a fair day's work; a boss therefore has unlimited opportunities for complaining about workers' inadequacies, and workers never really know what is expected of them. This can be remedied by the establishment after scientific investigation of a 'large daily task' as the amount to be done by a suitable worker under optimum conditions. For this they would receive a high rate of pay – much higher than the average worker would receive in 'unscientific' factories. They would also suffer a loss of income if they failed to achieve this performance.

2. THE SCIENTIFIC SELECTION AND PROGRESSIVE DEVELOPMENT OF THE WORKER

To earn this high rate of pay workers would have to be scientifically selected to ensure that they possess the physical and intellectual qualities to enable them to achieve the output required. Then they must be systematically trained to be 'first class'. Taylor believes that every worker could be first class at some job. It was the responsibility of management to develop workers, offering them opportunities for advancement which would finally enable them to do 'the highest, most interesting and most profitable class of work' for which they could become first class.

3. THE BRINGING TOGETHER OF THE SCIENCE OF WORK AND THE SCIENTIFICALLY SELECTED AND TRAINED WORKERS

It is this process that causes the 'mental revolution' in management; Taylor maintains that almost invariably the major resistance to scientific management comes from the side of management. The workers, he finds, are very willing to cooperate in learning to do a good job for a high rate of pay.

4. THE CONSTANT AND INTIMATE COOPERATION OF MANAGEMENT AND WORKERS

There is an almost equal division of work and responsibility between management and workers. The management takes over all the work for which it is better fitted than the workers (that is, the specification and verification of the methods, time, price and quality standards of the job) and the continuous supervision and control of the workers doing it. As Taylor saw it, there should be hardly a single act done by any worker which is not preceded and followed by some act on the part of management. With this close personal cooperation, the opportunities for conflict are almost eliminated since the operation of this authority is not arbitrary. Managers are continually demonstrating that their decisions are subject to the same discipline as the workers are asked to accept, namely the scientific study of the work.

By 'science' Taylor means systematic observation and measurement, an example that he often quotes being the development of 'the science of shovelling'. He is insistent that, although shovelling is a very simple job, the study of the factors affecting efficient shovelling is quite complex. So much so that a worker who is phlegmatic enough to be able to do the job and stupid enough to choose it is extremely unlikely to be able to develop the most efficient method alone. But this is in fact what is hoped will happen. The scientific study of shovelling involves the determination of the optimum load that a first-class worker can handle with each shovelful. Then the correct size of shovel to obtain this load, with different materials, must be established. Workers must be provided with a range of shovels and told which one to use. They must then be placed on an incentive payment scheme which allows them to earn high wages (double what they would earn in unscientific firms) in return for high output.

The insistence on maximum specialization and the removal of all extraneous elements in order to concentrate on the essential task are fundamental to Taylor's thinking. He applies these concepts to management too. He considers that the work of a typical factory supervisor is composed of a number of different functions (such as cost clerk, time clerk, inspector, repair boss, shop disciplinarian); he believes that these could be separated out and performed by different specialists who would each be responsible for controlling different aspects of the work and the workers. He calls this system 'functional management' and likens the increased efficiency that it would bring to that obtained in a school where classes go to specialist teachers for different subjects, compared with a school in which one teacher teaches all subjects. He also formulates 'the exception principle' which lays down that management reports should be condensed into comparative summaries giving in detail only the exceptions to past standards or averages – both the especially good and the especially bad exceptions. Thus the manager would obtain an immediate and comprehensive view of the progress of the work.

Taylor's methods have been followed by many others, among them Gantt, Frank and Lillian Gilbreth, Bedaux, Rowan and Halsey. They have developed his thinking into what is now called 'work study' or 'industrial engineering'. But even in his lifetime Taylor's ideas led to bitter controversy over the alleged inhumanity of his system, which was said to reduce workers to the level of efficiently functioning machines. In fairness to Taylor, it must be said that his principles were often inadequately understood. For example, few managements have been willing to put into practice one of his basic tenets – that there should be no limit to the earnings of a high-producing worker; many incentive schemes involve such limits. This may inhibit the 'mental revolution' Taylor sought, which requires that 'both sides take their eyes off the division of the surplus as the all-important matter and together turn their attention towards increasing the size of the surplus'.

BIBLIOGRAPHY

AITKEN, H. G. J., *Taylorism at Watertown Arsenal*, Harvard University Press, 1960.
TAYLOR, F. W., *Scientific Management*, Harper & Row, 1947.

Harry Braverman and the 'Labour Process' Debate

Harry Braverman (1920–1976) was an American Marxist theorist who was concerned to analyse the effects of the modern capitalist economy on the organization of work. He was stimulated to this by what he regarded as the unrealistic nature of much of what was written about productive labour. Braverman himself had very practical experience to bring to his analysis: he was trained as a craftsman coppersmith and worked at that trade and at pipe fitting and sheet-metal work. He was employed in a naval shipyard, a railroad repair shop and two sheet steel plants – in all of which he experienced the impact of technological change on craft employment. In later years as a journalist, book editor and then publishing executive, he again had experience of the impact of modern technology – this time on administrative work such as marketing, accounting and book production routines. His basic thesis is that, in a capitalist economy, all these changes act to de-skill work and to remove more and more power away from workers and into the hands of owners and managers. His book expounding this theme, *Labour and Monopoly Capitalism: The Degradation of Work in the Twentieth Century*, was awarded the 1974 C. Wright Mills Prize of the Society for the Study of Social Problems.

Braverman uses as a framework for analysing the nature of the capitalist system that presented by Karl Marx in *Capital*, Volume 1 (published in 1867), and applies it to modern work and its organization. Marx used the term the 'labour process' to refer to the ways by which raw materials are transformed into goods by human labour using tools and machines. In a capitalist system, by definition, the tools and machines are not owned by the workers but by the capitalists, and so the resulting goods become commodities to be sold on the market for the owners' profit. Workers themselves also have only a commodity to offer: their labour in exchange for wages. In this system it is inevitable that owners will exploit workers (that is, obtain as much as possible as a contribution to profit while paying as little as possible in return as wages).

In modern terms, according to Braverman, this requires managers (as representatives of owners) to design and redesign work in order to achieve competitive levels of profit. They need to have maximum control of workers and to be looking continually for ways of increasing that control. Typically, this has been achieved by increasing the division of labour into smaller and smaller, less and less demanding, fragments of tasks. In this way increased output may be obtained from a workforce which is cheaper, since it is less skilled and less trained. Ford-type mass production epitomizes the results. For example, car workers on an assembly line who drive to their place of work will have already exercised their highest level of skill for that day.

This de-skilling and the abolition of craft ownership of work lead to alienation. This is another reason for the owning class (and its representatives – the managers) to need to control the working class. They are seen as untrustworthy members of an opposing class who are likely to obstruct, undermine or otherwise resist the legitimate capitalist objective of maximizing profit. From this point of view, ways of organizing the labour and production process are not rationally determined in order to increase objective efficiency; rather organizations take the form they do in order to enhance the domination of capital over labour.

The prime advocate of this approach to efficiency in the organization of production was F. W. Taylor (see earlier in this chapter). Braverman sees so-called 'scientific management' as the classic and inevitable method used to control labour in growing capitalist enterprises. It is not scientific, of course, since it does not attempt to discover what is the actual case, but accepts management's view that it has a refractory workforce which has to be kept under control. It is not a 'science of work' but a 'science of the management of others' work under capitalist conditions'. Its three basic tenets are (1) that knowledge of the labour process must be gathered in one place, (2) that it must be the exclusive preserve of management and not available to the workers, and (3) that this monopoly of knowledge must be used by management to control each step of the labour process. In total contrast to craft working, Taylor advocated a complete separation of conception from execution.

Braverman insists that scientific management is in full flow as the dominant approach to capitalist organization of the labour process. He is very dismissive of those social science writers of the 'human relations' approach (see Mayo, Likert and McGregor, Herzberg and so on, in Chapter 6) who insist on the need to humanize work and improve the quality of working life. In industry these ideas are relegated to the sidelines of the personnel and training departments, with little real impact on the management of workers or work. In production departments, where the labour process is actually carried out and controlled, Taylorism reigns supreme. Indeed, it is being extended to an even wider range of occupations, such as clerical and administrative routines which are continually being de-skilled with the use of new computer technology. Braverman rejects the idea that automation is qualitatively different in the skill demands it makes of workers as compared to mechanization. He argues that it, too, will decrease skill, as will any other technological development. This result is not a matter of a particular technology, but of how it is inevitably used to increase the control of the labour process by capital in the interests of profit.

The de-skilling and cheapening of such white collar jobs as those of clerks and computer operators lead to an increase in the alienated working class. In this situation of 'monopoly capitalism' (that is, where giant corporations control the markets), new commodities are brought into being to shape the consumer to the needs of capital. All of society becomes a gigantic marketplace in the pursuit of profit. Printing and television, for example, become vehicles largely for marketing rather than for information and education. Thus, there is not only the degradation of work but also the degradation of family and community.

In the aftermath of Braverman's book, Marxist sociologists have continued to discuss the adequacy of its vision. Two particular issues have been taken up. The first concerns the inevitability of de-skilling on Taylorist lines in capitalist production. Braverman argued that this was the one classic form which gave both cheapness and control in the labour process, and therefore was inevitable. Later writers have suggested that de-skilling may not be universal and that work under capitalism can take a variety of forms. Managements may use different ways to achieve their objectives of control. In an historical survey of workplace relations, Richard Edwards argues that, although a hierarchy has remained constant, various additional forms of control have been used (for example coercive, technical, bureaucratic) depending upon the struggle of owners, workers and others to protect and advance their interests.

A second criticism has focused on Braverman's argument that the de-skilling of white collar workers will lead to an increase in the working class. As Graeme Salaman argues, this neglects the important element of the subjective identification of workers. This means that even de-skilled administrators and computer operators, for example, consider themselves – and therefore act and vote – as middle class.

BIBLIOGRAPHY

BRAVERMAN, H., *Labour and Monopoly Capitalism: The Degradation of Work in the Twentieth Century*, Monthly Review Press, 1974.

EDWARDS, R., *Contested Terrain: The Transformation of the Workplace in the Twentieth Century*, Heinemann, 1979.

SALAMAN, G., *Working*, Tavistock Publications, 1986.

Mary Parker Follett

Mary Parker Follett (1868–1933) was born in Boston and educated at Harvard and Cambridge. She was a student of philosophy, history and political science and wrote a number of works on political science including *The New State* and *Creative Experience*. In Boston she was very active in social work, taking a leading part in establishing evening classes and recreational centres for young people. She helped to develop youth employment bureaux which led her to study industry and management. She gained a reputation as a writer and as an independent member of statutory wage boards. She spent most of the last five years of her life studying and lecturing in England. Her collected papers have been issued posthumously under the title *Dynamic Administration* (edited by H. C. Metcalf and L. Urwick).

Follett holds very strongly that there are principles common to all spheres of administration. She became interested in business administration when she found that managers in industry were facing the same problems (of control, power, participation and conflict) as administrators in the public service. She felt that these problems were being more actively tackled by managers than by administrators. Business was a ferment of new ideas and experiments were bolder.

Follett is interested in general questions about the working of organizations, of which the two most basic are: (i) what do you want employees to do? and (ii) how do you scientifically control and guide employees' conduct in work and social relations? For answers to these questions she looks to an analysis of the fundamental motives involved in human relationships – particularly the reactions of the individual within the social group. Her writings are an attempt to provide an outlook on management in which organizations, leadership and power are dealt with as human problems. She was one of the first to appreciate the value of the then new tool of psychology. The problems for her are essentially those of reconciling individuals and social groups. Management must attempt to understand how these groups are formed and why and how to weld them together into a community of commitment and experience, so that the general purpose of the group is also the common aim of all its members.

Follett postulated four fundamental principles of organization:

1. COORDINATION BY DIRECT CONTACT

The responsible people must be in direct contact regardless of their positions in the organization. 'Horizontal' communication is as important as 'vertical' chains of command in achieving coordination.

2. COORDINATION IN THE EARLY STAGES

The people concerned should be involved in policy or decisions while these are being formed and not simply brought in afterwards. In this way the benefits of participation will be obtained in increased motivation and morale.

3. COORDINATION AS THE 'RECIPROCAL RELATING' OF ALL FACTORS IN A SITUATION

All factors have to be related to one another, and these interrelationships must themselves be taken into account.

4. COORDINATION AS A CONTINUING PROCESS

'An executive decision is a moment in a process.' So many people contribute to the making of a decision that the concept of final or ultimate responsibility is an illusion. Rather, combined knowledge and joint responsibility are critical. Authority and responsibility should derive from the actual function to be performed, not from one's place in the hierarchy.

It was Follett's belief that differences could be made to contribute to the common cause if they were resolved, not by domination or by compromise, but by 'integration'; thus, from the conflict of ideas and attitudes a new advance towards a common objective could emerge. She regarded as fundamental the joint study of facts and the bringing of objective differences into the open. From this would emerge the 'law of the situation' which would govern the orders to be given and the attitudes of groups and individuals to these orders. She felt it important to ensure that the work people are required to do be based on the objective requirements of the situation – not on the personal whim of a particular manager. 'The head of the sales department does not give orders to the head of the production department or vice versa. Each studies the market and the final decision is made as the market demands.' In this way an 'integrative unity' would be established in which all managers accept responsibility as a result of wishing to make their particular contributions to the best of their ability. All would fundamentally receive orders only from a personal realization and acceptance of what needs to be done. 'One *person* should not give orders to another *person*, but both should agree to take their orders from the situation.'

The idea of the organization as an 'integrative unity' may seem at variance with the traditional concepts of power, responsibility and leadership. Follett tries to show that these concepts, viewed in this new light, if anything strengthen the idea of unity. In the process, the notions of 'power *with*' rather than 'power *over*', of joint responsibility and *multiple* leadership are developed. Leaders must become aware of the groups in which they work and must regard their job as being concerned with drawing out the abilities and contributions of individual members. They must know how 'to create a group power rather than express a personal power'.

The basis of Follett's thinking is the concept of partnership. The core of her contribution is the proposition that in a democratic society the primary task of management is so to arrange the situation such that people cooperate readily of their own accord.

BIBLIOGRAPHY

FOLLETT, M. P., *The New State*, Longmans, 1920.
FOLLETT, M. P., *Creative Experience*, Longmans, 1924.
FOLLETT, M. P., *Dynamic Administration*, Pitman, 1941.

Peter F. Drucker

Peter Drucker (1909–2005) was born in Austria. He qualified in law and was a journalist in Germany until the advent of the Nazis. After a period in London, in 1937 he moved permanently to the USA, becoming an American citizen in 1943. He has been an economic consultant to banks and insurance companies and an adviser on business policy and management to a large number of American corporations. He was for many years at New York University Business School and from 1971 until his death was Clarke Professor of Social Science at Claremont Graduate University, California. In 1987 the University named its Management School after him. In 2002 he was awarded the Presidential Medal of Freedom for his contribution to American life.

Drucker has published over 30 books on business topics and is the external author who has contributed the largest number of articles to the Harvard Business Review. His writings have made him one of the leading contemporary thinkers on management issues – the doyen of management gurus.

Drucker's work begins with a view of top management and its critical role in the representative institution of modern industrial society, namely the large corporation. He identifies management as the central problem area, and the manager as the dynamic element in every business who provides the integration of the inevitably disparate parts. Managers through their control of the decision-making structure of the modern corporation breathe life into the organization and the wider society. The manager is given human and material resources to work with, and from them must fashion a productive enterprise from which springs the wealth of society.

This is becoming increasingly true as we operate in an era of knowledge technology, making human beings central to effective performance in organizations. Yet managers, while becoming ever more basic resources of a business, are the scarcest, the most expensive and the most perishable. Given this, it becomes extremely important that managers should be used as effectively as is possible at the present state of knowledge about the practice and functions of management. It is not just a question of efficiency, that is, doing things right; effectiveness is doing the right things. 'There is nothing so useless as doing efficiently that which should not be done at all.'

It is only possible to arrive at prescriptions for effectiveness if we first understand the role of the manager in the organization, that is, if we know what the job of management is. There are two dimensions to the task of management – an economic dimension and a time dimension. Managers who are responsible for business organizations must always put economic performance first; this is not the case for all administrators. The second dimension, time, is one which is present in all decision-making systems. Management always has to think of the impact of a decision on the present, the short-term future and the long-term future.

Management is the job of organizing resources to achieve satisfactory performance – to produce an enterprise from material and human resources. This does not necessarily mean profit maximization. Profit is not the cause of business behaviour, or the rationale of business decision making in the sense of always attempting to achieve the maximum profit. Rather profit is a test of the validity or success of the business enterprise. The aim of any business must be to create and keep customers, and by doing so achieve sufficient profit to cover the risks that have been taken.

The central question is thus how best to manage a business to ensure that sufficient profits are made, and that the enterprise is successful over time. Although it is possible to state the overall aims in a fairly precise and simple way, any on-going functioning organization has a variety of needs and goals. It is not realistic to think of an enterprise having a single objective. Effective management always involves a juggling act, balancing the different possible objectives, deciding the priorities to be put on the multiple aims that an organization has. Because of this, and due to the complex nature of business as exemplified by the large number of types of specialists involved, management by objectives (MBO) is vital. This is essential in the process of ensuring that informed judgement takes place. MBO forces managers to examine available alternatives and provides a reliable means for evaluating management performance.

Specifically, objectives in a business enterprise enable management to explain, predict and control activities in a way which single ideas like profit maximization do not. First, they enable the organization to explain the whole range of business phenomena in a small number of general statements. Secondly, they allow the testing of these statements in actual experience. Thirdly, it becomes possible to predict behaviour. Fourthly, the soundness of decisions can be examined while they are still being made rather than after the fact. Fifthly, performance in the future can be improved as a result of the analysis of past experience. This is because objectives force one to plan in detail what the business must aim at and to work out ways of effectively achieving these aims. MBO involves spelling out what is meant by managing a business. By doing this and then examining the outcome over time, the five advantages outlined above are realized.

This still leaves the problem of what the detailed objectives of a business enterprise should be. 'Management by objective works if you know the objectives. Ninety percent of the time you don't.' There are eight areas in business where performance objectives must be set: market standing; innovation; productivity; physical and financial resources; profitability; manager performance and development; worker performance and attitude; and public responsibility. In deciding how to set objectives for these areas it is necessary to take account of possible measures and lay down a realistic time span. Measures are important because they make things visible and real; they tell the manager what to focus attention upon. Unfortunately measurement in most areas of business is still at a very crude level. As far as the timespan of objectives is concerned, this depends on the area and the nature of the business. In the lumber business, today's plantings are the production capacity of fifty years' time; in parts of the clothing industry a few weeks' time may be the long-range future.

Perhaps the most important part of the MBO process is the effect that it has on the manager personally. It enables the organization to develop its most important resource – management. It is a key part of the process of MBO that the manager fully participates in negotiating the setting of personal goals. This is because managerial self-control is developed, leading to stronger motivation and more efficient learning. It is the essence of this style of management that all managers arrive at a set of realistic objectives for the units under their control, and for themselves. These objectives should spell out the contribution that the manager will make to the attainment of company goals in all areas of the business.

It is always necessary that the objectives set should be checked by higher levels of management to make sure that they are attainable (neither too high nor too low). But it is a degradation of the process if the goals are simply imposed from above. The importance as a motivator of individual managerial involvement in the setting of objectives cannot be over-stressed. If the manager is really going to be able to develop and take proper advantage of the system, information must be given directly to enable self-measurement of performance. This is very different from the situation in some companies where certain groups (for example accountants) act as 'secret police' on behalf of the chief executive.

The necessity of individual managers setting their own objectives stems from the nature of modern business, and what Drucker calls three forces of misdirection: the specialized work of most managers, the existence of a hierarchy, and the differences in vision that exist in businesses. All these raise the possibility of breakdown and conflicts in the organization. 'Most of what we call management consists of making it difficult for people to get their work done.'

MBO is a way of overcoming these deficiencies by relating the task of each manager to the overall goals of the company, thus encouraging integration. By doing this it takes note of a key aspect of modern business operations; management is no longer the domain of one person. Even the chief executive does not operate in isolation. Management is a group activity, and the existence of objectives emphasizes the contribution that each individual manager makes to the total group operation. The problem of a chief executive is that of picking the best managerial group; the existence of objectives with their built-in evaluation system enables better choices to be made.

MBO enables an executive to be effective. An important point is that effectiveness can be learned. Drucker insists that the self-development of effective executives is central to the continued development of the organization as the 'knowledge worker' has become the major resource. The system of objectives allows managers to evaluate their performance and by so doing strengthens the learning process. This is done by showing where the particular strengths of the individual are, and then building on them to produce effective decision-making patterns. The regular review of objectives and performance enables managers to know where their most effective contribution is made, how it is made, and as a result develop skills in these areas.

Overall then, MBO helps to overcome some of the internal forces which threaten to divide the organization by clearly relating the task of each manager to the overall aims of the company. The result is that organizational goals can be reached by having 'common people achieve uncommon performance'.

With his emphasis on the long-term effects of management decisions, Drucker has been very well aware of the inevitably changing nature of the environment in which organizations function and has warned: 'The only thing we know about the future is that it will be different.' His latest view is: 'We can say with certainty or 90 per cent probability that the new industries that are about to be born will have nothing to do with information.'

Throughout his writings he has been very early in alerting managements to changes that are taking place. For example, that knowledge has succeeded physical power as the basis for effectiveness; that we are operating in a society where continual learning is necessary for all; that Japan will rise as an economic power and then stagnate; that economic organizations cannot do all that is required for modern society. The Drucker Foundation for Non-profit Management (now called The Leader to Leader Institute) was established to apply his ideas in that sector, and he worked with such organizations as the Red Cross, the Girl Guide movement and evangelical churches.

Drucker has always insisted that there must be an ethical basis to management, in his own case based on Protestant Christianity. For example, maximizing profit at all costs is not acceptable in the long run. Managers who reap large bonuses by laying off workers are storing up problems for society. And he maintained that top management's pay should not be more than twenty times that of workers. This aspect of his ideas has not gone unchallenged by managers.

BIBLIOGRAPHY

DRUCKER, P. F., *The Practice of Management*, Harper & Row, 1954.
DRUCKER, P. F., *Managing in Turbulent Times*, Heinemann, 1980.
DRUCKER, P. F., *Managing the Non-Profit Organization*, Butterworth-Heinemann, 1990.
DRUCKER, P. F., *Management Challenges for the 21st Century*, Butterworth-Heinemann, 1999.
DRUCKER, P. F., *The Essential Drucker*, Butterworth-Heinemann, 2001.

Alfred P. Sloan

Alfred Sloan (1875–1966) spent 45 years in the General Motors Corporation of America, then the largest industrial corporation in the world. For 23 of those years, from 1923 until 1946, he was the Chief Executive Officer of the Corporation, continuing as Chairman of the Board until 1956. As such he was the person with the greatest influence on the way in which General Motors developed. He was largely responsible for the creation of the present form of the organization and of the methods of its top management; through this achievement he has had considerable influence on the methods of management of many large industrial and other enterprises whose developments are analysed by Chandler (see Chapter 1).

Sloan, an engineer by training, was the epitome of the professional manager. In this he contrasted very strongly with the founder of General Motors, William Durant, who had a highly personal style of management akin to his great rival in the American motor industry, Henry Ford. Durant was a genius at creating enterprises but was much less capable of carrying them on, a bankers' trust and later the du Pont Company acquiring control before General Motors became financially independent. Sloan, on the other hand, although he had a considerable fortune by personal standards (now administered by the Sloan Foundation), never owned more than one per cent of the stock of the Corporation. He was thus in Weber's terms (see Chapter 1) the bureaucratic administrator who succeeded the charismatic founder. In 1963 Sloan published *My Years with General Motors* in which he gave a history of the top management problems of the Corporation and his methods of handling them. In this he demonstrated the way in which technical, financial, organizational and personal factors interact in the management of large enterprises.

The recurrent theme of Sloan's book is the necessity of dealing with the one major problem which faces any large multi-operation enterprise: the appropriate degree of centralization or decentralization of authority for decision making. The centralizing approach has the advantages of flexibility and perhaps speed, but places an enormous weight on the top executive who may evince genius in many decisions, but will also be haphazard, irrational and apathetic with regard to others. This was the Henry Ford approach. The decentralizing approach has the advantage of allowing decisions to be made closer to the operational bases of the enterprise, but runs the real danger that decisions will be taken with regard to the best interests of the particular operating division itself without concern for those of the corporation as a whole. This was the William Durant method. He brought many companies into the General Motors Corporation (including the roller bearing company owned by Sloan) and allowed their managements to operate much as before, with little regard to the rather nebulous concept of the corporation as a whole. The management history of General Motors is one of attempting to find the right balance between these two extremes in an industrial environment of constant change and continuous, but fluctuating, growth.

A telling example of the extreme decentralization in the early days is the description given by Sloan of the method of cash control. Each operating unit controlled its own cash, depositing all receipts in its own accounts and paying all bills from them. There was no income coming directly to the Corporation and no effective procedure for getting cash from the points where it happened to be to others where it was needed. When the Corporation needed funds to pay dividends, taxes and other charges, the treasurer had to request cash from the operating divisions. But the divisions wanted to keep as much cash as possible to satisfy their own peak requirements, their financial staff being highly adept at delaying the reporting of cash in hand. The treasurer would thus have to guess how much cash a division was holding and decide how much of this he would try to retrieve from them. He would visit them, discuss other general matters and then casually, at the end of the conversation, bring up the topic of cash. The division would always express surprise at the amount that he wanted and occasionally would try to resist the transfer of such a large amount. Since the effects of this bargaining situation were that funds were not efficiently utilized over the Corporation as a whole, a centralized cash control system was set up. General Motors Corporation accounts were established and controlled by the central finance staff; all receipts were credited to them and all payments made from them. Transfers between one account and another could be made quickly and easily across the whole country when cash needed in one place was available in another. Minimum and maximum balances for each local account were set, inter-corporation settlements were facilitated and forward planning of cash was developed, all by the central staff.

Centralization can thus clearly bring great advantages, and systems of coordination for purchasing, corporate advertising, engineering and so on were set up. But there is also a clear need for decentralization if the central directing staff is not to stifle division managements. The controversy over the 'copper-cooled engine' which rent the Corporation in the early 1920s well illustrates this. The research section of the central staff had developed a revolutionary air-cooled engine and, with the strong backing of the then Chairman, Pierre du Pont, was pressing that all production should be turned over to this type. The operating divisions were resistant since they regarded the development as unproven on a production-and-use basis. Sloan did not regard himself as technically competent to take a view on the merits of the engine but, from a purely managerial analysis, he came to the conclusion that for the central direction of the corporation to force the change on unwilling division managements would in effect mean undertaking the operating management of the divisions – a degree of centralization which was inappropriate and basically unworkable. He therefore threw his weight behind the divisions, proposing that a special subsidiary of the research division be formed to develop and manufacture cars based on the new engine. Although the development eventually proved unworkable with the engineering technology then available, the Corporation learned a great deal from this controversy about the correct balance between the centre and the divisions.

Top management, according to Sloan, has the basic tasks of providing motivation and opportunity for its senior executives: motivation by incentive compensation through stock option plans, and opportunity through decentralized management. But coordination is also required, and good management rests on a reconciliation of centralization and decentralization. It was through his attempts to obtain the correct structural balance between these extremes that Sloan enunciated his seemingly paradoxical principle of 'coordinated decentralization'. His aim was coordinated control of decentralized operations. Policy coordination is achieved through committees. It is evolved in a continuous debate to which all may contribute and is basically an educational process. Executive administration is the clear responsibility of individuals who carry out the evolving policy. Many policy groups were established in the Corporation, but none of them detracted from the executive functions – indeed, they were the means of controlling them.

For such a system of coordinated control of decentralized operations to work, one further element is needed. Committees have to be supplied with adequate facts on which to base policies, and executive management similarly has to be based on fact. Time and time again throughout his tenure of office, Sloan emphasized this. Improved systems had to be developed to correct the fact that debates were being conducted on conjectures, decisions were taken on superficial evidence and only inadequate information was available. Through his influence General Motors pioneered many new techniques for obtaining managerially relevant information, particularly in financial control, through the use of return on capital as a measure of efficiency and in the statistical forecasting of market demand.

BIBLIOGRAPHY

SLOAN, A. P., *My Years with General Motors*, Doubleday, 1963; Sidgwick & Jackson, 1965.

Thomas J. Peters
and Robert H. Waterman

Tom Peters and Bob Waterman had been partners in McKinsey and Company the leading management consultancy firm, for many years when they undertook a study of excellence in American business. Their report, *In Search of Excellence*, became the most popular management book of the 1980s with up to 5 million copies sold worldwide. Both Peters and Waterman each founded and now run their own organizations, to develop and propagate their ideas.

Peters and Waterman were concerned to examine and draw lessons from companies which were big (that is, had annual turnovers of more than $1 billion) and which were well established (that is, more than 20 years old). From the Fortune 500 list of the largest US companies, 43 companies were chosen which satisfied a number of performance criteria. They had to be of above average growth and financial return over a 20-year period, and have a reputation in their business sector for continuous innovation in response to changing markets. For all these firms, a full study of the information published on them over 25 years was carried out. In addition, about half the cases were the subject of extensive interview studies of the top managers involved; more limited interviews were conducted in the remaining half of the sample.

The companies designated as excellent by this process include such leading names as Boeing, Hewlett-Packard, IBM, Johnson & Johnson, McDonald's, Procter & Gamble and 3M. It is not claimed for these firms, and for the others classified as excellent, that they are without fault; they have made plenty of well-publicized mistakes. But overall they have performed well over long periods, and they are in a good position to continue as innovative in the future.

The interviews were concerned with top management organizing for success and how this is tackled in these excellent companies. Peters and Waterman soon decided that they could not stick to the formal aspects of managing: the organization chart, the budget plan, the balance sheet, the control graph. These highly analytical tools and concepts are inherently conservative. They lead to detailed forecasting and planning, and tight control: cost reduction becomes the priority and not revenue enhancement, for example. Above all, the philosophy behind the use of these narrowly rational techniques is to abhor mistakes, and therefore it does not value experimentation.

Such an approach cannot capture the distinctive nature of the excellent firms who innovate. A much wider range of processes must be considered including those that will be classified as informal, intuitive, irrational, intractable, but which cannot be ignored. Indeed they must be managed, as they have as much or more to do with the way companies excel (or fail), as do the formal structures and strategies.

Together with their colleagues Richard Pascale and Anthony Athos, Peters and Waterman developed a set of concepts to focus on what happens in the process of organizing, which became known as the McKinsey 7-S Framework. This is a series of seven interdependent aspects of organizing, all conveniently beginning with the letter 's': structure, strategy, systems (and procedures), style (of management), skills (corporate strengths), staff (people) and shared values (culture). On the basis of this framework Peters and Waterman developed a set of eight attributes which characterize all excellent innovative US companies.

1. A BIAS FOR ACTION

Even though these companies may be analytical in their approach to decision making, they are not paralysed by the analysis. They have a 'can do' and 'let's try' approach which favours experimentation. Managers do not rely on the formal information and control systems. They get out of their offices and keep in touch informally; 'MBWA – Management By Wandering Around', it is called at Hewlett-Packard. An open-door policy at all levels is typical, as is the organizational fluidity which allows the setting up of small task forces (mainly of volunteers), with short deadlines, who are expected to come up with an answer to a problem *and then implement their proposals.*

2. CLOSE TO THE CUSTOMER

These companies offer good products because they do not regard the customer as a bloody nuisance, best ignored. They regularly listen to their customers, from whom they get some of their best product ideas. They have what amounts to an obsession about customer services. IBM, for example, trains its salesmen not to be salesmen but 'customer problem solvers'. Its claim to give the best customer service of any company in the world is backed up by a fleet of special assistants (including some of the best salesmen) who are on three-year secondments doing only one thing: dealing with every customer complaint within 24 hours.

3. AUTONOMY AND ENTREPRENEURSHIP

The innovative companies foster many leaders and many innovators throughout the organization. 3M, for example, is a hive of 'product champions', who have been allowed to be creative and who are feverishly trying to make their idea successful. Top management does not try to control so tightly that everyone feels stifled. They support practical risk taking and they encourage internal competition. They have large numbers of innovations on the go and they can tolerate it when, inevitably, many fail – that is how they ensure that some succeed. The comparison with Burns' organic system of management (see Chapter 2) is very clear.

4. PRODUCTIVITY THROUGH PEOPLE

The excellent companies treat the ordinary members of the organization as the basic source of quality and productivity gains. They do not regard capital investment and labour substitution as the fundamental source of efficiency improvement. They strongly oppose an 'us-them' attitude in industrial relations and they treat workers as people. They are not soft; the people orientation has a tough side. They are very performance conscious, but the personal achievements stem from mutually high expectations and peer review rather than exhortation and complicated control systems.

McDonald's, for example, compare a well-run restaurant to a winning baseball team and always refer to workers as 'crew members'. They believe that senior managers should be out in the field paying attention to employees, to training, to the standard of service offered. They work hard to restrain and cut the corporate management, believing that the less there is, the better. Their commitment to productivity through people is illustrated by the 'McDonald's Hamburger University', out of which many crew members graduate, and the annual competition for the best 'All-American Hamburger Maker'.

5. HANDS-ON, VALUE DRIVEN

The basic philosophy of the excellent firms, the shared values of all the participants, may sound very soft and abstract, but it has far more to do with their achievements than economic resources, technological developments, organizational structure or control systems. All of these factors have to change over the years but the philosophy must be established and maintained from the top to bottom of the firm. Those at the top work hard to maintain the values in a very public hands-on way. Their chief executives are famed throughout the company for getting involved in the actual processes (design, selling and so on) thus publicly demonstrating their commitment to high standards.

This explicit understanding of, and commitment to, a system of values is probably the single most important key to excellence. Less successful firms either do not know what their values are, or have a set of objectives but seem only to get fired up about quantitative ones (for example earnings per share, growth measures). These can motivate the top 10, 50, even the top 100 managers, but larger firms need to propagate clear values throughout the whole organization. The content of the dominant beliefs is narrow in scope, but exhibited by all the excellent firms. It includes a belief in being the best producer (whether the product is an aircraft, a hamburger or an advertising campaign) and in giving superior quality and service. The importance of the nuts and bolts of doing the job well, of informal methods of improving communication to achieve goals, of economic growth and profits, also feature strongly.

6. STICK TO THE KNITTING

Excellent companies do not wish to become conglomerates. 'Never acquire a business you don't know how to run' was how a retiring chairman of Johnson & Johnson put it to his successor. They have seen the way corporations like ITT have suffered through trying to spread into new business sectors by large acquisition. Excellent companies expand mainly through internally generated diversification, one manageable step at a time.

7. SIMPLE FORM, LEAN STAFF

As big as these companies are, the underlying structural forms and systems are elegantly simple. Top-level staffs are lean: corporate staffs of fewer than a hundred people running multi-billion dollar enterprises. Complicated structures which blur the lines of authority, such as matrix organizations, are eschewed. The straightforward divisional form, with the product divisions having all the functions of a business, is used. The hiving off of successful new products into separate divisions is encouraged and rewarded at surprisingly small volumes (for example at about $20 million turnover at 3M).

8. SIMULTANEOUS LOOSE-KNIT PROPERTIES

The excellent companies are both centralized and decentralized. For the most part they have pushed autonomy downwards, to the division, to the product development team, to the shop floor. On the other hand they are fanatical centralists around the few core values they see as key to the enterprise: quality, reliability, action, regular informal communication, quick feedback. These are ways of exerting extremely tight control and ensuring that nothing gets very far out of line. The attention to the customer is one of the tightest properties of all – not through massive forms and large numbers of control variables but through self- and peer-discipline making this the focus of activity. Thus the soft concept of a philosophical value is, in fact, harder in its impact than setting target ratios in a control system. As one chief executive said: 'It's easy to fool the boss, but you can't fool your peers.'

These findings, Peters and Waterman underline, show that the excellent companies were, above all, 'brilliant on the basics'. They do not let techniques substitute for thinking, or analysis impede action. They work hard to keep things simple in a complex world. They tolerate some chaos in return for quick action and regular innovation. They prize their values as their most essential asset.

One conclusion that Peters and Waterman came to, rather reluctantly, was that associated with almost every excellent company was a strong leader who was instrumental in forming the culture of excellence in the early stages of the firm's development. Even so, they strongly believe that firms can change towards excellence.

Yet Peters starts a later book, *Thriving on Chaos*, with the statement: 'There are no excellent companies!' This is because the business world is changing so fast that no company is safe, not even those earlier designated as excellent, many of which have been in difficulties. All firms must continue to face up to the need for a revolution in organizations by emphasizing a new set of basic aims. These are enhanced responsiveness through greatly increased flexibility and continuous short-cycle innovation aimed at creating new markets for both new and mature products of world-class quality and service.

To help in achieving the necessary changes, Peters proposes 45 specific prescriptions across five major business areas (customer responsiveness, fast-paced innovation, flexibility through empowering people, loving change and building new systems). For example, one of the ten prescriptions for 'creating total customer responsiveness' is 'be an internationalist'. Even small firms must early on look for business opportunities abroad: selling, designing, manufacturing. A prescription under learning to love change is 'create a sense of urgency', and one for building systems for a world turned upside-down is 'revamp the chief control tools'.

These aims may sound a tall order, but firms have no choice but to change and innovate in order to survive. If managers doubt this, they should look at what their fastest growing competitors are doing and see the writing on the wall.

BIBLIOGRAPHY

PETERS, T. J., *Thriving on Chaos: A Handbook of Management Revolution*, Macmillan, 1988.
PETERS, T. J. *The Pursuit of WOW*, Macmillan, 1994.
PETERS, T. J., *The Tom Peters Seminar*, Vintage Books, 1994.
PETERS, T. J., *Re-imagine! Business Excellence in a Disruptive Age*, Dorling Kindersley, 2003.
PETERS, T. J. and WATERMAN, R. H., *In Search of Excellence: Lessons from America's Best-Run Companies*, Harper & Row, 1982.
WATERMAN, R. H, *Adhocracy: The Power to Change*, Norton, 1992.

William Ouchi

William Ouchi is an American professor of Japanese extraction who works at the Graduate School of Management, University of California, Los Angeles. For Ouchi the key issue facing American (and generally Western) business is how its managers react to one fact – 'the Japanese know how to manage better than we do'.

Ouchi and his collaborators have carried out detailed studies of the way in which Japanese companies operate, both in Japan and in the US. He has identified a particular Japanese organizational culture (related to, and deriving from, the general culture of Japanese society) which is more conducive to greater productivity than typical Western organizational cultures.

He characterizes that work culture by using words which may sound abstract, soft, even wet to Western managerial ears, but whose working out is the key to Japanese success. In comparison to Western firms, Japanese organizational culture is based on more trust, more subtlety and more intimacy in work relationships.

That Japanese workers and managers trust their superiors considerably more than Western employees do is an important key to productivity and growth. For example, both American and Japanese managers want to be successful, but for the Japanese this means taking a much longer-term view. For an American, success might be a healthy bottom-line figure at the end of this financial quarter, even if that causes problems or losses in other parts of the organization: 'That's their problem!' might be a typical reaction. Japanese managers are willing to accept sacrifices if the firm's overall profitability will be maximized, trusting in the knowledge that future opportunities will arise from which they can achieve recognition and recompense. In any case, their take-home salary will be enhanced by the overall performance of the firm, not their particular section of it.

Greater subtlety in relationships is demonstrated by superiors who know the personalities of their staff and can use this knowledge to put together work teams of maximum effectiveness, without being hampered by professional or trade-union work rigidities. Intimacy is shown by the caring, the support and the disciplined unselfishness which make possible effective social life even at work. In the West, this characteristic has traditionally been thought appropriate to the family only perhaps with the addition of a few lifelong friends. In Japan, with the tradition of lifelong employment, economic and social life are integrated into a whole. People who live in a company dormitory, play in a company sports team, serve on the same company committees and working parties – and know that they will continue to do so for the rest of their working lives – necessarily become more intimate in taking each other into account. They cannot, for example, afford selfish and dishonest behaviour since they have to live long and closely with the consequences.

The most important characteristic of Japanese organization is lifetime employment since it is the rubric under which many facets of life and work are integrated. Lifetime employment, although desired by workers and a goal of employers, is not universal in Japan. It applies to male employees only; women are expected to retire on marriage. Even for males, not all firms can create the economic stability necessary to support such a system, but all large companies and government departments operate it. A pool of new employees is recruited by an organization straight from school and university once a year, even though there may typically not be work for all of them immediately. Thereafter, promotion is entirely from within, and those with experience of one company will not be considered for employment by another. Once hired, the new employee will remain with the company until the mandatory retirement age of 55. This relatively low age acts to create opportunities for younger people to progress. Until retirement, an employee will not be dismissed for anything less than a major criminal offence; dismissal is a harsh punishment since such a person has no possibility of finding work in a comparable major organization but must turn to small low-wage firms. Thus the pressures to be aware of what the organization requires and to fit in with it are very strong.

Managers, on the other hand, do not stop work at the age of 55. On retirement, in addition to getting a lump sum gratuity, managers are placed in one of the satellite supply firms which surround each major company. The job there, a part-time one for about ten years, would be to help ensure that supplies are to the quality and time required by the major firm. This is an important task since the firm relies on one supplier completely for each particular component; there is no concept of dual sourcing of supplies.

This approach is very different from that in the West, with its labour markets for all levels of jobs and experience, and with changes between firms being perfectly acceptable. The existence of these labour markets requires that managers in particular look for opportunities for rapid promotion; concomitant with this is a relatively rapid evaluation of performance.

On the other hand, Japanese managers (male, with extremely rare exceptions) have the security of lifelong employment. They are part of a system which has a very slow performance and evaluation pattern. For the first ten years of his organizational life, a manager there will expect to receive the same increases in pay and the same promotions as everyone else who entered the firm at the same time. This discourages short-term games since the manager has no reason to promote his career at someone else's expense; it also encourages an open attitude to cooperation. The typical open-plan nature of the Japanese office, with several managerial levels in the same room, also encourages openness since everybody can see who is interacting with whom, who is listened to, who has influence, and so on.

Lifelong employment also allows non-specialized career paths. A beginning manager will be sent to serve in all the departments of the business. This is not just a short period of secondment before embarking on a specialism, as in some Western traineeships, but a varied career progression lasting several decades. In the West this might well hamper a manager, who would not have sufficient experience in a specialism with which to enter the job market. Generalists, with a great knowledge of one company and its workings in many areas, are not so marketable to other companies. In Japan they do not need to be.

One important effect of the generalist experience, combined with a method of payment which is based on company-wide – not personal or departmental – achievement, is that organization structures can be much more flexible. There is much less emphasis on who precisely is responsible for a particular operation and much greater emphasis on communication and decision making by consensus. There is an intentional ambiguity about decision making which encourages collective responsibility. Important decisions therefore take longer to make since all the managers affected are consulted about possible options. When achieved in this fashion, consensus generates a great deal of commitment. This can be physically manifested in the fact that a document proposing a change in procedures may typically show the seal of approval of 20 or more managers before the director puts his final seal on it.

These manifestations of collective values run throughout Japanese organizational culture. It is an obvious fact of life to the Japanese that everything important happens as a result of teamwork and collective effort. By American standards, Japanese cost and managerial accounting systems are relatively underdeveloped. Profit centres, transfer pricing, the untangling and allocation of costs of common services to particular departments are all much less important in Japanese firms. The overall achievement is paramount, not the relative position of the component parts.

A US company operating in Japan found that its suggestion scheme did not work until it withdrew its American practice of rewarding the individual who made the suggestion and offered a group bonus instead. This was used jointly by the group either for a family party or a group vacation, underlining the holistic concern of the culture.

The Japanese model of organization is thus very different from the American model in every important respect, as is summarized by the following list:

Japanese organizations	*American organizations*
Lifetime employment	Short-term employment
Slow evaluation and promotion	Rapid evaluation and promotion
Non-specialized career paths	Specialized career paths
Implicit control mechanisms	Explicit control mechanisms
Collective decision making	Individual decision making
Collective responsibility	Individual responsibility
Holistic concern	Segmented concern

American and Western organizations cannot turn into Japanese ones – and would not want to – because in their much more individually orientated culture they would find a lot of the collective emphasis stifling. However, are there at least some elements of the Japanese style that can be sensibly applied in the West? Ouchi thinks there are. He recounts an occasion when he was describing the style and got the response from one manager: 'Do you realize that IBM is exactly like that?' Other companies which have been identified as having some of these characteristics include Procter & Gamble, Eastman-Kodak, the armed forces and many smaller firms.

Ouchi uses the term 'Theory Z' to describe the Japanese model as adapted to the West, a terminology related to the Theory X and Theory Y of Douglas McGregor (see Chapter 6). Theory Z builds on and goes beyond McGregor's Theory Y by using insights from the workings of Japanese organizations. Thus, American Theory Z organizations have long-term employment (though not necessarily lifelong, Japanese style), extensive investment in the training of employees who thus develop specific company skills, and relatively slow promotion (by American standards – though nothing like the ten years of the Japanese). Although they have financial and operational analyses, they use soft information a great deal in making decisions and pay considerable attention to whether an option is suitable in the sense of fitting in with the culture of the company. This 'fitting-in' is very important, with the result that their management groups are much more homogenous, taking more holistic and egalitarian views.

On the other hand, Theory Z organizations find it very difficult to change except by modifying their cultures, which takes time. They inevitably experience a loss of professionalism, and they tend to be more sexist and racist in recruitment since they attempt to employ people like themselves. Even so, they are among the long-term organizational successes and are among the feeder companies that head-hunters look to, knowing that they develop an uncommonly high proportion of their young people into successful general managers.

In later work Ouchi and colleagues researched innovative North American school systems in Edmonton, Seattle, and Houston, and compared them with the three largest traditional school systems in New York, Los Angeles, and Chicago. They found that the systems that consistently performed best had the most decentralized management structures. In them, individual school principals were fully responsible and fully accountable for the performance of their schools. The best ones acted as entrepreneurs, shaping their educational programmes to the needs of the students and being responsive to the demands of the parents.

BIBLIOGRAPHY

OUCHI, W., *Theory Z; How American Business Can Meet the Japanese Challenge*, Addison-Wesley, 1981.
OUCHI, W., *Making Schools Work: A Revolutionary Plan to Get Your Children the Education They Need*, Simon and Schuster, 2003.

Rosabeth Moss Kanter

Rosabeth Moss Kanter is a Professor of Business Administration at the Harvard Business School and a consultant to many organizations. A sociologist working in the tradition of Max Weber (see Chapter 1), she has carried out a historical study of American work communes. She has been the recipient of a Guggenheim Fellowship, and of a McKinsey Award for a 1979 article in the *Harvard Business Review*, on 'Power Failure in Management Circuits'. Her detailed study of the human aspects of the functioning of a major present-day US manufacturing company, *Men and Women of the Corporation*, was the 1977 winner of the C. Wright Mills Award for the best book on social issues.

The study focused on three key roles in the company (code-named the Industrial Supply Corporation – 'Indsco'): those of managers, secretaries and wives. The managers, with a small minority of exceptions, were men; the secretaries and the wives were women, and Kanter's work analyses their relationships. It might seem strange to consider wives as part of the corporation, but in fact (although not in theory) this is how they were defined and treated. On the other hand, the husbands of the, relatively rare, female managers were not put in this position, being considered to be independent of Indsco.

Managers, particularly as they rise to the top, are required to cope with increasing uncertainty. Greater routinization applies primarily to the lower levels; managers have to be allowed to exercise discretion. They are therefore the recipients of the owners' and main board's trust. At Indsco, the top managers inevitably chose people like themselves in whom to put this trust. The managers spent a lot of time interacting with each other – between a third and a half of their time actually in meetings. Interacting with people like yourself is always easier, and there was a decided wish to avoid those with whom communication was felt to be uncomfortable. Deviants and non-conformists were suspect; those who dressed differently raised questions because of the messages they might be conveying. Predictability had the highest value. It was acceptable to be somewhat controversial, as long as the manager was consistent and fitted in with the basic values of hard work (staying late at the office if necessary or taking work home) and loyalty (being committed to a long-term career with the company).

Uncertainties of performance and the need for easy communication are great pressures for management to become a closed circle. Homogeneity is the prime criterion for selection, and social conformity a standard for conduct. Women were clearly put in the category of the incomprehensible and unpredictable and, with rare exceptions, were excluded. Many managers reported that they felt uncomfortable in dealing with them. 'It took more time', 'They changed their minds all the time' and 'I'm always making assumptions that turn out to be wrong', were typical comments. Some managers were prepared to admit that this was really saying something about themselves, but this then became another example of their preference for dealing with their own kind.

The secretary had a very distinctive role in the corporation. She has been defined as the 'office wife'. This is a revealing analogy because the term 'wife' denotes a traditional, not a bureaucratic relationship (using Weber's terms, see Chapter 1). The secretarial promotion ladder (a bureaucratic component of the role) was very short; most women got there before the age of 30 and were then stuck. The only way forward was an enhancement in the status of her boss. This determined both the formal rank and the actual power of the secretary: the task remained more or less the same at all levels.

The secretary, therefore, had to live her organizational life through her boss. In Weber's terms this is the patrimonial traditional pattern, even though it is embedded in a formal bureaucratic system. Very untypically in a bureaucracy where people normally work with those just above and just below themselves in status and salary, the boss–secretary relationship allows two people working closely together to have very wide discrepancies in remuneration. The relationship encourages considerable dependency, and secretaries are expected to show loyalty and devotion to their bosses. They are expected to value non-material rewards such as prestige, personal feelings of being wanted and 'loved', and having a salary rather than wages (even though that salary may be less than many wages).

Although the corporate wife had no official employment relationship with Indsco, she still had a clear career progression. There were three phases, each with its own problems. The first was the technical phase, corresponding to the husband's specialist or early managerial job. At that stage he is engaged in a job, extremely demanding of time and energy, in which she can play no part. Conversely, he is under-involved at home, and she tends to leave him out of the activities there. This mutual exclusion is the major strain and resentment.

The second, managerial, phase of the wife's career came when the husband entered middle and upper management and she was expected to perform social and hostess duties. At this stage her behaviour, her social adequacy, has a considerable bearing on the progress of her husband's career. Friendships are no longer just a personal matter but have business implications – as, for example, when an old friendship between two of the managers and their wives had to be dropped because one manager now far outranked the other. Gossip is important, and every wife is faced with the problem as to how far she is going to let her true feelings determine her social life, and how far to let her relationships be determined by company political considerations.

The third career phase was the institutional one, with the husband at the top of the organization or in a position where he must represent it to the outside. Here the issue for both husband and wife is the public nature of almost all their activities. What for others would be defined as pleasure (playing golf, attending a symphony concert, giving a party) are part of the business, and indeed allowable for tax as a business expense. Charitable and community service activities, where the wife's role is especially prominent, may generate useful business. The corporation and its needs and relationships pervade the couple's whole life. Yet, because so much of the top manager's work is concerned with evaluating and being evaluated on personal grounds of trust and integrity the wife is faced with the task of carrying out these activities as though they were highly personal, not ritualistic and contrived. Her job is to contribute to the image of her husband as a whole real man. Top wives have also to suppress their private beliefs, and one wife, for example, told how proud she was that she never at any time during her husband's career unburdened herself of her private views to anyone.

From her study of Indsco, Kanter sees three important general needs for change in the modern industrial corporation: improving the quality of working life (to stem the steady decrease in the numbers of those who say that their jobs are satisfying), creating equal employment opportunities for women and minorities, and opening opportunities for releasing aspirations for employees to make better use of their talents in contributing to the corporation. To achieve these objectives, changes in organization structures are needed.

One way to enhance opportunities would be to open the circle of management to promotion from a wider range of personnel (for example women, clerical workers). This should be based on their appraised competences to do such jobs, and ignore the segregated and restricted career paths which trap them into lower-level jobs. Changes would be required in the appraisal, promotion and career systems and in the design of jobs. Ways need to be found to create intermediate jobs which would act as career bridges into management.

Then empowering strategies, concerned with flattening the hierarchy, decentralization and creating autonomous work groups, are necessary. Number-balancing strategies would aim to raise the proportion of women and other minorities in higher jobs. It is important to combat tokenism by ensuring that several such group members, not just a single representative, are hired and later promoted at the same time. All these strategies for change are required if affirmative-action policies are to be effective.

But Kanter is well aware of the difficulties in getting change in large corporations and this led her on to a study of 'change masters' – corporate entrepreneurs who are capable of anticipating the need for, and of leading, productive change. She carried out an in-depth study of ten major companies, each with a reputation for progressive human resource policies; the companies included General Electric, General Motors, Honeywell, Polaroid and Wang Laboratories.

By examining in detail 115 innovations and the factors which encouraged them, Kanter found a crucial distinction between organizations which can and do innovate, and those whose style of thought is against change and prevents innovation. Innovative firms have an 'integrative' approach to problems. They have a willingness to see problems as wholes and in their solutions to move beyond received wisdom, to challenge established practices. Entrepreneurial organizations are willing to operate at the edges of their competence, dealing with what they do not yet know (for example new investments, new markets, new products). They do not measure themselves by the standards of the past, but by their visions of the future.

They contrast very strongly with firms with a 'segmentalist' approach. These see problems as narrowly as possible, independently of their context. Companies like this are likely to have segmented structures: a large number of compartments strongly walled off from one another – production department from marketing department, corporate managers from divisional managers, management from labour, men from women. As soon as a problem is identified, it is broken up and the parts dealt with by the appropriate departments. Little or no effort is given to the problem as an integrated whole. As a segmentalist manager, you are not going to start dealing with others' aspects of the problem and you would regard it as a personal failure if they were to start worrying about yours. So entrepreneurial spirit is stifled and the solution is unlikely to be innovative. It will follow the solid structure laid down. (This analysis is comparable to the organic versus mechanistic distinction of Burns, see Chapter 2.)

In describing cases of integrative organizations where innovations thrive, Kanter suggests a number of important elements necessary to reduce the segmentalism apparent in so many non-innovative, older, troubled firms. The aim is to reawaken the spirit of enterprise and arouse the potential entrepreneurs that exist in all organizations. The methods include encouragement of a culture of pride in the firm's own achievements, reduction of layers in the hierarchy, improvement of lateral communication, and giving more information about company plans. Decentralization is very important, as is the empowerment of entrepreneurial people lower down the organization to have the authority and the resources to exploit their ideas – even if this means cutting across established segments and boundaries.

In later books Kanter elaborates the need for organizations to change in order to be successful. They have to employ the four 'f's: being focused, fast, friendly and flexible. The *focused* aspect means developing internal synergies in leaner, more integrated organizations. This involves encouraging cooperative efforts in a less diversified business that can apply one unit's competence to another's problems. They should also be *fast* in actively promoting 'newstreams', that is, creating official channels to speed the flow of new business possibilities within the firm. Thus the opportunities for innovation extend well beyond the R & D department, and many more people at more levels should be given the chance to lead new projects, encouraging 'interpreneurship'. *Friendly* companies find it easier to establish working alliances with other organizations. This allows them to extend their range without increasing in size. It gives them information access, windows on technology, speed of action and mutual accommodation to innovation. *Flexible* organizations have given up bureaucracy and reduced hierarchy and work flexibly with a smaller fixed core of employees and a larger number of partnership ties.

This all adds up to a new approach of *post-entrepreneurial management* based on three principles:

1. Minimize obligations and maximize options. Keep fixed costs low and use variable means to achieve goals.
2. Derive power through influence and alliances rather than through full control or total ownership.
3. Keep things moving by encouraging continuous regrouping of people, functions and products to produce innovative combinations.

In this way, top mangers will inspire in their employees the confidence that is necessary to turn an organization around towards an upward cycle of success.

BIBLIOGRAPHY

KANTER, R. M., *Men and Women of the Corporation*, Basic Books, 1977.

KANTER, R. M., 'Power Failure in Management Circuits', *Harvard Business Review* (July–August 1979), 65–75; reprinted in D. S. Pugh (ed.), *Organization Theory*, 5th edn, Penguin, 2007.

KANTER, R. M., *The Change Masters: Corporate Entrepreneurs at Work*, Allen & Unwin, 1984.

KANTER, R. M., *When Giants Learn to Dance*, Simon & Schuster, 1989.

KANTER, R. M., *World Class*, Simon & Schuster, 1995.

KANTER, R. M., *Confidence*, Random House, 2004.

Karl E. Weick

Karl Weick's lively view of managing and of organizing, active words which he prefers to the more static words 'management' and 'organization', matches the liveliness of his personal interests, which he says range from jazz big-bands to railroading. In its essentials, his is the view of an American psychologist who has used his discipline imaginatively to deepen the understanding of this field of endeavour. Weick is Rensis Likert Collegiate Professor of Organizational Behavior and Psychology at the University of Michigan.

As he sees organizations, they are 'sensemaking systems', which incessantly create and recreate conceptions of themselves and of all around them that seem sensible and stable enough to be manageable. Their members continually reaffirm to one another the truths of this reality as they see it, and the correctness of what should be done about it. Sensemaking is more than interpretation. It includes generating what is interpreted. People build up a view of themselves and what is going on, and at the same time interpret what was their own view in the first place. As Weick frequently puts it: 'People know what they think when they see what they say.'

So sensemaking is rolling hindsight. It is a continual weaving of sense from beliefs, from implicit assumptions, from tales from the past, from unspoken premises for decision and action, and from ideas about what will happen as a result of what can be done. Once put into words, it is constrained and framed by those same words because they are only approximately what they refer to. Often words have multiple meanings, so all the time people are working with puns. Further, words are inclined to convey discrete categories: they are not equal to depicting the unbroken, complex flow of life in organizations.

The sense that is made is shaped also by selective perception, that is, by noticing some things and not others. Commitments that have been made then have to be justified retrospectively. There is a constant process of putting together reasoned arguments and arguing about them, most obviously in meetings which have a value as sensemaking occasions. However, the sense that is made has its limits. People with time to spend on a problem at a meeting make sense of it in a way most understandable to themselves, so others become less able to follow what is afoot. Showing up at meetings therefore produces a situation that is manageable only by those who have been showing up.

The whole sensemaking process gives ostensible orderliness to what is going on, and has gone on. The development of a 'generic sensemaking', within which individuals differ yet sufficiently concur, maintains a sense of organization.

Organizational sensemaking has at least seven distinguishing characteristics. It is:

1. *grounded in identity construction,* for sensemakers perpetually redefine their notion of themselves;
2. *retrospective,* a never-ending reconstruction of experience. We are in the position of explorers who never know what they are exploring until it has been explored;
3. *enactive of sensible environments,* because people make sense of their worlds. By doing so they create, or enact, a part of the very environment they face. They implant their own reality. So an organization imposes on the environment that imposes on it, and the bigger it becomes the more it runs into what it has itself enacted. A manufacturer which defines itself as the monopoly supplier of a product will by that enactment hamper itself from perceiving that innovative substitutes are a threat to its market. Most firms in the Swiss traditional watch industry, for example, just did not enact their environment to include cheap digital watches, and so suffered;
4. *social,* since it occurs with and in relation to other people inside and outside the organization;
5. *ongoing,* as it never stops and therefore never starts. Sensemaking is always in process;
6. *focused on and by extracted cues,* that is, growing from familiar points of reference. Controlling these cues is a source of power, since controlling what others respond to frames the view they will take and what they will do;
7. *driven by plausibility rather than accuracy,* for 'the sensible need not be sensable'. People go along with what to them is plausible and credible even if it cannot be checked. It might also have some accuracy, but since an equivocal and changing world has always moved on before a precise account of it can be formulated, absolute accuracy is impossible. Hence accuracy takes second place to acceptability, to a version good enough to guide action for the time being.

Weick makes use of a published study on the knitwear industry in Scotland to illustrate these points – a number of small manufacturers in and around one town making cashmere sweaters. The managers of each see their own firms as having a distinct identity, signified by colour and design of product, within an industry having a collective high-quality identity that distinguishes it from other makers of sweaters. The industry claims to have a business strategy centred on a specific high-income market, a strategy which has developed retrospectively from experience of sales rather than one which has been planned with foresight. The sales agents whom the firms employ sell classically designed clothes, and therefore feed back information from that particular market which confirms the prior beliefs that the makers hold about it. Thus the latter constantly re-enact their environment, affirming this by social (including sociable) contacts in and between firms, the whole an ongoing process during which cues from designers, trade shows and shops, as well as from the agents, reinforce the particular way in which the situation is perceived and so sustain its plausibility.

This is a long-established industry where sensemaking is moulded by hand-craft traditions. In younger organizations with professionally qualified employees, sensemaking has freer range, especially when innovative, non-routine decisions are to be made. Here the enactment of environments and the self-fulfilling prophecies that result from this should be most conspicuous. If, however, these newer organizations follow the current fashion and set up self-managed teams, their sensemaking will become less generic and more fragmented. Each team will make sense of things in its own way.

Excellent illustrations of the impact of the enacted nature of organizational sensemaking are given by an examination of crisis situations. These are so complex that the enactments of the individuals involved will inevitably be partial, and their interactions may well exacerbate the crisis. Weick uses the example of the industrial disaster at the Union Carbide plant in Bhophal, India, to show how it was the preconceptions of everybody involved, from senior managers to operators, that determined which action was taken. Their enacted views of their situation led to disaster. He wryly quotes the operating manual. After telling operators to dump the gas into a spare tank if a leak cannot be stopped, this reads: 'There may be other situations not covered above. The situation will determine the appropriate actions.' In fact, it was the other way round: the actions of the managers and operators determined the disaster situation. For example, after early safety violations had been corrected, top management regarded the plant as safe. This preconception allowed them to undertake methods of reducing the operating costs of 'a safe plant' in ways which, in the event, contributed to the disaster. Again, the operators had long dismissed an operating gauge as dysfunctional, having had trouble with it. They therefore neglected its correct reading in the disaster situation – a blind spot which had an important bearing on their attempts to make sense of what was happening. This is not to blame them; we often cannot know what 'the appropriate action' should be until we are involved in doing something, seeing what happens and making sense of it.

Paradoxically, if sensemaking constructs relatively stable interpretations, this will render a flexible organic form of organization (see Burns, Chapter 2) steadily less so, and steadily less effective if it continues to be in an unstable environment. This might account for the tendency of organic organizations to drift towards the mechanistic form.

Whatever the form of organization, some of its elements will be tightly coupled together whilst the coupling of others will be comparatively loose. Weick derives the concept of *loose coupling* from work by March (see Chapter 5) and others. It means that, if some of the parts or activities in an organization change, the effect of this on other parts or activities will be limited, or be slow to show, or both. The mutual influence of loosely coupled systems is low.

Loose coupling facilitates adaptation. In a loosely coupled organization there can be differential change, some aspects changing faster or more than others, so that overall there is a flexible response by the organization. Because bonds *within* loosely coupled sub-assemblies are stronger than those *between* them (for example, within workgroups or departments as against between workgroups or departments), there is both stability and flexibility.

Whatever the form of organization, it will have to work with ambiguous, uncertain, equivocal and changing information. Despite their façade of numbers and objectivity and accountability, organizations and those who manage them wade amidst guesswork, subjectivity and arbitrariness. Weick feels that language could better reflect this constant ambiguous flux by making more use of verbs and less of nouns. Indeed, he urges people to 'stamp out nouns': to think of managing rather than management, of organizing rather than organization, as noted earlier.

He offers managers and others in organizations ten further 'pieces of advice':

1. *Don't panic in the face of disorder.* Some degree of disorder is necessary so that disorderly, ambiguous information can be taken in and coped with, rather than tidily screened out.
2. *You never do one thing all at once.* Whatever you do has many ramifications, not just the one you have in mind. And whilst some consequences happen right away, others show up indirectly and much later.
3. *Chaotic action is preferable to orderly inaction.* When someone asks, 'What shall I do?' and is told 'I don't know, just do something', that is probably good advice. Since sense is made of events retrospectively, an action, any action, provides something to make sense of. Inaction is more senseless.
4. *The most important decisions are often the least apparent.* Decisions about what is to be retained in files, in databases, in memories indeed, provide the basis for future action. Such decisions may not be conspicuous, yet they sustain the past from which the future is begun.
5. *There is no solution.* As there are no simple answers, and rarely is anything right or wrong, learn to live with improvisation and just a tolerable level of reasonableness.
6. *Stamp out utility.* Good adaptation now rules out some options for the future. Concentrating overmuch on utility now can rule out sources of future utility. Resources and choices are used up. Better to retain some noise and variability in the system, even at a cost to present efficiency, so that fresh future repertoires of action may be opened up.
7. *The map is the territory.* When the managers' map of what causes what, drawn from past experience, is superimposed on the future, it becomes for them the territory that it maps. Simplification though it is, such a map has been worked over more than any other product has, and is as good a guide as can be had.
8. *Rechart the organizational chart.* Do not be boxed in by its conventional form. See things as they work out and people as they are to you. See the chart in the way that it functions. For example, in the box on the chart for chairman write 'hesitancy'; in the box for general manager write 'assertiveness', and so on, in the way people come over to you.

9. *Visualize organizations as evolutionary systems.* See what is evolving, and what you can and should change. Likewise, recognize what is not, and you cannot.
10. *Complicate yourself!* Consider different causes, other solutions, new situations, more complex alternatives, and take pleasure in the process of doing so.

Weick does his best to follow his own tenth piece of advice and to always move on, towards other ways of looking at organizing and organizers.

BIBLIOGRAPHY

WEICK, K. E., *The Social Psychology of Organizing*, Addison-Wesley, 1969; 2nd edn, 1979.
WEICK, K. E., 'Enacted sensemaking in crisis situations', *Journal of Management Studies*, 25 (1988), 305–17; reprinted in D. S. Pugh (ed.), *Organization Theory*, 5th edn, Penguin, 2007.
WEICK, K. E., *Sensemaking in Organizations*, Sage, 1995.
WEICK, K. E., *Making Sense of the Organization*, Blackwell, 2001.

5 Decision Making in Organizations

The task of administration is so to design this environment that the individual will approach as close as practicable to rationality (judged in terms of the organization's goals) in his decisions.
HERBERT A. SIMON

An organization is a collection of choices looking for problems, issues and feelings looking for decision situations in which they might be aired, solutions looking for issues to which they might be the answers, and decision makers looking for work.
JAMES G. MARCH

An administrator often feels more confident when 'flying by the seat of his pants' than when following the advice of theorists.
CHARLES E. LINDBLOM

It makes more sense to talk about participative and autocratic situations than it does to talk about participative and autocratic managers.
VICTOR H. VROOM

An organization can be considered as a set of games between groups of partners who have to play with each other.
MICHEL CROZIER

Hierarchy is divisive, it creates resentment, hostility and opposition ... Paradoxically, through participation, management increases its control by giving up some of its authority.
ARNOLD S. TANNENBAUM

Although writers have considered a range of aspects of organizational functioning, there has been a continuing school of thought which maintains that it is the analysis of decision making which is the key to understanding organizational management processes.

This approach was inaugurated by Herbert Simon and his colleagues at Carnegie-Mellon University. For Simon, management is decision making. His one-time colleague James March develops this approach to consider the non-rationality of decision processes, while Charles Lindblom looks at decision making in relation to public policy and discovers a 'science of muddling through'.

Victor Vroom proposes a theory of appropriate decision-making styles; Michel Crozier examines the nature of the power which is at the basis of the decision-making game, and Arnold Tannenbaum analyses the distribution across organizational levels of the power to control decision making.

Herbert A. Simon

Herbert Simon (1916–2001) was a distinguished American political and social scientist whose perceptive contributions have influenced thinking and practice in many fields. He began his career in public administration and operations research, but as he took appointments in successive universities his interests encompassed all aspects of administration. He was Professor of Computer Science and Psychology at Carnegie Mellon University Pittsburgh, where he and his colleagues have been engaged in fundamental research into the processes of decision making, using computers to simulate human thinking. Herbert Simon's outstanding intellectual contribution was publicly recognized when, in 1978, he was awarded the Nobel Prize for Economics.

For Simon management is equivalent to decision making. His major interest has been an analysis of how decisions are made and of how they might be made more effectively.

He describes three stages in the overall process of making a decision:

1. finding occasions calling for a decision – the intelligence activity (using the word in its military sense);
2. inventing, developing and analysing possible courses of action – the design activity;
3. selecting a particular course of action from those available – the choice activity.

Generally speaking, intelligence activity precedes design, and design activity precedes choice; but the sequence of stages can be much more complex than this. Each stage can in itself be a complex decision-making process. The design stage can call for new intelligence activities. Problems at any stage can generate a series of sub-problems which in turn have their intelligence, design and choice stages. Nevertheless in the process of organizational decision making, these three general stages can always be discerned.

Carrying out decisions is also regarded as a decision-making process. Thus after a policy decision has been taken, the executive having to carry it out is faced with a wholly new set of problems involving decision making. Executing policy amounts to making more detailed policy. For Simon, then, all managerial action is essentially decision making.

On what basis do administrators make decisions? The traditional theory of economists assumed complete rationality. Their model was of 'economic man' (which, of course, embraced woman) who deals with the real world in all its complexity. He selects the rationally determined best course of action from among all those available to him in order to maximize his returns. But clearly this model is divorced from reality. We know that there is a large non-rational element in people's thinking and behaviour. The need for an administrative theory is precisely because there are practical limits to human rationality. These limits to rationality are not static but depend upon the organizational environment in which the individual's decision takes place. It then becomes the task of administration so to design this environment that the individual will approach rationality in decisions as closely as practicable as judged in terms of the organization's goals.

In place of economic man Simon proposes a model of 'administrative man'. While economic man maximizes (that is, selects the best course from those available), administrative man 'satisfices' – looking for a course of action that is satisfactory or good enough. In this process decision makers are content with gross simplifications, taking into account only those comparatively few relevant factors which their minds can manage to encompass. 'Most human decision making, whether individual or organizational, is concerned with the discovery and selection of satisfactory alternatives; only in exceptional cases is it concerned with the discovery and selection of optimal alternatives.' Most decisions are concerned not with searching for the sharpest needle in the haystack but with searching for a needle sharp enough to sew with. Thus administrators who satisfice can make decisions without searching for all the possible alternatives and can use relatively simple rules of thumb. In business terms they do not look for 'maximum profit' but 'adequate profit', not 'optimum price' but 'fair price'. This makes their world much simpler.

What techniques of decision making are then available? In discussing this problem, Simon makes a distinction between two polar types of decisions: *programmed* and *non-programmed* decisions. These are not mutually exclusive but rather make up a continuum stretching from highly programmed decisions at one end to highly unprogrammed decisions at the other. Decisions are programmed to the extent that they are repetitive and routine or to the extent that a definite procedure has been worked out to deal with them. Thus they do not have to be considered afresh each time they occur. Examples would be the decisions involved in processing a customer's order, determining an employee's sickness benefit or carrying out any routine job.

Decisions are unprogrammed to the extent that they are new and unstructured or where there is no cut-and-dried method for handling the problem. This may either be because it has not occurred before, or because it is particularly difficult or important. Examples would be decisions to introduce a new product, make substantial staff redundancies or move to a new location. All these decisions would be non-programmed (although entailing many programmed sub-decisions) because the organization would have no detailed strategy to govern its responses to these situations; it would have to fall back on whatever general capacity it had for intelligent problem solving.

Human beings are capable of acting intelligently in many new or difficult situations, but they are likely to be less efficient. The cost to the organization of relying on non-programmed decisions in areas where special-purpose procedures and programmes can be developed is likely to be high; thus an organization should try to programme as many of its decisions as possible. The traditional techniques of programmed decision making are habit, including knowledge and skills, clerical routines and standard operating procedures, together with the organization's structure and culture, that is, its system of common expectations, well-defined information channels, established sub-goals and so on The traditional techniques for dealing with non-programmed decisions rely on the selection and training of executives who possess judgement, intuition and creativity. These categories of techniques have been developed over thousands of years (the building of the pyramids must have involved the use of many of them). But since the Second World War, Simon argues, a complete revolution in techniques of decision making has got under way, comparable to the invention of powered machinery in manufacture.

This revolution has been due to the application of such techniques as mathematical analysis, operational research, electronic data processing, information technology and computer simulation. These were first used for completely programmed operations (for example mathematical calculations, accounting procedures) formerly regarded as the province of clerks. But more and more elements of judgement (previously unprogrammed and the province of middle management) can now be incorporated into programmed procedures. Decisions on stock control and production control have been in the forefront of this development. With advances in computer technology, more and more complex decisions will become programmed. Even a completely unprogrammed decision, made once and for all, can be reached via computer techniques by building a model of the decision situation. Various courses of action can then be simulated and their effects assessed. 'The automated factory of the future', Simon maintains, 'will operate on the basis of programmed decisions produced in the automated office beside it.'

BIBLIOGRAPHY

MARCH, J. G. AND SIMON, H. A., *Organizations*, Wiley, 1958.
SIMON, H. A., *The New Science of Management Decision*, Harper & Row, 1960.
SIMON, H. A., *The Shape of Automation*, Harper & Row, 1965.
SIMON, H. A., *Administrative Behaviour*, 3rd edn, Free Press, 1976.

James G. March

James March is Emeritus Professor of International Management at Stanford University, California, his breadth of mind being indicated by his additional links with the departments of Political Science and of Sociology. His interests have long focused upon decision making in organizations, beginning with his early work at Carnegie Mellon University. Its renowned contributors to the understanding of decision making also include Herbert Simon (see previously in this chapter) and Richard Cyert (1921–1998), both former colleagues of March.

March brings to his lively analyses of decision making a unique blend of the logical and the poetical. His work is logical in argument, poetical in imagery and expression. He feels that decision making can be understood in much the same non-rational way as a painting by Picasso or a poem by T. S. Eliot. It is far from a rationally controlled process moving steadily to a culminating choice. The confusion and complexity surrounding decision making are underestimated. Many things are happening at once. Views and aims are changing, and so are alliances between those concerned. What has to be done is not clear, nor is how to do it. In this topsy-turvy world where people do not comprehend what is going on, decisions may have little to do with the processes that supposedly make them, and organizations 'do not know what they are doing'.

It is a world in which there are cognitive, political and organizational limits to rationality. Cognitively, attention is the key scarce resource. Individuals cannot attend to everything at once, nor can they be everywhere at once. So they attend to some parts of some decision making, not to all of it. What they attend to depends upon the alternative claims upon them, since giving attention to one decision means overlooking others. As March puts it, 'every entrance is an exit somewhere else'. Therefore timing is crucial, timing when to join in and which matters to raise.

March shares with his former colleague Simon the conception of bounded rationality. Not only is attention scarce, but mental capacity is limited. The mind of the decision maker can only encompass so much. It can only cope with a limited amount of information and with a limited number of alternatives (see also Lindblom, next in this chapter).

That being so, even if decision making is intended to be rational, there are severe bounds to its rationality. Decisions will be taken knowing much less than in principle could be known.

Along with scarce attention and bounded rationality come erratic preferences. People change their minds as to what they want. Even if they know what they want, they may ignore their own preferences and follow other advice or other traditions.

Or they may state their preferences in an ambiguous way. Their preference may also conflict with the preferences of others.

Here the cognitive limits to rationality connect with the political limits. March and his other former colleague Cyert recognize that a firm, and indeed any other kind of organization, is a shifting multiple-goal political coalition. 'The composition of the firm is not given; it is negotiated. The goals of the firm are not given; they are bargained.' The coalition, to use their word, includes managers, workers, stockholders, suppliers, customers, lawyers, tax collectors and other agents of the state, as well as all the sub-units or departments into which an organization is divided. Each has its own preferences about what the firm should be like and what its goals should be. Hence negotiation and bargaining rather than detached rationality are endemic.

This is where the political limits to rationality connect with the organizational limits. These are the limits set by *organized anarchies*. Though all organizations do not have the properties of organized anarchy all of the time, they do for part of the time and especially if they are publicly owned or are educational, such as universities, colleges and schools. Organized anarchies have 'three general properties'. First, since preferences are unclear, the organization discovers its goals from what it is doing rather than by defining them clearly in advance. Second, since it has 'unclear technology', 'its own processes are not understood by its members' and it works by trial and error more than by knowing what it is doing. Third, since there is 'fluid participation', who is involved in what is constantly changing? Take a college, for instance. Pronouncements on strategy are more reviews of what courses are already taught than statements of future goals; new teaching techniques such as video games are tried without knowing whether they will work and without their being understood by authorizing committees; what such committees do understand and approve depends on who turns up to meetings.

Given these cognitive, political and organizational characteristics, decision-making processes are bound to be affected. Not only in those organizations prone to organized anarchy, but even in business firms, such decision processes have four peculiarities:

1. quasi-resolution of conflict
2. uncertainty avoidance
3. problemistic search
4. organizational learning.

Quasi-resolution of conflict is the state of affairs most of the time. The conflicts inherent in the political nature of organizations and therefore in the making of decisions are not resolved. Rather there are devices for their quasi-resolution which enable them to be lived with. One such device is 'local rationality'. Since each sub-unit of a department deals only with a narrow range of problems – the sales department with 'how to sell', the personnel department with 'how to recruit' and so on – each can at least purport to be rational in dealing with its 'local' concerns. Of course, these local rationalities can be mutually inconsistent (as when accounting's insistence on remaining within budget destroys marketing's advertising campaign), so they may not add up to overall rationality for the organization as a whole.

A second such device can ease this difficulty. It is 'acceptable level decision rules'. The acceptable level of consistency between one decision and another is low enough for divergences to be tolerable. What is needed is an outcome acceptable to different interests rather than one that is optimal overall. Third, 'sequential attention to goals' also helps. As the conflicts between goals are not resolved, attention is given first to one goal and then to another in sequence. For example, smooth production may first be emphasized; then priority may switch to satisfying customers by design variations which in turn disrupt production.

Uncertainty avoidance, too, pervades decision making. All organizations must live with uncertainty. Customer orders are uncertain, so are currency fluctuations, so is future taxation and so on. Therefore decision making responds to information here and now and neglects the uncertainties of longer-term forecasting. Pressing problems are dealt with and planning for the longer run not attempted. Market uncertainties are avoided by exclusive contracts with customers and by conforming with everyone else to recognized pricing and negotiating practices.

For the same reason *search is problemistic* and short-sighted. The occurrence of a problem spurs a search for ways to deal with it, and once a way is found then search stops. Far-sighted regular search, such as the steady accumulation of market information, is relatively unimportant. Such information is likely to be ignored in the urgency of any particular sales crisis. Moreover, search is 'simple-minded'. When a problem arises, search for a solution is concentrated near the old solution. Radical proposals are brushed aside and a safer answer is found not much different from what went before (see Lindblom, next). When an American university sought a new dean to head a major faculty, for instance, prominent outsiders were passed over and an established insider chosen because of fears that outsiders might make too many changes. Business organizations, too, regularly choose both managers and workers who will fit into existing set-ups with least disruption.

Finally, decision-making processes are learning processes. In them, *organizational learning* takes place. Decision makers do not begin by knowing all they need to know. They learn as they go. They learn what is thought practicable and what is not, what is permissible and what is not. By trial and error they find out what can be done and adapt their goals to it.

Perhaps it should not be surprising that all this leads March, together with Cohen and Olsen, to propose a *garbage-can model of organizational choice*, famed for its name as well as for its thesis. For when people fight for the right to participate in decision making and then do not exercise it, when they request information and then do not use it, when they struggle over a decision and then take little interest in whether it is ever carried out, something curious must be going on.

The opportunity or the need to arrive at a decision, to make a choice, can be seen as 'a garbage can into which various kinds of problems and solutions are dumped by participants as they are generated'. There may be several garbage cans around each with a different label.

In the model so vividly depicted, a decision is an outcome of the interplay between *problems, solutions, participants* and *choices*, all of which arrive relatively independently of one another. Problems can arise inside or outside the organization. Solutions exist on their own irrespective of problems (people's preferences wait for their moment to come, the computer waits for the question it can answer). Participants move in and out. Opportunities for choices occur any time that an organization is expected to produce a decision (for example when contracts must be signed or money must be spent).

Decisions come about by resolution, by oversight or by flight. If by resolution, then deliberate choice resolves the problem, though this is likely to take time. If by oversight, the choice is made quickly, incidentally to other choices being made. If by flight, the original problem has gone (flown) away leaving a choice which can now be readily made but solves nothing. Probably most decisions are made by oversight or flight, not by resolution.

Whether or not a decision emerges is due to the 'temporal proximity' of inputs into the garbage can. That is, a decision happens when suitable problems, solutions, participants and choices coincide. When they do, solutions are attached to problems and problems to choices by participants who happen to have the time and energy to make them. So the decision that is taken may be more or less 'uncoupled' from the apparent process of making it, being due to other coincidental reasons.

Seen like this, 'an organization is a collection of choices looking for problems, issues and feelings looking for decision situations in which they might be aired, solutions looking for issues to which they might be the answer, and decision makers looking for work'. Though this may be the situation anywhere, nowhere is it more prevalent than in an organized anarchy such as a university.

March admits that this picture may be overdrawn, but contends that it is real enough to mean that the rational 'technology of reason' should be supplemented with a 'technology of foolishness'. Sometimes people *should* act *before* they think so that they may discover new goals in the course of that action. They *should* make decisions with consequences for the future, in the knowledge that they do not know what will be wanted in the future. In terms of ostensible rationality, this is foolish. But decision making needs scope for foolishness. Playfulness allows this. Playfulness is a deliberate (but temporary) suspension of the normal rational rules so that we can experiment. We need to play with foolish alternatives and inconsistent possibilities. We need to treat goals as hypotheses to be changed, intuitions as real, hypocrisy as a transitional inconsistency, memory as an enemy of novelty, and experience not as fixed history but as a theory of what happened which we can change if that helps us to learn. From time to time we should be foolishly playful inside our garbage cans.

BIBLIOGRAPHY

COHEN, M. D., MARCH, J. G. and OLSEN, J. P., 'A Garbage Can Model of Organizational Choice,' *Administrative Science Quarterly*, 17, (1972), 1-25.
CYERT, R. M. and MARCH, J. G., *A Behavioural Theory of the Firm*, Prentice Hall, 1963.

MARCH, J. G., *Decisions and Organizations*, Blackwell, 1988.
MARCH, J. G., *A Primer on Decision Making*, Free Press, 1994.
MARCH, J. G., *The Pursuit of Organizational Intelligence*, Blackwell, 1999.
MARCH, J. G. and OLSEN, J. P., *Ambiguity and Choice in Organizations*, 2nd edn, Oxford University Press, 1980.

Charles E. Lindblom

Charles Lindblom is Stirling Professor Emeritus of Political Science and Economics at Yale University, and is a former director of the Yale Institution for Social and Policy Studies. He has served in a wide variety of academic and political posts including those of Guggenheim Fellow and economic adviser to the US Aid Mission to India.

Lindblom asks how decisions should be made and how they are made. His description and explanation of how they are made are framed primarily in terms of public administration and political systems, but pertain to all forms of organizations. How do administrators and managers, indeed all who have to face substantial decisions, go about them: by root or by branch?

Lindblom supposes an instance of public policy. An administrator has to formulate policy with respect to inflation (this could as easily be a marketing director formulating a firm's pricing policy). To go to the root of the matter, one should attempt to list all possible variables however many there might be, such as full employment, reasonable business profits, protection of savings, stable exchange rates and so on. Then one should attempt to calculate how much a change in each of the variables is worth in terms of a change in each of the others. This done, the administrator can try to evaluate the alternative outcomes of the virtually infinite number of possible combinations. To do this would require gathering prodigious amounts of information. It would also require reconsideration of fundamentals of theory from total central planning on the one hand to a completely free market on the other. The information and the alternatives, if ever they could be fully amassed, would be beyond comprehension.

Instead the administrator could remain content with the comparatively simple goal of a period of stable prices. In this case most of the social values may be disregarded and attention focused only on what is directly and immediately relevant. One would compare only a limited range of alternatives, most already familiar from previous occasions, and avoid recourse to theory or fundamental questioning. One could then make a decision which would have some partial success for a time.

The first approach to a policy decision described above aspires to the *rational deductive ideal*. This requires that: all values be ascertained and stated precisely enough for them to be arranged in order of priority; that principles then be derived which would indicate what information is necessary for every possible policy alternative to be compared with every other; that full information on each be obtained; and that logical calculative deduction then lead to the best alternative.

This is an ideal of science – the complete deductive system – transferred to the field of values and application. Superficially, it corresponds to good-sense notions of care and comprehensiveness. Its contemporary techniques are operations research, systems analysis, PPB (Planning–Programming–Budgeting) and the like. If followed, it would produce a *synoptic approach* to decision making.

Yet it is difficult to find examples of this synoptic approach. Its advocates cannot point to where it has been applied. It is more an ideal than something actually accomplished, for it fails to adapt to what are in reality two troublesome characteristics of decisions – decision makers and decision making.

Decision makers need a way to proceed that takes account of these characteristics. They face situations in which the sheer multiplicity of values, and differences in formulating them, prevent their being exhaustively listed. Indeed, if any such attempt at listing were made, values and priorities would be changing whilst it was being done. The process would be endless. In any case, because of the different partisan interests in any decision, decision making has to proceed by 'mutual partisan adjustment', and so has to accommodate (but not necessarily reconcile) the many values of differing interests and cannot rank one above the other in explicit priority.

Decision makers also need a way to proceed that is adapted to their own limited problem-solving capacities (see Simon, earlier in this chapter). Mentally they could not cope with the deluge of information and alternatives implied in the synoptic approach. As Lindblom puts it, 'the mind flees from comprehensiveness'. In practice, their mental capacities are unlikely to be so stretched, for usually information is incomplete and inadequate, if only because the cost of finding out everything there is to know would be insupportable. Further, the presumption that what there is to know is finite and can be found out also presumes that facts and values occupy separate compartments, whereas in actuality they are inseparable. Different facts draw attention to different values, and values reinterpret facts. Likewise, the systems of variables with which decision makers have to contend cannot be closed off to allow the finite analysis demanded by the synoptic approach, for there are always further interactions in fluid and open systems. Problems arise and extend in many forms.

Therefore the strategy for making decisions that is commonly used by analysts and decision makers is not synoptic. Lindblom terms what they actually do as the *strategy of disjointed incrementalism*, a way of proceeding by *successive limited comparisons* that is far removed from the synoptic approach as required by the rational deductive ideal.

Although disjointed incrementalism cannot be the only set of adaptations used to deal with the practical difficulties of decision making, Lindblom suggests that it is the most prevalent. It makes changes in small increments by disjointed or uncoordinated processes (an increment is 'a small change in an important variable', but there is no sharp line between the incremental and the non-incremental, which is a matter of degree along a continuum). It makes an indefinite and apparently disorderly series of small moves away from the ills of the day rather than towards defined goals. It leaves many aspects of problems seemingly unattended.

In summary disjointed incrementalism is incremental, restricted, means oriented, reconstructive, serial, remedial and fragmented.

Instead of rationally rooting out all the possibilities, the analyst or decision maker simplifies the problem by contemplating only the margins by which – if altered – circumstances might differ. Marginal and therefore comprehensible change is examined and only a restricted number of alternatives is considered. Furthermore, the task is made manageable by considering only a restricted number of consequences for each alternative. The more remote or imponderable possibilities are ignored even if they are important, for to include them might prevent any decision from being made at all.

While the conventional view is that means are adjusted to ends, the comparatively means-oriented strategy of disjointed incrementalism accepts the reverse. Ends are adjusted to means. This works both ways in a reciprocal relationship. Thus if the cost of the means of attaining the objective increases, either other means can be found or the end objective can be changed so that it is brought within the means. Objectives can be fitted to policies as much as policies to objectives. This merges into the strategy's fourth feature – its active reconstructive response. Information is revised and reinterpreted, proposals are redesigned and values are modified, continually. As problems are examined, they are transformed.

The strategy's serial procedure is evident in its long chains of policy steps. There are never-ending series of attacks on more or less permanent (though perhaps slowly changing) problems. These problems are rarely solved, only alleviated. The decision maker does not look for some elusive solution, but instead for appropriate moves in a series that is expected to continue. The strategy therefore has a remedial orientation that identifies situations or ills from which to move *away*, rather than goals to move *towards*. Improvements here and there are preferred to grand aims.

Finally disjointed incrementalism is fragmented by the way analysis and evaluation go ahead at different times, or at the same time in many places. In the political sphere, a government policy may be under study at various times in several government departments and agencies, in universities and in private firms and institutions (just as the policy of a single firm, for example, may be looked at by several of its departments, by its major customer and by its bankers). Whereas the synoptic approach would try to coordinate these efforts rationally disjointed incrementalism accepts their lack of coherence in return for the advantage of diversity. One may find what another misses. An overly controlled approach could 'coordinate out of sight' a potentially useful variety of contributions.

In these several ways the strategy of disjointed incrementalism scales problems down to size. It limits information, restricts choices and shortens horizons so that something can be done. What is overlooked now can be dealt with later. The strategy recognizes diverse values, but discourages intransigence by those involved because its reconstructive nature avoids rules or principles, which if defined could provoke firm stands by different parties.

The result is what Lindblom has called the *science of muddling through* – a practical and sophisticated adaptation to the impossibility of attaining the synoptic ideal. As he says, administrators often feel more confident when flying by the seat of their pants than when trying to follow the advice of theorists. Disjointed incrementalism is a working strategy and not merely a failure of synoptic method. It has the virtues of its own defects, which carry it pragmatically through.

On the face of it, the strategy looks conservative. It attempts small changes which do not have far-reaching consequences. Yet radical changes may be needed. However, Lindblom points out that it is logically possible to make changes as quickly by small frequent steps as it might be by more drastic and therefore less frequent steps. Each incremental step may be relatively easy because it is not fraught with major consequences, and at least it is a step that can be taken, whereas the enormity of a fully synoptic consideration can deter decision makers from making even a beginning, so that it achieves no movement at all.

In later work, Lindblom has mounted a critique of the workings of the modern capitalist market system. While it is the best system for creating wealth and encouraging innovations, it is not very efficient at managing social processes, such as democracy or social justice, which cannot be evaluated in monetary terms. So democracy becomes 'polyarchy' (equivalent to 'oligarchy' in economic activity) where the choices of the population are restricted to the two, simplified options as offered by opposing political parties. Thus serious consideration of complex social and political issues is restricted to elite groups at the top of society.

BIBLIOGRAPHY

LINDBLOM, C. E., 'The Science of Muddling Through', *Public Administration Review*, 19 (1959), 79–88.
LINDBLOM, C. E., *The Policy-Making Process*, Prentice-Hall, 1968.
LINDBLOM, C. E., *The Market System*, Yale University Press, 2001
LINDBLOM, C. E. and BRAYBROOKE, D., *A Strategy of Decision*, Free Press, 1963.
LINDBLOM, C. E. and COHEN, D. K., *Usable Knowledge: Social Science and Social Problem Solving*, Yale University Press, 1979.

Victor H. Vroom

Victor Vroom has been involved for many years in research, teaching and consulting on the psychological analysis of behaviour in organizations. A Canadian by birth, he has been at McGill University, a number of US universities and is currently Searle Professor of Organization and Management and Professor of Psychology at Yale University. His interest in the effects of personality on participation in decision making began early, his doctoral dissertation on this topic winning him the Ford Foundation Doctoral Dissertation Competition in 1959. He has also won the McKinsey Foundation Research Design Competition and the J. M. Cattell award of the American Psychological Association.

Vroom's dissertation corroborated previous findings that participation in decision making has positive effects on attitudes and motivation. But in addition it showed that the size of these effects was a function of certain personality characteristics of the participants. Authoritarians and persons with weak independence needs are unaffected by the opportunity to participate, whereas egalitarians and those with strong independence needs develop more positive attitudes and greater motivation for effective performance through participation. The study did point out that there are a number of different processes related to participation which might be affected differently.

Much more recently, Vroom (in collaboration with P. W. Yetton and A. G. Jago) has explored in much greater depth the processes of management decision making and the variations in subordinate participation which can come about. Possible decision processes which a manager might use in dealing with an issue affecting a group of subordinates are as follows (though there are some variations if the issue concerns one subordinate only):

AI   You solve the problem or make the decision yourself, using information available to you at that time.

AII   You obtain the necessary information from your subordinate(s), then decide on the solution to the problem yourself. You may or may not tell your subordinates what the problem is when getting the information from them. The role played by your subordinates in making the decision is clearly one of providing the necessary information to you, rather than generating or evaluating alternative solutions.

CI   You share the problem with relevant subordinates individually getting their ideas and suggestions without bringing them together as a group. Then you make the decisions that may or may not reflect your subordinates' influence.

CII   You share the problem with your subordinates as a group, collectively obtaining their ideas and suggestions. Then you make the decision that may or may not reflect your subordinates' influence.

GII   You share a problem with your subordinates as a group. Together you generate and evaluate alternatives and attempt to reach agreement (consensus) on a solution. Your role is much like that of chairperson. You do not try to influence the group to adopt *your* solution and you are willing to accept and implement any solution that has the support of the entire group.

Processes AI and AII are designated *autocratic* processes, CI and CII *consultative* processes, and GII a *group* process. (GI applies to single subordinate issues.) Having identified these processes, Vroom and Yetton's research programme then proceeded to answer two basic questions:

1. What decision-making processes should managers use to deal effectively with the problems they encounter in their jobs? This is a normative or prescriptive question. To answer it would require setting up a logical model with a series of steps or procedures by which managers could rationally determine which was the most effective process to inaugurate.

2. What decision-making processes do managers use in dealing with their problems and what factors affect their choice of processes and degree of subordinate participation? This is a descriptive question. The answer is important in delineating how far away from a rational approach managers are in their decision making. We could then ask what activities of training or development could lead managers to a more effective decision-making style.

It is in their answer to the first question that Vroom and his collaborators have made a most distinctive contribution. They have developed a detailed normative model of decision-making processes based on rational principles consistent with existing evidence on the consequences of participation for organizational effectiveness. They begin by distinguishing three classes of consequences which influence decision effectiveness:

1. The quality or rationality of the decision. Clearly a process which jeopardized this would be ineffective.

2. The acceptance or commitment on the part of subordinates to execute the decision effectively. If this commitment were necessary, then processes which did not generate it would be ineffective even though they gave a high quality decision.

3. The amount of time required to make the decision. A decision process which took less time, if it were equally effective, would normally be preferable to one which took longer.

These consequences generate a set of rules for the model which may then be applied to the characteristics of whichever managerial problem is under consideration. The model will then indicate which of the decision processes is appropriate to the particular case. The model can be expressed in the form of a decision tree as shown on page 204. In this Decision Model, the problem characteristics are presented as questions. The manager starts at the left-hand side and moves to the right along the path determined by the answer to the question above each column. At the final point of the line the model shows which of the decision processes should be used to reach, in the least time, a quality decision which will be found acceptable.

As will be seen from the Decision Model, all decision processes (autocratic, consultative, group) are applicable in some circumstances; how often each should be used will depend on the type of decisions that the manager has to take. The normative model requires that in order to be rational and effective, all managers have to be able to operate across the whole range. In later work Vroom and Jago have elaborated the model to give greater discrimination among options and thus allow more detailed and more effective targeting of the decision process to the manager's problem. They have also made the more elaborate model available for use via a computer program.

The research undertaken by Vroom and his collaborators to answer their second question – how do managers actually behave? – is based on two methods. In the first, many managers were asked to recall decision problems and how they tackled them in terms of the questions of the Decision Model. The second method involved many managers assessing a set of standardized problem descriptions and giving their preferred solutions.

The most striking finding of these descriptive studies was that, while there certainly were average differences between managers in their use of various decision processes, these were small in comparison with the range of processes used by each individual manager. No managers indicated that they would use the same process for all decisions; most used all five of the decision processes described above under some circumstances. 'It makes more sense to talk about participative and autocratic situations than it does to talk about participative and autocratic managers.'

The descriptive research also enabled a comparison to be made between what managers do (or say they would do) and what the model would designate as rational behaviour. On average, a typical manager was found to use the same decision process as that required by the Decision Model in 40 per cent of situations. In a quarter of cases they used a process which is called 'feasible' in that it satisfied the constraints of the model in protecting decision quality and acceptability, but would not be the least time consuming. In only about one-third of the situations did the typical manager initiate a process which would risk either quality or acceptability. In addition it was found that the constraints necessary to achieve acceptability were much more frequently ignored than those necessary to achieve quality.

Vroom has designed a leadership development programme based on his normative model to enable managers to analyse their own decision processes against those of the model and see where they depart from the rational constraints for effective decision making. The model proposes far greater variation for each

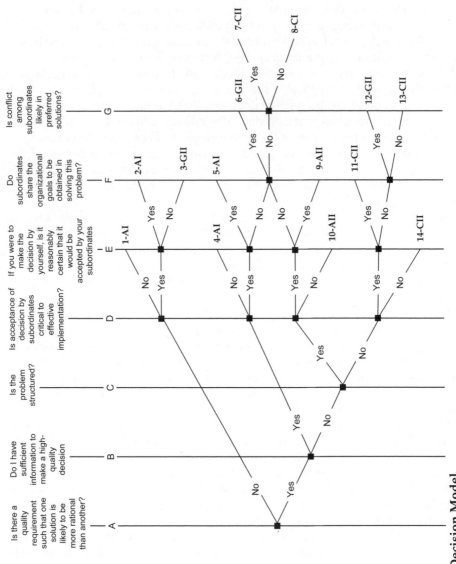

Decision Model
Source: Vroom and Yetton (1973).

problem situation than the typical manager exhibits. Using the model as a basis for making decisions would require such a manager to become both more autocratic and more participative according to the problem (cf. Fiedler in Chapter 6 for an opposing view on this issue).

BIBLIOGRAPHY

VROOM, V. H., *Some Personality Determinants of the Effects of Participation*, Prentice-Hall, 1960.
VROOM, V. H 'A New Look at Managerial Decision Making', *Organizational Dynamics*, 5 (1974), 66–80.
VROOM, V. H and JAGO, A. G., *The New Leadership: Managing Participation in Organizations*, Prentice-Hall, 1988.
VROOM, V. H and YETTON, P. W., *Leadership and Decision-Making*, University of Pittsburgh Press, 1973.

Michel Crozier

The distinctly French view of organizations contributed by Michel Crozier arises both from his French birth and experience and from the many periods he has spent in the US. These periods away from France give him a perspective on his own society. From 1961 to 1993 he was Director of the Centre for the Sociology of Organizations in Paris, under the auspices of the Centre National de la Recherche Scientifique (CNRS). He has a long record of research in France covering a wide range of organizations and administrative and social problems, but with an emphasis on studies of public administration and state-owned industries. However, his early training in sociology was in the US, and he has spent many subsequent periods at Stanford and Harvard.

Although Crozier's view has its origins in research in France, it pertains to bureaucracies everywhere. He does not see them as monolithic rational structures, but as systems in which, despite all efforts at control, individuals and groups of individuals have room for manoeuvre. There is constant interaction between the system and the actors in the system.

This view is distinctively founded on the concept of the *power game*. An organization is seen as a series of enmeshed power games, an 'ensemble' of games. This idea is no mere colourful image. Games are very real to those in organizations. Indeed, an organization is not so much the direct creation of deliberate design as the result of the ensemble of games. The game channels power relationships and enables cooperation, reconciling the freedom of those in the organization with the constraints it places upon them.

Games are played between groups of partners of many kinds, for example between superiors and subordinates such as managers and workers, or between departments and sections. The players evolve different strategies which govern what they do. Superiors may follow a strategy of 'divide and rule'; subordinates may follow a defensive strategy to protect whatever scope they may have to do things in their own way, free of interference from bosses or new regulations; occupational groups such as maintenance engineers may follow conservative (or aggressive) strategies towards technical modernization, and so on. Crozier calls this a *strategic model* of organization.

Players go so far but not too far in pursuing their strategies. While all are free to enjoy whatever advantage can be gained from a strategy rationally designed to serve their interests, the continuance of the organization is necessary for them to be able to play at all. These are not life-and-death struggles but games for position within a system; therefore limits are accepted. These are the rules of the game which players must respect if it is to continue. They are not formally set-down rules, but principles which can be discovered by analysing the players' recurrent behaviour, in the same way as their strategies can be seen in what they do. There may not be complete consensus on the rules and some players may be endeavouring to change them, but they are sufficiently acknowledged and persistent for newcomers to learn them and to absorb the associated norms and values which define acceptable and unacceptable strategies.

The players in a game are far from equal – some are more powerful than others – and their roles also differ between one game and the next, so that players who are powerful in one may be weak in another. However, their strategies share a common fundamental objective – to gain whatever advantage is possible, within the constraining rules of the game, by restricting the choices of alternatives open to others while preserving or enhancing their own choices. The aim is to manoeuvre others into positions where their actions can be circumscribed, while retaining one's own freedom of action. All attempt to defend and extend their own discretion and to limit their dependence, while placing others in the reverse position.

The most revealing case among those described by Crozier is that of the maintenance workers in what he terms the 'Industrial Monopoly' – the French nationalized tobacco industry. At the time of Crozier's research, at the end of the 1950s and beginning of the 1960s, this was dispersed throughout the country in a large number of small and very similar factories. Each employed in the order of 350 to 400 people of which perhaps one-third were direct production workers. These workers were women whose job it was to operate the semi-automatic machines turning out cigarettes and so on.

The organization was very stable, and each small factory worked in a controlled environment. Finance, raw material procurement, distribution and sales were all centrally controlled from Paris, so each local plant could get on with its task of production, unimpeded by problems. Except one. Machine stoppages.

These stoppages occurred because of breakdowns and because of variations in the tobacco leaf which required the constant adjustment of machines. They were the only major impediment that could not be dealt with by impersonal bureaucratic rules or bureaucratic actions from Paris. Yet if machines stopped, work stopped and the factory stopped making what it was there to do. Who could do something about it? Only the dozen or so male maintenance workers under the factory's technical engineer who alone knew how to set and repair the machines. No bureaucrat in Paris, no local factory director, not even the production workers on the machines knew what they knew. These maintenance workers acquired the tricks of their trade from one another and kept them to themselves. They did not explain what they did to anyone else. In their eyes it was an unforgivable sin for a production worker herself to 'fool around' with the machine or tinker with it beyond operating it in the normal way. Thus the maintenance workers succeeded in making the production workers directly, and everyone else indirectly, dependent upon themselves. Everyone else was constrained by the maintenance workers being the only ones able to deal with stoppages, whilst they themselves preserved their freedom of choice over what to do.

They could do so because they were powerful; they were powerful because of their 'control over the last source of uncertainty remaining in a completely routinized organizational system'. Machine stoppages occurred unpredictably and the repair was in their hands. This gave them power, because those who face and cope with uncertainties have power over others who are dependent upon their choices. In the long run, power is closely related to those uncertainties on which the life of an organization depends, the strategies of the groups in power games being aimed at controlling the 'ultimate strategic sources of uncertainties'. *Uncertainty explains power.*

The maintenance workers therefore had power because, whilst everything else was under bureaucratic control, the uncertain machine stoppages were not. These had to be dealt with on the spot as they happened. They presented the maintenance workers with an opportunity which was conspicuous because it was the sole cause of uncertainty in each factory. In other organizations the sources of uncertainty may not be so obvious, but in all organizations they come and go, and as they do so the power of those who tackle them waxes and wanes. Maintenance workers are only one example: the same applies to the rise and fall of financial experts, of production control specialists and so on.

Why is it then that powerful experts are not able to cling to power indefinitely? If the uncertainty continues and with it their know-how, they could indeed keep their grip on power, but this is unlikely because their success becomes self-defeating. The rationalization inherent in organizations breeds constant attempts to bring areas of uncertainty within the range of formal controls; experts are themselves agents of the rationalization that diminishes their own power. The more they succeed in recording their own know-how in bureaucratic procedures and regulations, the more their own power to deal with the uncertainties themselves is curtailed. Their choices become restricted. Therefore the maintenance workers in the tobacco factories strove to keep their rules of thumb to themselves and to prevent them from becoming bureaucratized. Even though officially laid-down instructions for the setting and maintenance of machines were kept at head office in Paris, these were totally disregarded by the maintenance workers; neither could copies be found in the factories themselves. For *the routinization of uncertainty removes power.*

This principle shapes strategies up and down hierarchies as well as between occupational groupings. The battle between superiors and subordinates involves a basic strategy by which subordinates resist rules which encroach upon their discretion, whilst pressing for rules which will limit the discretion of their superiors.

It is possible for opposed strategies to interlock in a series of bureaucratic vicious circles which block change. Administrators try to extend bureaucratic regulation; those subjected to it resist. The directors of the tobacco factories typically pressed for the modernization of procedures, whilst the technical engineers resisted anything that might weaken the position of their maintenance workers. Crozier sees French society as a whole as an example of this, for its tendencies to bureaucratic centralization and impersonality provoke protective strategies by those affected, and these strategies in turn provoke greater bureaucratization. In every branch of administration each level of hierarchy becomes a layer protected from those above and beneath. Those beneath restrict communication to those above and stall any threatening changes, while those above make ill-informed decisions which are not carried out as intended but from the consequences of which they are shielded.

This gives rise to a peculiar rhythm of change in bureaucratic organizations, certainly in France and perhaps elsewhere too. It is an alternation of long periods of stability with very short periods of crisis and change. Conflicts are stifled until they explode. Crises are therefore endemic to such bureaucracies but necessary to them as a means for change. At such times in French bureaucracies, personal authority supersedes the rules as someone is able to force some change out of the crisis. *Authoritarian reformer figures* wait amid the bureaucratic routine for that moment of crisis when the system will need them.

Yet Crozier is optimistic; with reforms in training and recruitment for French public administration and in its caste system, he believes the elites could be opened up. He argues that the large organizations of the modern world are not necessarily inimical to change, for change has never been faster, being fastest in those societies with the largest organizations. But there is always a risk that bureaucratic structures will lead to forms of power games which block the changes that are needed.

BIBLIOGRAPHY

CROZIER, M., *The Bureaucratic Phenomenon*, Tavistock Publications and University of Chicago Press, 1964.

CROZIER, M., 'Comparing Structures and Comparing Games', in G. Hofstede and S. Kassim (eds), *European Contributions to Organization Theory*, Van Gorcum, 1976.

CROZIER, M. and FRIEDBERG, E., *Actors and Systems*, University of Chicago Press, 1980.

UNIVERSITY OF ... CHESTER
LIBRARY

Arnold S. Tannenbaum

Arnold Tannenbaum did not begin as the social psychologist he later became. His first degree was in electrical engineering from Purdue University. He went on to take his PhD at Syracuse University and to join the staff of one of the leading and longest-established American social science institutes, the Institute for Social Research not far from Detroit, where he has worked ever since as researcher, teacher and consultant. He is Research Scientist Emeritus at the Institute's Survey Research Center and Emeritus Professor in the Department of Psychology at the University of Michigan.

In the small text published in 1966, Tannenbaum set out clearly the view of organizational functioning that has shaped his work for many years. 'Hierarchy is divisive, it creates resentment, hostility and opposition. Participation reduces disaffection and increases the identification of members with the organization.' What is more: 'Paradoxically through participation, management increases its control by giving up some of its authority.'

Early in his research career, Tannenbaum found that in trade unions the more effective and active local branches had both more influential officers and more influential members – at first sight an impossibility. An impossibility, that is, if control of an organization was thought of as a given quantity, something divisible so that if one person had more then another had less; but not impossible if control of an organization was elastic so that everyone could have more. It is this possibility that shapes Tannenbaum's view of what organizations can be.

His work has focused on control, for organizations are a means whereby the behaviour of large numbers of individuals is controlled. That is, people have to work together more or less as they are intended to if the aims of the organizations are to be achieved, whether that organization is a trade union, a firm, a welfare agency, a cooperative or an Israeli kibbutz, a financial institution, a brokerage firm or a branch of the American League of Women Voters – all examples of organizations which Tannenbaum and his colleagues or others following their lead have studied. Control is any process by which a person or group of persons determines (that is, 'intentionally affects') the behaviour of another person or group; in other words, causes someone else to do what they want them to do. In an organization this may be by orders or by persuasion, by threats or by promises, through written communications or through discussion, even indirectly by fixing the speed of a machine that someone else must keep up with or by programming a computer to produce information they must deal with – or by any other means having such an effect.

The way of representing control used in studies by Tannenbaum and his colleagues over many years is to ask members of organizations how much influence they and others have. They are asked a question worded typically as follows: 'How much say or influence does each of the following groups have over what goes on (in the organization)?' The groups referred to are hierarchical echelons such as managers, supervisors and workers; the groupings can be varied as appropriate. This simple question is capable of yielding a great amount of information since even with only three groups – managers, supervisors and workers – those in each can rate the influence of both the other two groups and of themselves, so that a large number of cross-checking ratings are obtained. If four, five or six groupings are used, the information is greater again. The wording of the question can also be varied to refer more specifically to the influence over what others do or to policy, for example.

Members of organizations respond to the question by ticking one of five categories for each group, in the form shown below.

	Little or no influence	*Some influence*	*Quite a bit of influence*	*A great deal of influence*	*A very great deal of influence*
Managers	–	–	–	–	–
Supervisors	–	–	–	–	–
Workers	–	–	–	–	–

The degrees of influence are scored from one to five so that a tick under 'Little' scores one, a tick under 'Some' scores two, and so on with 'A very great deal' scoring five.

Responding to such a question in this way gives a representation of how actual influence is perceived by those involved. A second and equally large amount of information is obtained by asking the same question again but with the word 'does' replaced by 'should'. This gives preferred or ideal influence.

The impact of Tannenbaum's work and its interpretation are heightened by the way in which the results can be plotted on what are called control graphs. Various different averagings of scores can be plotted, but usually the influence ratings given to each group by all the others and by itself are added and its mean score calculated. In the example above, this would give a mean score out of five for managers, another for supervisors, and another for workers which could then be plotted on a control graph in which the three hierarchical groups were placed evenly along the lateral axis in hierarchical order. A simplified but not unrepresentative hypothetical result might look like the graph shown on page 212.

The lines are drawn through the three graph points for the mean scores for each group (managers, workers, supervisors) on the vertical control (influence score) axis.

The immediate visual impact of a control graph is from the slope of the lines, its most obvious if not necessarily most significant feature. In the graph, the two solid lines represent the actual (as against ideal) distributions of control in two hypothetical companies. Tannenbaum interprets such left-to-right slopes as showing a hierarchical distribution in which there is a sharp reduction in control from one level to the next down the hierarchy. In their actual hierarchies of control Companies A and B show the classical view of the industrial firm. Tannenbaum finds that in practically all manufacturing organizations in Western industrialized nations, all employees – whether bosses or subordinates – report the steeply graded hierarchy that he sees as divisive and fraught with resentment and hostility.

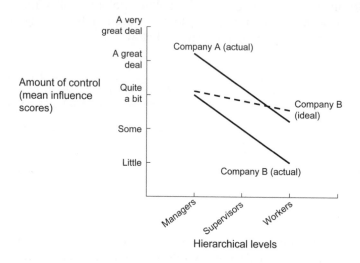

This may be unavoidable in large-scale manufacturing: even ideal slopes (plots of the responses to the 'should' question) do not fundamentally challenge the basic hierarchy of control. No one in manufacturing organizations suggests anything other than that upper levels should have more control than lower levels – the slope does not flatten out nor tip the other way – but the *degree* of differentiation is challenged. The ideal slope is often less steep. Lower-level employees frequently feel that they should have more say in what goes on, as in the hypothetical ideal slope for Company B which reveals a desire for more democratic practices than those indicated by the actual slope.

Further, not only might the steeply graded hierarchies in large-scale industrial organizations be levelled out to some degree, but it is also possible to manage them in ways that mitigate the hierarchy's negative effects. American supervisors, for example, treat their subordinates more as equals, with relative informality, as compared to the typical authoritarian approach in Italian plants.

Tannenbaum recognizes that Italian workers may be more concerned with changing the system than with the possibility of working better. Certainly a nation's socio-economic system is embodied in forms of organization which affect hierarchy. The slope of control graphs from former Yugoslavia (which had workers' councils) and from Israeli kibbutzim (which have collective ownership and elected managers) are not as steep as those from capitalistic Western enterprises. This is not to say that the Yugoslavs and Israelis could or should be copied everywhere else, for Yugoslav managers could be authoritarian and the kibbutz system is probably only possible in small-scale units.

The type of membership that is appropriate to the purpose of the organization also affects control. In organizations that depend on a voluntary membership (such as American trade unions and the American League of Women Voters), the rank and file exert much greater influence than do the paid employees in industry; similar results in Brazilian development banks staffed by highly educated professionals suggest that professionalization has the same effect because these members are relied on to do their work with less direct control, and more attention is paid to their views.

However, though the slope of the line in a control graph is its most instantly obvious feature, it does not in Tannenbaum's view depict the most important characteristic of an organization which, he says, is the *total control* exercised within it, as depicted on the graph by the *area* beneath the line. In the graph both companies have identical hierarchical slopes but since the line for Company A is higher than that for Company B, the area beneath the line for Company A (that is, between the line and the lateral axis at the base of the graph) is greater. In other words, the influence scores for all groups are greater, so that everyone has more control. Here is the visual representation of the apparent paradox that lower-level employees such as workers can have greater control and yet not detract from the control exercised by managers. Indeed, managers too may then have greater control. This is possible because the total amount of influence – the size of the 'influence pie' – can be expanded and so be greater in one organization than in another because control is not a zero-sum process.

The reason for this is that leaders are also the led. Superiors depend upon their subordinates to get things done. Authoritarian bosses who take a zero-sum view assume a fixed amount of total control and cling to what they perceive as their rightful major share of it. They may look as if they are dominating everyone, but their actual influence on what others do may be very restricted. Subordinates in this situation will also take a zero-sum view and will defend their share from encroachment. Conflict and minimal cooperation are likely to result. If superiors assume an expandable amount of total control, they can communicate readily with subordinates, welcome opinions and take up suggestions; in other words, invite influence over themselves. At the same time, the involvement of subordinates in what is being done means that the superiors' influence expands also, for they are more likely to do what needs to be done.

Research results show that a greater amount of control exists in Japanese mining and manufacturing companies compared with equivalent American organizations. 'Progressive' dioceses in the Roman Catholic church (that is, those where the bishop is rated as positive to democratizing decision making) have more total control than conservative ones, as do plants incorporating self-managing socio-technical groups (see Trist, Chapter 6) compared with conventional factories.

In terms of morale and productivity, greater organizational effectiveness is likely to be linked more to increasing the total amount of control than to democratizing its hierarchical distribution, because all concerned are more fully controlled and in control through interlocking influence. This is true as much of privately owned American firms as it is of collectively owned Israeli kibbutzim.

Tannenbaum's research challenges the commonplace view that control is and should be unilateral, from the leaders to the led. Leaders have greater control when the led also have greater control. Though diminishing the slope of hierarchies can be important, too much attention is paid to this 'power equalization' and too little to the possibilities of expanding the total. The evidence suggests that people are more interested in exercising greater control themselves than in exactly how much others may have.

The strength of Tannenbaum's challenging perspective is that it is based on a uniquely sustained series of research projects in many countries, using standard methods, which have confirmed his results again and again.

BIBLIOGRAPHY

TANNENBAUM, A. S., *Social Psychology of the Work Organization*, Wadsworth (California) and Tavistock, 1966.

TANNENBAUM, A. S., *Control in Organizations*, McGraw-Hill, 1968.

TANNENBAUM, A. S., 'Controversies about Control and Democracy in Organizations', in R. N. Stern and S. McCarthy (eds), *The International Yearbook of Organizational Democracy*, Vol. 111, Wiley, 1986.

TANNENBAUM, A. S., KAVCIC, B., ROSNER, M., VIANELLO, M. and WIESER, G., *Hierarchy in Organizations*, Jossey-Bass, 1974.

6   People in Organizations

Management succeeds or fails in proportion as it is accepted without reservation by the group as authority and leader.
ELTON MAYO

The entire organization must consist of a multiple overlapping group structure with *every* work group using group decision-making processes skilfully.
RENSIS LIKERT

The average human being learns, under proper conditions, not only to accept but to seek responsibility.
DOUGLAS MCGREGOR

The 9,9 orientation to the management of production and people aims at integrating these two aspects of work under conditions of high concern for both.
ROBERT R. BLAKE and JANE S. MOUTON

The successful manager must be a good diagnostician and must value a spirit of enquiry.
EDGAR H. SCHEIN

The primary functions of any organization, whether religious, political or industrial, should be to implement the needs of man to enjoy a meaningful existence.
FREDERICK HERZBERG

The closest approximation to the all-round good leader is likely to be the individual who intuitively or through training knows how to manage his environment so that the leadership situation best matches his leadership style.
FRED E. FIEDLER

Only organizations based on the redundancy of functions (as opposed to the redundancy of parts) have the flexibility and innovative potential to give the possibility of adaptation to a rapid change rate, increasing complexity and environmental uncertainty.
ERIC TRIST

As society changes, so must its organizations; as organizations change, so must their pay systems.
EDWARD E. LAWLER

Organizations are systems of interdependent *human beings*. Although this has been recognized implicitly by the writers in the previous sections, and explicitly by some, their main concern has been with the 'formal system' – its aims, the principles on which it should be constituted to achieve them, and the methods by which it should function. People have then been considered as one of the essential resources required to achieve the aims. But people are a rather special sort of resource. They not only work for the organization – they *are* the organization.

The behaviour of the members of an organization clearly affects both its structure and its functioning, as well as the principles on which it can be managed. Most importantly, human beings affect the aims of organizations in which they participate – not merely the methods used to accomplish them. The writers in this chapter are social scientists specifically concerned to analyse the behaviour of people and its effects on all aspects of the organization. They have studied human attitudes, expectations, value systems, tensions and conflicts and the effects these have on productivity, adaptability, cohesion and morale. They have regarded the organization as a 'natural system' (an organism whose processes have to be studied in their own right) rather than as a 'formal system' (a mechanism designed to achieve particular ends).

Elton Mayo is the founding father of the 'Human Relations' movement which brought into prominence the view that workers and managers must first be understood as human beings. Rensis Likert and Douglas McGregor reject the underlying assumptions about human behaviour on which formal organizations have been built and propose new methods of management based on a more adequate understanding of human motivation, while Robert Blake and Jane Mouton describe a form of management which shows equally high concern for both production and people.

Edgar Schein's concern has been to understand and manage the relationship between the individual's career and the organization's culture. Frederick Herzberg determines how people's characteristically human needs for growth and development may be satisfied in work.

Fred Fiedler analyses appropriate styles of leadership for effectiveness in differing situations. Eric Trist and his colleagues at the Tavistock Institute demonstrate the utility of designing groups and organizations to take account of human and social, as well as technical, concerns. Edward Lawler highlights an aspect of this approach in emphasizing the impact of payment systems upon the motivation and performance of organizational members.

Elton Mayo and the Hawthorne Investigations

Elton Mayo (1880–1949) was an Australian who spent most of his working life at Harvard University, eventually becoming Professor of Industrial Research in the Graduate School of Business Administration. In this post he was responsible for the initiation and direction of many research projects, the most famous being the five-year investigation of the Hawthorne works of the Western Electric Company in Chicago. Immediately prior to his death, Mayo was consultant on industrial problems to the British government.

Elton Mayo has often been called the founder of both the Human Relations Movement and of industrial sociology. The research that he directed showed the importance of groups in affecting the behaviour of individuals at work and enabled him to make certain deductions about what managers ought to do.

Like most of his contemporaries, Mayo's initial interests were in fatigue, accidents and labour turnover, and the effect on these of rest pauses and physical conditions of work. One of his first investigations was of a spinning mill in Philadelphia where labour turnover in one department was 250 per cent compared with an average of 6 per cent in all the other departments. Rest pauses were introduced by Mayo and production and morale improved. When the operatives took part in fixing the frequency and duration of the pauses, a further improvement was registered and morale in the whole factory also rose. At the end of the first year, labour turnover in the department concerned was down to the average for the rest of the mill. The initial explanation was that, in breaking up the monotony of the job, the rest pauses improved the mental and physical conditions of the workers. However, after subsequent investigations, Mayo modified his explanation.

The major investigation which led to this modification and which laid the basis for a great many subsequent studies was the Hawthorne Experiment carried out between 1927 and 1932. Prior to the entry of Mayo's team, an inquiry had been made by a number of engineers into the effect of illumination on workers and their work. Two groups of workers had been isolated: the lighting conditions for one had been varied and for the other held constant. No significant differences in output were found between the two; indeed whatever was done with the lighting, production rose in both groups.

At this point the industrial research team directed by Mayo took over. The first stage of their inquiry is known as the 'relay assembly test room'. Six female operatives, engaged in assembling telephone relays, were segregated in order to observe the effects on output and morale of various changes in their conditions of work during five years of experiment. A continuous record of output was kept. At first a special group payment scheme was introduced, whereas previously the women had been grouped with a hundred other operatives for incentive payment purposes. A total of more than ten changes introduced at various times included rest pauses in several different forms (varying in length and spacing), shorter hours and refreshments. Before putting the changes into effect, the investigators spent a lot of time discussing them with the women. Communication between the workers and the research team was very full and open throughout the experimental period. Almost without exception, output increased with each change made.

The next stage in the experiment was to return to the original conditions. The operatives reverted to a 48-hour six-day week, no incentives, no rest pauses and no refreshment. Output went up to the highest yet recorded. By this time it had become clear, to quote Mayo, 'that the itemized changes experimentally imposed ... could not be used to explain the major change – the continually increasing production'. The explanation eventually given was that the women experienced a tremendous increase in work satisfaction because they had greater freedom in their working environment and control over their own pace-setting. The six operatives had in fact become a social group with their own standards and expectations. By removing the women from their normal work setting and by intensifying their interaction and cooperation, informal practices, values, norms and social relationships had been built up, giving the group high cohesion. Also, the communication system between researchers and workers was extremely effective; this meant that the norms of output were those that the women felt the researchers desired. The supervisors also took a personal interest in each worker and showed pride in the record of the group. As a result, workers and supervisors developed a sense of participation and established a completely new working pattern. Mayo's generalization was that work satisfaction depends to a large extent on the informal social pattern of the work group. Where norms of cooperativeness and high output are established because of a feeling of importance, physical conditions have little impact.

However, this is the explanation arrived at in later years. At the time of the actual experiment, the women's continually increasing output was regarded as something of a mystery, leading to an inquiry into conditions in the factory at large. This took the form of an interview programme. It was quickly realized that such a programme told the researchers little about actual conditions in the factory, but a great deal about the attitudes of various employees. The major finding of this stage was that many problems of worker–management cooperation were the result of the emotionally based attitudes of the workers rather than of objective difficulties in the situation. Workers, thought Mayo, were activated by a 'logic of sentiment', whereas management was concerned with the 'logic of cost and efficiency'. Conflict is inevitable unless this difference is understood and provided for.

The third stage of the investigation was to observe a group performing a task in a natural setting, that is, a non-experimental situation. A number of male employees in what became known as the 'bank wiring observation room' were put under constant observation and their output recorded. It was found that they restricted their output; the group had a standard for output and this was not exceeded by any individual worker. The attitude of the members of the group towards the company's financial incentive scheme was one of indifference. The group was highly integrated, with its own social structure and code of behaviour which clashed with that of management. Essentially this code consisted of solidarity on the part of the group against management. Not too much work should be done: that would be rate-busting; on the other hand, not too little work should be done: that would be chiselling. There was little recognition of the organization's formal allocation of roles. This was confirmation of the importance of informal social groupings in determining levels of output.

Taken as a whole, the significance of the Hawthorne investigation was in discovering the informal organization which, it is now realized, exists in all organizations. It demonstrated the importance to individuals of stable social relationships in the work situation. It confirmed Mayo's wider thinking that what he calls the 'rabble hypothesis' about human behaviour (that each individual pursues only narrow rational self-interest) was completely false. It confirmed his view that the breakdown of traditional values in society could be countered by creating a situation in industry conducive to spontaneous cooperation.

For Mayo, one of the major tasks of management is to organize such spontaneous cooperation, thereby preventing the further breakdown of society. As traditional attachments to community and family disappear and as the workplace increases in importance, the support given to people by traditional institutions must now be given by the organization. Conflict, competition and disagreement between individuals are to be avoided by management understanding its role as providing the basis for group affiliation. From the end of the Hawthorne project to his death, Mayo was interested in discovering how spontaneous cooperation could be achieved. It is this which has been the basis of the Human Relations Movement – the use of the insights of the social sciences to secure the commitment of individuals to the ends and activities of the organization.

The impact of Hawthorne and Mayo on both management and academics has been tremendous. It led to a fuller realization and understanding of the human factor in work situations. Central to this was the discovery of the informal group as an outlet for the aspirations of the worker. His work also led to an emphasis on the importance of an adequate communication system, particularly upwards from workers to management. The investigation showed, to quote Mayo, that 'management succeeds or fails in proportion as it is accepted without reservation by the group as authority and leader'.

BIBLIOGRAPHY

MAYO, E., *The Human Problems of an Industrial Civilization*, Macmillan, 1933.
MAYO, E., *The Social Problems of an Industrial Civilization*, Routledge & Kegan Paul, 1949.
ROETHLISBERGER, F. J. and DICKSON, W. J., *Management and the Worker*, Harvard University Press, 1949.

Rensis Likert and Douglas McGregor

Rensis Likert (1903–1981) was an American social psychologist who in 1949 established the Institute of Social Research at the University of Michigan. Until his retirement in 1969, he was thus at the head of one of the major institutions conducting research into human behaviour in organizations. On his retirement he formed Rensis Likert Associates, a consulting firm, to put his ideas about the management of organizations into wider practice. His books are based on the numerous research studies which he and his colleagues conducted, his last book being jointly written with his research collaborator and wife, Jane Gibson Likert.

Douglas McGregor (1906–1964) was a social psychologist who published a number of research papers in this field. For some years he was president (that is, chief executive) of Antioch College and he has described how this period as a top administrator affected his views on organizational functioning. From 1954 until his death, he was Professor of Management at the Massachusetts Institute of Technology.

'Managers with the best records of performance in American business and government are in the process of pointing the way to an appreciably more effective system of management than now exists,' proclaims Likert. Research studies have shown that departments which are low in efficiency tend to be in the charge of supervisors who are 'job-centred'. That is they 'tend to concentrate on keeping their subordinates busily engaged in going through a specified work cycle in a prescribed way and at a satisfactory rate as determined by time standards'. This attitude is clearly derived from Taylor (see Chapter 4) with his emphasis on breaking down the job into component parts, selecting and training people to do them, and exerting constant pressure to achieve output. Supervisors see themselves as getting the job done with the resources (which includes the people) at their disposal.

Supervisors with the best record of performance are found to focus their attention on the human aspects of their subordinates' problems and on building effective work groups which are set high achievement goals. These supervisors are 'employee-centred'. They regard their jobs as dealing with human beings rather than with the work; they attempt to know them as individuals. They see their function as helping them to do the job efficiently. They exercise general rather than detailed supervision and are more concerned with targets than methods. They allow maximum participation in decision making. If high performance is to be obtained, a supervisor must not only be employee-centred, but must also have high performance goals and be capable of exercising the decision-making processes to achieve them.

In summarizing these findings, Likert distinguishes four systems of management:

- System 1 is the exploitive authoritative type where management uses fear and threats, communication is downward, superiors and subordinates are psychologically far apart, most decisions are taken at the top of the organization, and so on.
- System 2 is the benevolent authoritative type where management uses rewards, subordinates' attitudes are subservient to superiors, information flowing upward is restricted to what the boss wants to hear, policy decisions are taken at the top though decisions within a prescribed framework may be delegated to lower levels, and so on.
- System 3 is the consultative type where management uses rewards; occasional punishments and some involvement is sought; communication is both down and up, but upward communication other than that which the boss wants to hear is given in limited amounts and only cautiously. In this system subordinates can have a moderate amount of influence on the activities of their departments since broad policy decisions are taken at the top and more specific decisions at lower levels.
- System 4 is characterized by participative group management. Management gives economic rewards and makes full use of group participation and involvement in setting high performance goals, improving work methods, and so on; communication flows downwards, upwards and with peers and is accurate; subordinates and superiors are very close psychologically. Decision making is undertaken throughout the organization largely through group processes; it is integrated into the formal structure by regarding the organization chart as a series of overlapping groups with each linked to the rest of the organization by means of persons (called 'linking pins') who are members of more than one group. System 4 management produces high productivity, greater involvement of individuals and better labour–management relations.

In general, high-producing managers are those who have built the personnel in their units into effective groups, whose members have cooperative attitudes and a high level of job satisfaction through System 4 management. But there are exceptions. Technically competent, job-centred, tough management can achieve high productivity (particularly if backed up by tight systems of control techniques). But the members of units whose supervisors use these high-pressure methods are likely to have unfavourable attitudes towards their work and the management, and to have excessively high levels of waste and scrap. They also show higher labour turnover and greater labour–management conflict as measured by work-stoppages, official grievances and the like.

Management, according to Likert, is always a relative process. To be effective and to communicate, leaders must always adapt their behaviour to take account of the persons whom they lead. There are no specific rules which will work well in all situations, but only general principles which must be interpreted to take account of the expectations, values and skills of those with whom the manager interacts. Sensitivity to these values and expectations is a crucial leadership skill, and organizations must create the atmosphere and conditions which encourage all managers to deal with the people they encounter in a manner fitting to their values and their expectations.

To assist in this task, management now has available a number of measures of relevant factors which have been developed by social scientists. Methods are available to obtain objective measurements of such variables as:

- the degree of member loyalty to an organization;
- the extent to which the goals of groups and individuals facilitate the achievement of the organization's goals;
- the level of motivation among members;
- the degree of confidence and trust between different hierarchical levels and between different sub-units;
- the efficiency and adequacy of the communication process;
- the extent to which superiors are correctly informed of the expectations, reactions, obstacles, problems and failures of subordinates – together with the assistance they find useful and the assurance they wish they could get.

These measures and others enable an organization to know at any one time the state of the system of functioning human beings which underpins it (called the 'interaction-influence system'); whether it is improving or deteriorating and why, and what to do to bring about desired improvements. This objective information about the interaction-influence system enables problems of leadership and management to be depersonalized and the 'authority of facts' to come to the fore. In this way the 'law of the situation' (see Mary Parker Follett, Chapter 4) will determine which actions need to be taken. A much wider range of human behaviour can now be measured and made objective, whereas previously impressions and judgements had to suffice.

Douglas McGregor examines the assumptions about human behaviour which underlie managerial action. The traditional conception of administration (as exemplified by the writings of Fayol, Chapter 4) is based upon the direction and control by management of the enterprise and its individual members. It implies certain basic assumptions about human motivation, which McGregor characterizes as 'Theory X':

> The average human being has an inherent dislike of work and will avoid it if possible. Thus management needs to stress productivity, incentive schemes and 'a fair day's work' and to denounce 'restriction of output'. Because of this human characteristic of dislike of work, most people must be coerced, controlled, directed and threatened with punishment to get them to put forth adequate effort towards the achievement of

organizational objectives. The average human being prefers to be directed, wishes to avoid responsibility, has relatively little ambition and wants security above all.

Theory X has persisted for a long time (although it is not usually stated as baldly as this). It has done so because it has undoubtedly provided an explanation for *some* human behaviour in organizations. There are, however, many readily observable facts and a growing body of research findings (such as those described by Likert) which cannot be explained on these assumptions. McGregor proposes an alternative 'Theory Y', with the underlying principle of 'integration' replacing direction and control. The assumptions about human motivation of Theory Y are:

1. The expenditure of physical and mental effort in work is as natural as play or rest. The ordinary person does not inherently dislike work: according to the conditions it may be a source either of satisfaction or punishment.
2. External control is not the only means for obtaining effort. People will exercise self-direction and self-control in the service of objectives to which they are committed.
3. The most significant reward that can be offered in order to obtain commitment is the satisfaction of the individual's self-actualizing needs (compare Argyris, see Chapter 7). This can be a direct product of effort directed towards organizational objectives.
4. The average human being learns, under proper conditions, not only to accept but to seek responsibility.
5. Many more people are able to contribute creatively to the solution of organizational problems than do so.
6. At present the potentialities of the average person are not being fully used.

McGregor develops an analysis of how the acceptance of Theory Y as the basis for running organizations would work out. He is particularly concerned with effects on performance appraisals, salaries and promotions, participation and staff–line relationships. On this last topic he makes the important point that there will be tension and conflict between staff and line as long as staff departments are used as a service to top management to *control* the line (which is required by Theory X). With Theory Y the role of the staff is regarded as that of providing professional help to *all levels* of management.

The essential concept which both Likert and McGregor are propounding is that, to be effective, modern organizations must regard themselves as interacting groups of people with 'supportive relationships' to each other. In the ideal, all members will feel that the organization's objectives are of personal significance to them. They will regard their jobs, which contribute to those objectives, as meaningful, indispensable and difficult. Therefore, in order to do their jobs effectively, they need and obtain the support of their superiors. Superiors in turn regard their prime function as giving such support to make their subordinates effective.

In later work Likert and Likert extend the System 1 to 4 classification by identifying the 'System 4 Total Model Organization' (System 4T). This designation refers to organizations which have a number of characteristics in addition to those of System 4, including:

- high levels of performance goals held by the leader and transmitted to subordinates;
- high levels of knowledge and skill of the leader with regard to technical issues, administration and problem solving;
- the capacity of the leader to provide planning, resources, equipment, training and help to subordinates.

System 4T is also characterized by an optimum structure in terms of differentiation and linkages, as well as stable group-working relationships.

System 4T is currently the best method for dealing with conflict because of its approach in obtaining appropriate data related to group needs (thus removing person-to-person conflict) and engaging in group decision making in order to resolve differences in the best interests of the entire organization. If members of one or both of the two groups show an inability to use group decision-making techniques sufficiently well, then higher levels must provide further training in group processes. The interaction-influence system will develop a capacity for self-correction, since superiors recognize those groups which are not performing their linking-pin and problem-solving functions effectively and can arrange for coaching and training. Correction is possible because the failures are picked up not by after-the-fact data (for example falling production, rising costs, lower earnings), but through the interaction-influence system in the early stages before poor performance and conflict arise.

Likert's argument is that the nearer to System 4T the organization approaches, the more productivity and profits will improve and conflict be reduced. Likert also suggests a System 5 organization of the future in which the authority of hierarchy will disappear completely. The authority of individuals will derive only from their linking-pin roles and from the influence exerted by the overlapping groups of which they are members.

BIBLIOGRAPHY

LIKERT, R., *New Patterns of Management*, McGraw-Hill, 1961.
LIKERT, R., *The Human Organization: Its Management and Value*, McGraw-Hill, 1967.
LIKERT, R. and LIKERT, J. G., *New Ways of Managing Conflict*, McGraw-Hill, 1976.
MCGREGOR, D., *The Human Side of Enterprise*, McGraw-Hill, 1960.
MCGREGOR, D., *Leadership and Motivation*, MIT Press, 1966.
MCGREGOR, D., *The Professional Manager*, McGraw-Hill, 1967.

Robert R. Blake and Jane S. Mouton

Robert Blake (1918–2004) and Jane Mouton (d. 1987) were Chairman and President respectively of Scientific Methods, Inc. (now Grid International Inc.), an organization which provides behavioural science consultancy services to industry. Both were psychologists, trained in American universities. Blake first designed and tested the 'Managerial Grid' during his subsequent employment in industry.

Blake and Mouton start from the assumption that a manager's job is to foster attitudes and behaviour which promote efficient performance, stimulate and use creativity, generate enthusiasm for experimentation and innovation, and learn from interaction with others. Such managerial competence can be taught and it can be learned. Their managerial grid provides a framework for understanding and applying effective management.

The grid sets the guidelines for an approach to management which has been widely applied. It has been successful in North America, in Europe and in Asia; in production work, sales and R & D; in trade unions, and in military, government and welfare organizations. Its relevance appears to transcend both cultural boundaries and forms of organization. Moreover, it has been applied from supervisory jobs to executive levels.

The managerial grid results from combining two fundamental ingredients of managerial behaviour. One is concern for production; the other is concern for people. 'Concern for' does not mean a dedication to specific targets, nor does it mean results achieved in themselves. It means the general approach to management which governs the actions of managers – just how they concern themselves with production and with people.

Concern for production does not mean only physical factory products. The term 'production' can refer to the number of good research ideas proposed, the number of accounts processed, the volume of sales achieved, the quality of service given or of top policy decisions made, and so on. Concern for people similarly includes a whole range of concerns for friendships, for personal commitment to tasks, for someone's self-respect, for equitable payment and so on.

Any manager's approach to management will show more or less of each of these two fundamental constituents. A manager may show a high degree of production concern together with low people concern, or the other way around, or may be middling on both. Indeed all of these are common; it is also commonplace that none of these is satisfactory. Placing the two fundamentals as the axes of a graph enables a grid to be drawn which reveals very simply not only many typical combinations seen in the behaviour of managers every day but also the desirable combination of 'concern for', as shown in the figure.

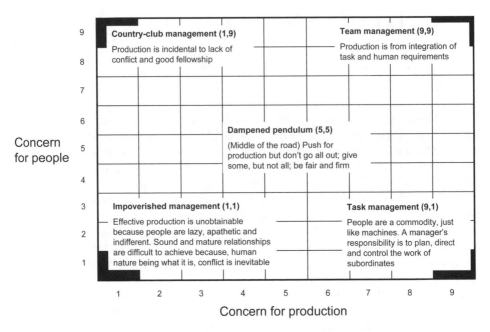

The Managerial Grid
Source: Blake and Mouton, 'The Managerial Grid', *Advanced Management Office Executive*, 1962, vol. 1:9.

Different positions on the grid represent different typical patterns of behaviour. The grid suggests that change could be towards both high concern for production (scores 9) and high concern for people (also scores 9) simultaneously; that is, to a 9,9 managerial style of 'team management'.

The grid indicates that all degrees of concern for production and concern for people are possible, but for simplicity five styles of management are picked out for illustration.

The 9,1 management style, or 'task management', focuses overwhelmingly on production. A 9,1 manager is an exacting taskmaster who expects schedules to be met and people to do what they are told, no more and no less. Anything that goes wrong will be viewed as the result of someone's mistake, and that someone must be found and that blame squarely placed. Supervisors make decisions. Subordinates carry them out. The manager should run the show, and disagreement is likely to be viewed as the next thing to insubordination. The 9,1 management style can achieve high production, at least in the short run, but it has a number of deficiencies. Any creative energies of subordinates go into how to defeat the system rather than how to improve it. Disagreements are ruled out and suppressed rather than settled. Subordinates do what is required, but no more, and seem obviously indifferent and apathetic. Win–lose thinking is eventually reflected in the development of trade unions and struggles between unions and managements. The 9,1 management style is prevalent in a competitive industrial society such as the US because inadequate education leaves many people unable to use more than limited skills and compelled to endure this kind of supervision.

The 1,9 managerial style, or 'country-club management' as it has been called, emphasizes exclusively concern for people. It does not push people for production, because 'you can lead a horse to water, but you can't make it drink'. People are encouraged and supported, and their mistakes are overlooked because they are doing the best they can. The key word is togetherness and informal conversation, coffee together, with a joke helping things along. The informal rule is 'no work discussions during breaks'. But country club management also has deficiencies. People try to avoid direct disagreements or criticisms of one another and production problems are glossed over. No one should be upset even if work is not going quite as it should. New ideas which might cause trouble or objectives which would cause strain are allowed to slide. The 1,9 style easily grows up in quasi-monopoly situations or when operating on a cost-plus basis; its ultimate end may be the complete closing of a non-competitive unit.

Little concern for either production or people results from 'impoverished management', the 1,1 style. It is difficult to imagine a whole organization surviving for long with this kind of management, but it is frequent enough in individual managers and supervisors. The 1,1 management style is characterized by the avoidance of responsibility or personal commitment, and by leaving people to work as they think fit. These leaders do just enough so that if anything goes wrong they can say 'I told them what to do – it's not my fault'. They minimize contacts with everyone, and are non-committal on any problems which come to them. The 1,1 approach typically reveals the frustrations of someone who has been passed over for promotion, shunted sideways, or has been in a routine job for years (as Argyris, Chapter 7, also suggests).

Managers frequently alternate between the 1,9 country-club style and the 9,1 task management style. They tighten up to increase output, 9,1 style, but when human relationships begin to suffer, the pendulum swings right across to 1,9 again. The middle of the managerial grid shows the 5,5 'dampened pendulum' style, typified by marginal shifts around the happy medium. This middle-of-the-road style pushes enough to get acceptable production, but yields enough to maintain acceptable morale. To aim fully for both is too idealistic. Such managers aim at a moderate carrot-and-stick standard, fair but firm, and have confidence in their subordinates' ability to meet targets. The 5,5 management style thus gives rise to 'splitting the difference' on problems, to attempting balanced solutions rather than appropriate ones.

Unlike 5,5 management and all the other styles, 9,9 team management style shows high concern for production and for people, and does not accept that these concerns are incompatible. The team manager seeks to integrate people around production. Morale is task related. Unlike 5,5 the 9,9 style tries to discover the best and most effective solutions, and aims at the highest attainable production to which all involved contribute and find their own sense of accomplishment. People satisfy their own needs through the job and working with others, not through incidental sociability in the country-club style. The 9,9 manager assumes that employees who know what the stakes are for them and others in what they are doing will not need boss direction and control (as Likert, previously in this chapter). The manager's responsibility is to see to it that work is planned and organized by those with a stake in it, not necessarily to do that task personally. Objectives should be clear to all and, though demanding, should be realistic. It is accepted that conflict will occur, but problems are confronted directly and openly and not as personal disputes. This encourages creativity. Sustained improvement of the form of organization and the development of those in it are both aims and likely outcomes of a 9,9 style.

Blake and Mouton reject most strongly a contingency approach to leadership and decision making (see Fiedler, later in this chapter, and Vroom, Chapter 5). Contingency theorists argue that particular leadership styles are appropriate to particular situations. This is to say that there are certain circumstances where a 9,1 or a 1,9 style would be the most effective. Blake and Mouton dispute this very static approach, for it does not appear to consider, for example, the adverse longer-term effects which a 9,1 style might have on the leader's health and career or on the development of subordinates.

The 9,9 leadership style is always the best since it builds on long-term development and trust. A leader whose subordinates expect or want 9,1 or 1,9 leadership should train them to understand and respond to 9,9. In this way their own development will be improved.

The 9,9 approach should be adopted with versatility, but its principles should be firmly retained.

In *Executive Achievement*, Blake and Mouton present eight case studies of top executives, using the Grid framework to analyse the limitations in leadership shown. Many of the habits which limit top management effectiveness have come about over the years in an unsystematic, even unthinking way. Leaders can be encouraged to think more about how to behave effectively and to gain personal insights into ways of changing. They are then better prepared to change towards 9,9 leadership because the bottom-line pay-off is so considerable.

For maximum effectiveness the whole culture of the organization must be changed to a 9,9 orientation, using a phased programme of organizational development. In Phase 1 the Managerial Grid is studied as a framework for understanding organizational behaviour through off-site training. Phase 2 focuses on the on-site training in problem solving methods of actual functioning teams as a whole. The same kind of application is made in Phase 3 but this time to inter-group work between units of the company where cooperation and coordination are necessary. Phase 4 is concerned with setting group goals for the optimum performance of the total organization. In Phase 5 the resulting changes are implemented, and Phase 6 measures these changes in order to consolidate them and set new goals for the future. Where evaluation of this programme has been carried out, the evidence points both to more successful organizations and to greater career accomplishments by individual managers.

BIBLIOGRAPHY

BLAKE, R. R. and MOUTON, J. S., *The Versatile Manager: A Grid Profile*, Irwin-Dorsey, 1981.
BLAKE, R. R.and MOUTON, J. S., *The Managerial Grid III*, Gulf Publishing, 1985.
BLAKE, R. R. and MOUTON, J. S., *Executive Achievement: Making it at The Top*, McGraw-Hill, 1986.

Edgar H. Schein

Edgar H. Schein has been for many years Professor of Management at the Sloan School of Management of the Massachusetts Institute of Technology, where he is now professor emeritus. A social psychologist by training, in his early years at MIT he was a junior colleague of Douglas McGregor (see previously in this chapter) whose personality and work had much influence on him. Working in that tradition, Schein has been an influential researcher, consultant and writer on issues concerned with organizational behaviour, particularly individual motivation, career dynamics and organizational culture.

Schein's analysis of motivation begins, like McGregor's, with an examination of the underlying assumptions that managers make about the people they manage. He suggests three sets of assumptions, roughly in order of their historical appearance, and adds a fourth which he considers more appropriate.

1. The *Rational-Economic Model* is the mental picture held by managers who consider workers to be primarily motivated by economic incentives as manipulated by the organization. The worker is essentially passive, lazy, unwilling to take responsibility and must therefore be controlled by the manager. This is the basis of Taylor's approach to management (see Chapter 4), which is expounded by McGregor (see earlier in this chapter) as Theory X. This approach led to the possibility of mass-production industry, but broke down when unions became powerful and jobs became more complex, requiring more of an employee than being just a pair of hands.
2. The *Social Model* developed from awareness of the worker's need for identity through relationships with others, particularly the working group. The group's norms and pressures have much more power over production than do formal incentive systems and management controls. The work of Mayo and the Hawthorne investigations (see earlier in this chapter) had an important impact in changing managerial ideas, as did the study of mining by Trist and his colleagues (see later in this chapter). The implications for managers are spelled out in Likert's work on the need for 'employee-centred' leadership and participative group management (see earlier in this chapter).
3. The *Self-Actualizing Model* is a further development which underlines the fact that organizations typically remove the meaning of any work that employees do. The inherent need of workers to exercise their understanding, capacities and skills in an adult way is thus frustrated, and alienation and dissatisfaction ensue. The analysis of the clinical psychologist, Abraham Maslow, has been

very influential here. He maintains that 'self-actualization' (the realization of one's distinctive psychological potential) is the highest form of human need, going beyond economic and social fulfilment. The implications of this approach are developed for managers in McGregor's Theory Y (see earlier in this chapter), Argyris's Model II (see Chapter 7) and Herzberg's Job Enrichment (see later in this chapter).

4. The *Complex Model*, developed by Schein, maintains that earlier theories are based on conceptions which are too simplified and generalized. Human needs fall into many categories and vary according to the person's stage of personal development and life situation. So motives will vary from one person to another, one situation to another, one time to another. Incentives can also vary in their impact: money for example, though usually satisfying basic economic needs, can also serve to satisfy self-actualization needs for some. What motivates millionaires to go on to make their second or fifth million? Employees are also capable of learning new motives through organizational experiences and can respond to different kinds of managerial strategies.

The most important implication for managers is that they need to be good diagnosticians. They should be flexible enough to vary their own behaviour in relation to the need to treat particular subordinates in particular situations in an appropriate way. They may need to use any one of the economic, social or self-actualizing models. They may use 'scientific management' in the design of some jobs, but allow complete group autonomy for workers to organize themselves in others. They would thus use a 'contingency approach' as exemplified by Lawrence and Lorsch (see Chapter 2), Vroom (see Chapter 5) and Fiedler (see later in this chapter), among others.

According to Schein the key factor which determines the motivation of individuals in organizations is the 'psychological contract'. This is the unwritten set of expectations operating at all times between every member of an organization and those who represent the organization to that member. It includes economic components (pay, working hours, job security and so on) but also more implicit concerns such as being treated with dignity, obtaining some degree of work autonomy, having opportunities to learn and develop. Some of the strongest feelings leading to strikes and employee turnover have to do with violations of these implicit components, even though the public negotiations are about pay and conditions of work.

The organization, too, has implicit expectations: that employees will be loyal, will keep trade secrets, will do their best on behalf of the organization, and so on Whether individuals will work with commitment and enthusiasm is the result of a matching between the two components. On the one side, their own expectations of what the organization will provide for them and what they should provide in return; on the other, the organization's expectations of what it will give and get. The degree to which these correspond will determine the individual's motivation. The degree of matching is liable to change and the psychological contract is therefore continually being renegotiated, particularly during the progress of an individual's career.

The 'career development perspective' taken by Schein identifies the continual matching process between the individual and the organization as the key to understanding both human resource planning for the organization and career planning for the individual. This matching is particularly important at certain key transition points in a career, such as initial entry into the organization, moving from technical to managerial work, changing from being 'on the way up' to 'levelling off' and so on.

A crucial element in the matching process is the nature of the *career anchor* that the individual holds. This is the self-perceived set of talents, motives and attitudes, based on actual experiences, which is developed by each individual, particularly in the early years of an organizational career. It provides a growing area of confidence within the individual's attitudes which anchors the interpretation of career and life options. Typical career anchors found by Schein in a detailed longitudinal study of MIT management graduates include those of technical competence, managerial competence, security and autonomy Career anchors affect the way individuals see themselves, their jobs and their organizations to a considerable extent. For example, one graduate using a technical competence anchor was, in mid-career, still only concerned with technical tasks. He refused to become involved in aspects of sales or general management even though he was now a director and part owner of the firm in which he worked. Another graduate, using managerial competence as an anchor, left one firm although his bosses were quite pleased with his performance. But he considered that he only actually worked two hours a day, and he was not satisfied with that.

The understanding of the dynamics of career development is important in enabling human resource planning and development to improve the matching processes between the needs of the individual and the organization so that early-, mid- and late-career crises can be dealt with more effectively.

A distinctive aspect of the way that an organization functions – which shapes its overall performance as well as the feeling which individuals have about it – is its *culture*. This is the pattern of basic assumptions developed by an organization as it learns to cope with problems of external adaptation and internal integration. These assumptions are taught to new members as the correct way to perceive, think and feel in order to be successful. They cover a wide range of issues: how to dress, how much to argue, how far to defer to the boss's authority, what to reward, what to punish, and so on. Organizations develop very wide differences on these topics.

Leaders play a key role in maintaining and transmitting the culture. They do this by a number of powerful mechanisms including what they pay attention to, measure and control; how they react to a range of crises; who they recruit, promote and excommunicate. All these send important messages about the kind of organization they are running. The key to leadership is managing cultural change.

The considerable difficulties that almost inevitably beset the establishment of an effective organization after a merger of two companies underline the need to understand the nature of cultural differences and how cultural change can be consciously managed. The big danger is that the acquiring company will impose not only its own structures and procedures, but also its own philosophy, value systems and managerial style on a situation for which it has no intuitive feel. Thus a large packaged-foods manufacturer purchased a chain of successful fast-food restaurants. They imposed many of their manufacturing control procedures on the new subsidiary, which drove costs up and restaurant managers out. These were replaced by parent-company managers who did not really understand the technology and hence were unable to make effective use of the marketing techniques. Despite ten years of effort they could not run the subsidiary profitably and had to sell it at a considerable loss.

Similar problems occur when organizations diversify into new product lines, new areas or new markets. Afterwards managers frequently say that cultural incompatibilities were at the root of the troubles, but somehow these factors rarely get taken into account at the time. One reason is that the culture of an organization is so pervasive that it is very difficult for members to identify its components in their immediate situation. They recognize their own characteristics only when they run up against problems due to differences in others. Schein presents a series of diagnostic procedures to enable managers (usually with the help of an outside consultant) to make explicit the cultural assumptions of their own organization and thus gain insight into their compatibility with those existing elsewhere.

BIBLIOGRAPHY

SCHEIN, E. H., *Career Dynamics: Matching Individual and Organizational Needs*, Addison-Wesley, 1978.
SCHEIN, E. H., *Organizational Psychology*, 3rd edn, Prentice-Hall, 1980.
SCHEIN, E. H., *Organizational Culture and Leadership*, 3rd edn, Wiley, 2004.

Frederick Herzberg

Frederick Herzberg (1923–2000) was Distinguished Professor of Management in the University of Utah. After training as a psychologist he studied Industrial Mental Health. For many years he has, with colleagues and students, been conducting a programme of research and application on human motivation in the work situation and its effects on the individual's job satisfaction and mental health. He questions whether current methods of organizing work in business and industry are appropriate for people's total needs and happiness.

Herzberg and his colleagues conducted a survey of 200 engineers and accountants representing a cross-section of Pittsburgh industry. They were asked to remember times when they felt exceptionally good about their jobs. The investigators probed for the reasons why they felt as they did, asking for a description of the sequence of events which gave that feeling. The questions were then repeated for sequences of events which made them feel exceptionally bad about their jobs. The responses were then classified by topic in order to determine what type of events led to job satisfaction and job dissatisfaction.

The major finding of the study was that the events that led to satisfaction were of quite a different kind from those that led to dissatisfaction. Five factors stood out as strong determinants of job satisfaction: achievement, recognition, the attraction of the work itself, responsibility and advancement. Lack of these five factors, though, was mentioned very infrequently in regard to job dissatisfaction. When the reasons for the dissatisfaction were analysed they were found to be concerned with a different range of factors: company policy and administration, supervision, salary, interpersonal relations and working conditions. Since such distinctly separate factors were found to be associated with job satisfaction and job dissatisfaction, Herzberg concludes that these two feelings are not the opposites to one another, rather they are concerned with two different ranges of human needs.

The set of factors associated with job dissatisfaction are those stemming from the individual's overriding need to avoid physical and social deprivation. Using a biblical analogy, Herzberg relates these to the 'Adam' conception of the nature of humanity. When Adam was expelled from the Garden of Eden he was immediately faced with the task of satisfying the needs which stem from his animal nature: the needs for food, warmth, avoidance of pain, safety, security, belongingness and so on Ever since then people have had to concern themselves with the satisfaction of these needs together with those which, as a result of social conditioning, have been added to them. Thus, for example, we have learned that in certain economies the satisfaction of these needs makes it necessary to earn money which has therefore become a specific motivating drive.

In contrast, the factors associated with job satisfaction are those stemming from people's need to realize their human potential for perfection. In biblical terms this is the 'Abraham' conception of human nature. Abraham was created in the image of God. He was capable of great accomplishments, of development, of growth, of transcending his environmental limitations, of self-realization. People have these aspects to their natures too; they are indeed the characteristically human ones. They have needs to understand, to achieve, and through achievement to experience psychological growth, and these needs are very powerful motivating drives.

Both the Adam and Abraham natures look for satisfaction in work, but they do so in different ranges of factors. The Adam nature seeks the avoidance of dissatisfaction and is basically concerned with the job environment. It requires effective company policies, working conditions, security, pay and so on and is affected by inadequacies in these. Since they are extrinsic to the job itself, Herzberg refers to them as 'job hygiene' or 'maintenance' factors. Just as lack of hygiene will cause disease but the presence of hygienic conditions will not, of itself, produce health, so lack of adequate 'job hygiene' factors will cause dissatisfaction, but their presence will not of itself cause satisfaction. Satisfaction in work is provided through the Abraham nature which is concerned with the job content of the work itself, with achievement, recognition, responsibility, advancement and so on These are the motivator or growth factors and their presence will cause satisfaction. Their absence will not cause dissatisfaction (if the job hygiene factors are adequate) but will lead to an absence of positive satisfactions. It is thus basic to Herzberg's approach that job satisfaction and job dissatisfaction are not opposites, since they are concerned with different factors in work serving different aspects of human nature. The opposite of job satisfaction, therefore, is not job dissatisfaction but simply no job satisfaction. The opposite of job dissatisfaction, similarly, is lack of job dissatisfaction.

This finding of the original study – that the factors associated with job satisfaction were basically different in kind from those associated with job dissatisfaction – has been repeated in several subsequent studies. Collating the information based on 12 different investigations, involving over 1600 employees in a variety of jobs in business and other organizations and in a number of countries, Herzberg presents results to show that the overwhelming majority of the factors contributing to job satisfaction (81 per cent) were the motivators concerned with growth and development. A large majority of the factors contributing to job dissatisfaction (69 per cent) involved hygiene or environmental maintenance.

How, then, may this 'motivation–hygiene' approach be used to increase the motivation and job satisfaction of employees? First, it is clear that this cannot be done through the job hygiene factors. Certainly, these can and should be improved as they will reduce job dissatisfaction, but adequate company policies, working conditions, pay and supervision are increasingly thought of as a right to be expected, not as an incentive to greater achievement and satisfaction. For this, the rewarding nature of the work itself, recognition, responsibility, opportunities for achievement and advancement are necessary. Herzberg recognizes that these are phrases that may be used nowadays in relation to jobs, but they are often used in a superficial way or as inspirational talk without much effective action. He therefore advocates an industrial engineering approach, based on the design of jobs, but from the opposite point of view from that of Taylor (see Chapter 4). Instead of rationalizing and simplifying the work to increase efficiency, the motivation–hygiene theory suggests that jobs be enriched to include the motivating factors in order to bring about an effective utilization of people and to increase job satisfaction.

The principles of *job enrichment* require that the job be developed to include new aspects which provide the opportunity for the employee's psychological growth. It is important that the new aspects are capable of allowing this. Merely to add one undemanding job to another (as is often the case with job enlargement) or to switch from one undemanding job to another (as in job rotation) is not adequate. These are merely horizontal job loading. In contrast, job enrichment calls for vertical job loading, where opportunities for achievement, responsibility, recognition, growth and learning are designed into the job. The approach would be to look for ways of removing some controls while retaining or increasing individuals' accountability for their own work; giving a person a complete natural unit of work; granting additional authority to an employee in the job; increasing job freedom; making reports directly available to the worker personally rather than to the supervisor; introducing new and more difficult tasks not previously undertaken, and so on.

A number of experiments have been reported by Herzberg and his colleagues where these changes have been introduced with considerable effect. For example, in a study of the job of 'stockholder correspondent' of a large corporation the following suggestions were considered but rejected as involving merely horizontal job loading: firm fixed quotas could be set for letters to be answered each day; the employees could type the letters themselves as well as composing them; all difficult inquiries could be channelled to a few workers so that the rest could achieve high rates of output; the workers could be rotated through units handling different inquiries and then sent back to their own units. Instead, changes leading to the enrichment of jobs were introduced: correspondents were made directly responsible for the quality and accuracy of letters which were sent out directly over their names (previously a verifier had checked all letters, the supervisor had rechecked and signed them and was responsible for their quality and accuracy); subject-matter experts were appointed within each unit for other members to consult (previously the supervisor had dealt with all difficult and specialized questions); verification of experienced workers' letters was dropped from 100 per cent to 10 per cent; and correspondents were encouraged to answer letters in a more personalized way instead of relying upon standard forms. In these ways, the jobs were enriched, with resulting increases in both performance and job satisfaction.

In other studies, laboratory technicians ('experimental officers') were encouraged to write personal project reports in addition to those of the supervising scientists and were authorized to requisition materials and equipment direct; sales representatives were made wholly responsible for determining the calling frequencies on their customers and were given a discretionary range of about 10 per cent on the prices of most products; factory supervisors were authorized to modify schedules, to hire labour against agreed manning targets, to appoint their deputies, and so on. In each case, the results in both performance and satisfaction were considerable.

The more subordinates' jobs became enriched, the more superfluous does on-the-job supervision in the old sense become. But this does not downgrade the supervisors' job: in the companies studied they found themselves free to develop more important aspects of their jobs with a greater managerial component than they had had time to before. It soon becomes clear that supervising people who have authority of their own is a more demanding, rewarding and enjoyable task than checking on every move of circumscribed automatons. For management the challenge is task organization to call out the motivators, and task support to provide adequate hygiene through company policy, technical supervision, working conditions and so on, thus satisfying both the Adam and the Abraham natures of humanity in work.

BIBLIOGRAPHY

HERZBERG, F., *Work and the Nature of Man*, World Publishing Co., 1966.
HERZBERG, F., 'One more time: How do you motivate employees?, *Harvard Business Review*, 46 (1968), 53–62.
HERZBERG, F., *Managerial Choice: To Be Efficient and To Be Human*, Dow Jones-Irwin, 1976.
HERZBERG, F., MAUSNER, B. and SNYDERMAN, B., *The Motivation to Work*, Wiley, 1959.
PAUL Jr, W. J., ROBERTSON, K. B. AND HERZBERG, F., 'Job enrichment pays off', *Harvard Business Review*, 47 (1969), 61–78.

Fred E. Fiedler

Fred Fiedler is Professor Emeritus of Psychology and Management at the University of Washington. For over four decades he has been concerned with a research and consulting programme into the nature of effective leadership which has been carried out in a large range of organizations including business concerns, governmental agencies (both civil and military) and voluntary organizations.

Fiedler's studies of leadership have concentrated on workgroups rather than the organization of which the group is a part. He assumes that those who are appointed leaders will have the requisite technical qualifications for the job (for example the Director of Product Development in a manufacturing firm will be an engineer; only qualified social workers will become Heads of Social Work Departments). He therefore asks what is it about leadership behaviour per se which leads to effective group working. Effectiveness is defined, in a very hardnosed way as how well the group performs the primary task for which it exists – for example, output levels for managers of manufacturing departments, students' standardized achievement-test grades for school principals.

Focusing on the behaviour of the leader, Fiedler identifies two main leadership styles. *Relationship-motivated leaders* get their major satisfaction from good personal relationships with others. Their self-esteem depends very much on how others regard them, and they are sensitive to, and very concerned about, what their group members feel. They encourage subordinates to participate and to offer ideas.

Task-motivated leaders, on the other hand, are strongly concerned to complete successfully any task they have undertaken. They run a 'tight ship' with clear orders and standardized procedures for subordinates and in their turn feel most comfortable working from their superiors' clear guidelines and operating procedures. If these are missing they will try to create them.

Fiedler has developed a very distinctive measure to classify these two styles or motivation patterns. His questionnaire measure asks leaders to review all the people with whom they have ever worked and identify the one with whom they could work least well. They are then asked to rate this 'least preferred co-worker' (LPC) on a number of characteristics.

Relationship-motivated leaders are those who will score these characteristics highly in spite of difficulties experienced with their LPC. Thus they may rate their choice as untrustworthy and inconsiderate, but will admit that the LPC was cheerful, warm and relaxed. Since relationships are important to them, this type of leader will make such detailed discriminations and attempt to treat their choice fairly.

Task-motivated leaders rate people in terms of their ability to contribute to the successful achievement of the group's task: on this they will rate their LPC very low indeed – and it will be a blanket negative evaluation. Thus the LPC would not only be unpleasant and disloyal, but also tense, boring, insincere and quarrelsome as well!

In all his work Fiedler emphasizes very strongly that *both* these leadership styles can be effective in appropriate situations. Thus he takes a contingency approach to leadership and rejects the conception that there is a best style that is appropriate for all situations (cf. Likert and McGregor, and Blake and Mouton, earlier in this chapter). Effective leadership will be contingent on the nature of the tasks which leaders face and the situations in which they operate.

The underlying concept which is used to characterize the situation of the leader is that of 'favourableness' in terms of the ability to exercise power and influence. The more power the leader has, the greater the influence and control; the less dependence on the goodwill of others, then the easier the leadership task will be. Three dimensions are used to analyse any leadership situation.

1. *Leader–member relations*: Leaders who have good relationships with their group members, who are liked and respected, will have more influence than those with poor relationships. Fiedler claims that this is the most important single dimension.
2. *Task structure*: Tasks or assignments which are spelled out with specific guidelines, or even programmed, give the leader more influence than tasks which are vague, nebulous and unstructured.
3. *Leader's position power*: Leaders who are able to reward and punish subordinates (through disciplining, setting pay, hiring and firing, and so on) have more power and are thus in a more controlling and favourable position than those who cannot.

Ordering leadership situations as being either high or low in relation to each of these three dimensions generates an eight-cell classification which is listed along the horizontal axis of the figure shown on page 240. This is the scale of favourableness for the leader.

An example of a leader in Octant 1, the most favourable situation, might be a construction superintendent building a bridge from a set of blueprints, who has personally hired the work crews and has their full support. The *technical* task may be difficult but, because it is structured and spelled out and the leader has good personal relations and strong power, the *leadership* task is the easiest and the leader has a great deal of control.

In contrast, an example of an Octant 8 situation might be that of a parent who has taken on the task of chairing a committee of the parent–teachers association to organize an outing 'so that everybody can have a good time'. Here the *technical* task is much easier than building a bridge, but the *leadership* task is much more difficult since it is very unstructured (how do you determine whether everybody has had a good time?), the parent has weak position power (not being able to order the committee to carry out instructions) and many may resent the appointment anyway (poor leader–member relations).

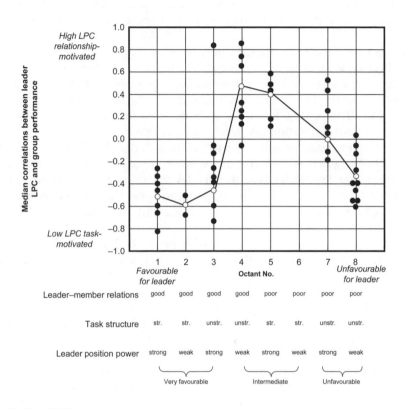

Source: Fiedler (1967).

In between these two extreme examples fall many leadership situations (classified as Octants 2 to 7) where some aspects of the situation are favourable to the leader but others are not.

The critical question to ask then becomes what kind of leadership (relationship-motivated or task-motivated) does each of these octants call for? The figure presents the results of Fiedler's wide-ranging studies, based on many hundreds of workgroups and covering the whole range of octants. The groups included bomber and tank crews, boards of directors, basketball teams and creative problem-solving groups. For each of the octants (shown on the horizontal axis) the vertical axis indicates the relationship between the leader's style and group performance. A median correlation above the mid-line shows that relationship-motivated leaders (that is, those with high LPC scores) tended to perform better than task-motivated leaders (that is, those with low LPC scores). A correlation below the mid-line indicates that task motivated leaders performed better than relationship-motivated leaders.

The findings presented in the figure (and which have been replicated by many further studies) demonstrate two important facts about effective leadership:

1. Task-motivated leaders tend to perform better in situations that are very favourable (Octants 1, 2, 3) and in those that are very unfavourable (Octants 7, 8) that is, where the correlations fall below the mid-line on the vertical axis. Relationship-motivated leaders tend to perform better in situations that are intermediate in favourableness. It is clear that both types of leadership styles perform well under some conditions and poorly under others. We cannot therefore speak of poor leaders or good leaders without examining the situation in which the leader functions.
2. The performance of the leader depends as much on situational favourableness as it does on the style of the person in the leadership position. The crucial factor is that the style of the leader and the work group situation should be matched. This leader match and its appropriate benefits can be obtained either by trying to change the leader's style or by trying to change the leadership situation.

Fiedler has consistently maintained that the first of the change options to achieve leader match (changing the leader's style) is unrealistic and that leadership training which attempts to do this (for example to increase openness or employee-centredness) has not been effective because the leadership-style motivational pattern is too ingrained a characteristic of the individual (see Vroom, Chapter 5, for an opposing view). From Fiedler's point of view, what appropriate training does – together with experience – is to give the leader more technical knowledge and administrative know-how. This allows more influence and control and thus the situation becomes more favourable. But the contingency approach indicates that in many of the octants a more favourable situation (for example moving from Octant 8 to Octant 4 by improving leader–member relations) requires a different leadership style. Hence while training and experience will improve the performance of one type of leader – where the new octant situation will now be matched to the style – it will *decrease* the performance of the other style type which has now lost its matching. Training must therefore be undertaken with a knowledge of leadership style in relation to leaders' situations, otherwise on average it is bound to have no effect.

Changing the situations in which leaders operate to those which call for their particular styles is a more appropriate way of achieving the leader match. Thus we might increase the favourableness of a task-motivated leader's situation to one which made a better match by giving more explicit instructions to work to and more authority to achieve the tasks (Octant 4 to Octant 1). *Decreasing* the favourableness of the situation in order to improve the leader's performance by a better match is not as unusual as might first appear. Managers are frequently transferred to more challenging jobs because they have become bored or stale. 'Challenging' could well mean that there are awkward people to work with and that authority is much diminished. But the move of a relationship-motivated leader from Octant 1 to Octant 6 would improve the match and the leader's subsequent performance.

In later work, the importance of a leader's cognitive ability is explored as an additional factor in determining the group's effectiveness. The task-motivated style works when linked to high leader intelligence and a supportive environment. To be successful, leaders, who are less intelligent in relation to their groups have to be relationship-motivated in order to draw on the resources of their followers. These are key considerations in determining where a leader should be placed. In general, successful organizations are those which give all leaders a full evaluation of their own characteristics and their group's performance, and which make them aware of the situations in which they perform best. Good leaders will create situations in which their cognitive capacity and leadership style are most likely to succeed.

BIBLIOGRAPHY

FIEDLER, F. E., *A Theory of Leadership Effectiveness*, McGraw-Hill, 1967.

FIEDLER, F. E., 'Situational Control and a Dynamic Theory of Leadership' in B. King et al. (eds), *Managerial Control and Organizational Democracy*, Wiley, 1978.

FIEDLER, F. E. and GARCIA, J. E., *New Approaches to Effective Leadership: Cognitive Resources and Organizational Performance*, Wiley, 1987.

FIEDLER, F. E., CHEMERS, M. M. and MAHAR, L., *Improving Leadership Effectiveness: The Leader Match Concept* (rev. edn), Wiley, 1977.

Eric Trist and the Work of the Tavistock Institute

Eric Trist (1909–1993) was a social psychologist who, for more than 20 years, was the senior member of the Tavistock Institute of Human Relations, London, a leading centre for the application of social science to social and industrial problems. He subsequently was a Professor at the University of Pennsylvania and at York University, Ontario. At the Tavistock, he conducted, with a number of colleagues (including F. E. Emery, A. K. Rice and E. J. Miller), a programme of combined research and consultancy investigations into group and organizational functioning. This combination of research and consultancy is referred to as 'action research'. The work of Trist and his colleagues uses a systems approach to understanding organizational behaviour.

In collaboration with K. W. Bamforth (an ex-miner), Trist studied the effects of mechanization in British coal mining. With the advent of coal-cutters and mechanical conveyors, the degree of technical complexity of retrieving coal was raised to a higher level. Mechanization made possible the working of a single long face in place of a series of short faces; however, this technological change had a number of social and psychological consequences for the work organization and the worker's place in it to which little thought was given before the change was introduced. The pattern of organization in short-face working was based on a small artisan group of a skilled man and his mate, assisted by one or more labourers. The basic pattern around which the work relationships in the longwall method were organized was a coalface group of 40 to 50 men, their shot-firer and 'deputies' (that is, supervisors). Thus in size and structure the basic unit in mining took on the characteristics of a small factory department, and in doing so disrupted both the traditional high degree of job autonomy and close work relationships, with a number of deleterious effects.

The mass production character of the longwall method necessitates a large-scale mobile layout advancing along the seam, basic task specialization according to shift, and very specific job roles with different methods of payment within each shift. In these circumstances there are considerable problems of maintaining effective communications and good working relations between 40 men spatially spread over 200 yards in a tunnel, and temporally spread over 24 hours in three successive shifts. From the production engineering point of view it is possible to write an equation that 200 tons equals 40 men over 200 yards over 24 hours, but the psychological and social problems raised are of a new order when the work organization transcends the limits of the traditional, small face-to-face group undertaking the complete task itself. The social integration of the previous small groups having been disrupted by the new technology and little attempt having been made to achieve any new integration, many symptoms of social stress occur. Informal cliques which develop to help each other out can only occur over small parts of the face, inevitably leaving some isolated; individuals react defensively, using petty deceptions with regard to timekeeping and reporting of work; they compete for allocation to the best workplaces; there is mutual scapegoating across shifts, each blaming the other for inadequacies (since, in the new system with its decreased autonomy, no one individual can normally be pinpointed to be at fault, scapegoating of the absent shift becomes self-perpetuating and resolves nothing). Absenteeism becomes a way of the miner compensating himself for the difficulties of the job.

This study of the effects of technological change led Trist to develop the concept of the working group as being neither a technical system nor a social system, but as an interdependent socio-technical system. The technological demands place limits on the type of work organization possible, but the work organization has social and psychological properties of its own that are independent of the technology. From this point of view it makes as little sense to regard social relationships as being determined by the technology as it does to regard the manner in which a job is performed as being determined by the social-psychological characteristics of the workers. The social and technical requirements are mutually interactive and they must also have economic validity, which is a third interdependent aspect. The attainment of optimum conditions for any one of these aspects does not necessarily result in optimum conditions for the system as a whole, since interference will occur if the others are inadequate. The aim should be joint optimization.

In further studies of mining, Trist found that it was possible, within the same technological and economic constraints, to operate different systems of work organization with different social and psychological effects, thus underlining the considerable degree of organizational choice which is available to management to enable it to take account of social and psychological aspects. A third form of operation, known as the 'composite longwall method', was developed which enabled mining to benefit from the new technology while at the same time allowing some of the characteristics of the shortwall method to be retained. In the composite system, groups of men are responsible for the whole task, allocate themselves to shifts and to jobs within the shift, and are paid on a group bonus. Thus the problems of overspecialized work roles and segregation of tasks across shifts, with consequent scapegoating and lack of group cohesion, were overcome. For example, it became common for a sub-group that had finished its scheduled work for a shift before time, to carry on with the next activity in the sequence in order to help those men on the subsequent shift who were members of their group. The composite longwall method was quite comparable in technological terms with the conventional longwall method, but it led to greater productivity, lower cost, considerably less absenteeism and accidents, and greater work satisfaction, since it was a socio-technical system better geared to the workers' social and psychological needs for job autonomy and close working relationships.

This socio-technical system approach was also applied to supervisory roles by Rice in studies of an Indian textile firm. He found that it was not enough to allocate to the supervisor a list of responsibilities (see Fayol, Chapter 4) and perhaps insist upon a particular style of handling workers (see Likert, earlier in this chapter). The supervisor's problems arise from a need to control and coordinate a system of worker–task relationships, and in particular to manage the 'boundary conditions', that is, those activities of one system which relate it to the larger system of which it forms a part. To do this effectively, there must be an easily identifiable arrangement of tasks so that the autonomous responsibility of the group for its own internal control can be maximized, thus freeing the supervisor for the key role of boundary management.

In an automatic weaving shed, for example, in which the occupational roles had remained unchanged since hand weaving, the activities of the shed were broken down into component tasks, with the number of workers required determined by work studies. Those in different occupational tasks worked on different numbers of looms; weavers operated 24 or 32, battery fillers charged the batteries of 48, smash hands served 75, jobbers 112, the bobbin carrier 224, and so on This resulted in the shift manager having to interact about the job regularly with all the remaining 28 workers on the shift, jobbers having to interact with 14, smash hands with 9, a weaver with 7, and so on, all on the basis of individual interactions aggregated together only at the level of the whole shift, with no stable internal group structure. Rice carried through a reorganization to create four groups of six workers with a group leader, each with an identifiable group task and a new set of interdependent work roles to carry it out. The boundaries of these groups were more easily delineated, and thus the work leader's task in their management facilitated. As a result there was a considerable and sustained improvement in efficiency and a decrease in damage.

These studies and others of the Tavistock Institute have led Emery and Trist to conceptualize the enterprise as an 'open socio-technical system'. 'Open' because it is concerned with obtaining inputs from its environment and exporting outputs to its environment, as well as operating the conversion process in between. They regard the organization not in terms of a closed physical system which can obtain a stable resolution of forces in static equilibrium, but in the light of the biological concept of an open system (due to von Bertalanffy) in which the equilibrium obtained by the organism or the organization is essentially dynamic, having a continual interchange across the boundaries with its environment. Indeed, they would regard the primary task of the management of an enterprise as a whole as one of relating the total system to its environment through the regulation of boundary interchanges, rather than that of internal regulation. A management which takes its environment as given and concentrates on organizing internally in the most efficient way is pursuing a dangerous course. This does not mean that top management should not be involved in internal problems, but that such involvement must be oriented to environmental opportunities and demands.

The problem is that environments are changing at an increasing rate and towards increasing complexity. Factors in the environment, over which the organization has no control or even no knowledge, may interact to cause significant changes. Emery and Trist have classified environments according to their degree of complexity from that of a placid, randomized environment (corresponding to the economist's perfect competition) to that of a 'turbulent field' in which significant variances arise, not only from the competitive organizations involved but also from the field (for example market) itself.

They present a case history of an organization which failed to appreciate that its environment was changing from a relatively placid to a relatively turbulent one. This company in the British food canning industry had, for a long period, held 65 per cent of the market for its main product – a tinned vegetable. On this basis the company invested in a new automatic factory, and in doing so incorporated an inbuilt rigidity – the necessity for long runs. But even while the factory was being built, several changes in the environment were taking place over which the organization had no control. The development of frozen foods and the increasing affluence which enabled more people to afford these presented consumers with an alternative. Greater direct competition came from the existence of surplus crops which American frozen food manufacturers sold off very cheaply due to their inappropriateness for freezing, their use by a number of small British fruit canning firms with surplus capacity due to the seasonal nature of imported fruit, and the development of supermarkets and chain stores with a wish to sell more goods under their house names. As the small canners provided an extremely cheap article (having no marketing costs and a cheaper raw material), they were able within three years to capture over 50 per cent of a shrinking market through supermarket own-label channels. This is a clear example of the way in which factors in the environment interact directly to produce a considerable turbulence in the field of the organization's operations which, in the case of the vegetable canning factory, required a large redefinition of the firm's purpose, market and product mix before a new dynamic equilibrium was reached.

Emery and Trist maintain that enterprises like the food canner tend to design their organization structures to fit simpler environments than the complex turbulent ones which they are actually facing. A new *design principle* is now required. Organizations by their very nature require what is known in systems theory and information theory as 'redundancy'. By this is meant duplication, replaceability, interchangeability, and resources needed to reduce error in the face of variability and change. The traditional technocratic bureaucracy is based on *redundancy of parts*. Segments are broken down so that the ultimate elements are as simple as possible; thus an unskilled worker in a narrow job who is cheap to replace and who takes little time to train would be regarded as an ideal job design. But this approach also requires reliable control systems – often cumbersome and costly.

An alternative design, based on the *redundancy of functions*, is appropriate to turbulent environments. In this approach individuals and units have wide repertoires of activities to cope with change and are self-regulating. For the individual they create roles rather than mere jobs; for the organization, they bring into being a *variety-increasing system* rather than the traditional control by variety reduction. For this approach to be achieved there has to be a continuing development of appropriate new values concerned with improving the *quality of working life* by keeping the technological determinants of worker behaviour to a minimum in order to satisfy social and psychological needs by the involvement of all concerned. Autonomous working groups, collaboration rather than competition (between organizations as well as within them) and reduction of hierarchical emphasis are some of the requirements for operating effectively in modern turbulence. The table below sets out the key features of the old and new approaches.

The socio-technical systems approach to achieving effective functioning in a turbulent environment as well as to improving the quality of working life has also been undertaken at a wider 'macro-social' level. For example, working with the Norwegian social psychologists E. Thorsrud and P. G. Herbst, the Tavistock group has studied the Norwegian shipping industry.

Features of Old and New Approaches

Old approach	New approach
The technological imperative	Joint optimization
People as extensions of machines	People as complementary to machines
People as expendable spare parts	People as a resource to be developed
Maximum task breakdown, simple narrow skills	Optimum task grouping, multiple broad skills
External controls (supervisors, specialist staffs, procedures)	Internal controls (self-regulating sub-systems)
Tall organization chart, autocratic style	Flat organization chart, participative style
Competition, gamesmanship	Collaboration, collegiality
Organization's purposes only	Members' and society's purposes also
Alienation	Commitment
Low risk taking	Innovation

Source: Trist (1981).

Many technological designs are available for sophisticated bulk carriers. The one chosen was that which best met the social and psychological needs of the small shipboard community that had to live together in isolated conditions, 24 hours a day for considerable periods, while also efficiently achieving its work tasks. A common mess and a recreation room were established; deck and engine-room crews were integrated, status differences between officers and men were reduced and even eliminated through the development of open career lines and the establishment of 'all officer' ships. Also training for future jobs onshore was initiated at sea.

Without these improvements in the quality of working life, too few Norwegians would have gone to sea to sustain the Norwegian Merchant marine which is critical for Norway's economy. Poorly educated and transient foreign crews could not cope with technically sophisticated ships, and alcoholism was dangerously high. These issues could not have been effectively tackled by any one single company; all firms in the industry, several seafaring unions and a number of maritime regulatory organizations all had to be involved in order to sustain the macro-social system development that was required.

The work of Trist and the Tavistock group has been most consistent in applying systems thinking over a large range of sites – the primary work system, the whole organization system and the macro-social domain. In doing so they have illuminated the dynamic nature of organizations and their functioning, the crucial importance of boundary management, and the need for a new approach to organizational design which can accommodate environmental change.

BIBLIOGRAPHY

EMERY, F. E. and THORSRUD, E., *Democracy at Work*, Martinus Nijhoff (Leiden), 1976.
EMERY, F. E. and TRIST, E. L., 'Socio-Technical Systems', in C. W. Churchman and M. Verhulst (eds), *Management Science, Models and Techniques*, vol. 2, Pergamon, 1946; reprinted in F. E. Emery (ed.), *Systems Thinking*, Penguin, 1969.
EMERY, F. E. and TRIST, E. L., 'The Causal Texture of Organizational Environments', *Human Relations*, 18 (1965), 21–32; reprinted in F. E. Emery (ed.), *Systems Thinking*, Penguin, 1969.
HERBST, P. G., *Alternatives to Hierarchies*, Martinus Nijhoff (Leiden), 1976.
RICE, A. K., *Productivity and Social Organization*, Tavistock, 1958.
TRIST, E. L., 'The Socio-Technical Perspective', in A. van de Ven and W. F. Joyce (eds), *Perspectives on Organization Design and Behaviour*, Wiley Interscience, 1981.
TRIST, E. L. and BAMFORTH, K. W., 'Some Social and Psychological Consequences of the Longwall Method of Coal Getting', *Human Relations*, 4, 3–38, 1951.

Edward E. Lawler

Edward E. Lawler is Distinguished Professor of Business and Director of the Center for Effective Organizations at the University of Southern California. An organizational psychologist, he has been concerned with a range of programmes of research and action research into management effectiveness, quality of working life, and innovative approaches to designing and managing organizations. His continuing interest in the psychological analysis of the part that pay and reward systems play in organizational effectiveness and organizational change led, in 1972, to his receiving a Distinguished Scientific Award from the American Compensation Association.

Lawler's interest in appropriate systems for pay and reward stems from his view, based on a considerable amount of research both of his own and of others, that compensation has an important influence on those behaviours which lead to organizational effectiveness. In a survey of research studies, four methods used to improve productivity were compared. Incentive payments yielded the highest average increase (30 per cent); goal-setting, including management by objectives (see Drucker, Chapter 4) and job enrichment (see Herzberg, earlier in this chapter), each had under 20 per cent, and participation only one-half per cent. Thus, argues Lawler, for any change to be effective (including participation) it should be linked to appropriate changes in payment systems.

This is because pay is vitally important to individuals in the organization. It not only enables them to satisfy their material needs and gives a feeling of security, but also, very important for many people, pay is seen as a mark of the esteem in which they are held. In addition it provides opportunities to engage in activities which are autonomously directed and independent of the work organization.

Why then, in spite of its importance both to organizations as a determinant of effectiveness and to individuals as a source of satisfaction, is pay so often an organizational problem? Studies have shown that in many organizations 50 per cent or more of employees are dissatisfied with their pay. In a major US sample survey, the percentage of people who agreed that they received good pay and fringe benefits dropped from 48 per cent to 34 per cent between 1973 and 1977.

There are a number of conclusions available from research which can explain this situation. Satisfaction with pay is a function of how much is received compared with how much the individual feels should be received. Ideas of what should be received are based on two factors.

The first factor is an evaluation of what contribution the individual makes in terms of skill, experience, age, amount of responsibility and so on. Typically individuals rate their personal contributions higher than other people rate them. (Surveys have shown that the average male employee rates his performance in the top 20 per cent of his grade!) They also consider that the contributions in which they are strong (for example, formal education, company loyalty) should be weighted most heavily, and those in which they are weak (for example seniority, difficulty of task) should be regarded as less important.

The second factor contributing to ideas of appropriate payment is a comparison of what other people in similar posts both within and outside the organization receive. Often there is a lack of correct information about the rewards of others, because this is an emotional issue and organizations keep secret the results of salary surveys, performance, appraisals and individual remuneration. On the whole, therefore, people tend to overestimate the pay of others doing similar work.

Not surprisingly, then, there is dissatisfaction with rewards which leads to reduced motivation, absenteeism, labour turnover and difficulties in recruitment. What can be done to attack these problems? Since dissatisfaction stems from relativities and comparisons, paying everybody more money will clearly not improve the situation. Lawler maintains that it is possible *within the same total wage bill* to redesign the payment and benefit system to obtain increased individual satisfaction and organizational effectiveness.

There are a number of major organizational characteristics which influence the nature of an appropriate compensation plan chosen for a particular enterprise:

1. ORGANIZATIONAL CLIMATE

Using the distinction made by Likert and McGregor (earlier in this chapter), it is clear that an organization with a participative climate (System 4, Theory Y) can use participative methods for disclosure of information, setting of objectives, generation of trust to allow changes and so on. In such an organization it might be agreed, for example, that an all-salary payment system is appropriate because sufficient trust and confidence in supervision exist that unfair advantage will not be taken by anyone through slacking, absenteeism and so on. An authoritarian climate on the other hand (System 1, Theory X) would do well to emphasize hard criteria, such as quantity of output and sales, since these can be monitored in detail and thus require a much lower level of trust and openness.

2. TECHNOLOGY

The distinctions by Woodward (Chapter 1) of unit, mass and process production will affect the payment system. Individual performance measures may be appropriate in unit and mass, but plant-wide measures are necessary for process industry. In non-industrial professional service organizations (for example hospitals, schools), attempts to tie rewards to measures of performance would likely result in increased bureaucratic behaviour. Joint goal setting would be more appropriate here.

3. SIZE AND ORGANIZATION STRUCTURE

The size of an organization will affect the possibilities; small enterprises can use company-wide indices of performance, thus emphasizing the common endeavour. For large organizations this is inevitably seen as irrelevant by an individual employee (unless right at the top). Decentralized organizations can link payment schemes to the performance of the sub-unit, but there must be real delegation of decision-making power to the sub-unit (for example factory) to affect its own performance, otherwise effort will be directed to defeating the control system, not to improving effectiveness.

The pay system must therefore fit the characteristics of an organization if it is to be effective. Appropriate merit pay plans for different types of organization are presented in the table on page 252.

The characteristics of the organization and the characteristics of the pay system must be matched in one of two ways: by choosing the correct system for present organizational characteristics or by changing the organization to fit the plan. Because pay is so important to individuals, is so tangible in its effects and has system-wide implications, simultaneously changing the pay system is crucial in ensuring that other changes are effective. For example, the continued administration of a traditional authoritarian pay system could well ensure that an avowed move to more participative management will be regarded as insincere and a management gimmick. Alternatively an appropriate new pay system can signal to all that a real change is taking place.

Many changes taking place in regard to work organizations have implications for new payment systems. For example, the workforce is becoming more heterogeneous, multi-cultural, with greater participation of women and of minority groups in more senior positions. People are becoming more educated and knowledgeable, less accepting of traditional authority and with an increasing desire for more influence at the workplace. The nature of organizations is changing (more service organizations and fewer manufacturing ones, large organizations are getting larger and more diversified, while numerous small businesses are coming into being) and so is the environment in which they operate. Slower economic growth and recession, together with all these other changes, will inevitably intensify people's concern with social equity and thus make it ever more imperative that payment systems should motivate performance and give individual satisfaction.

Lawler identifies a number of practices which are being introduced to deal with such changes. Of primary importance is the concept of *individualization of compensation systems*. Plans that use the same pay methods in all parts of the organization and give everybody the same benefits using the same basic rates for example, no longer fit both the diverse workforce and the diverse nature of organizations. More individual contracts with greater flexibility on working hours, pay–performance relationships, balance between salary and fringe benefits and so on are needed. This is already in place for managers at the top but will have to percolate further down the organizational levels to give people greater choice

Appropriate Merit Pay Plans for Various Types of Organizations

Authoritarian	Mass and unit	Large	Cent.	Individual basis; objective criteria
			Decent.	For workers – individual; for managers – group plan possible on profit centre basis; for all objective criteria
		Small	Cent.	Individual basis; objective criteria
			Decent.	For workers – individual; for managers – group plan possible on profit centre basis; for all objective criteria
	Process	Large	Cent.	None very appropriate; company-wide bonus possible for managers
			Decent.	Group plan based upon objective sub-unit performance criteria
		Small	Cent.	Organization-wide bonus plan
			Decent.	Group plan based upon objective sub-unit performance measures
	Professional service	Large	Cent.	None appropriate
			Decent.	None appropriate
		Small	Cent.	None appropriate
			Decent.	None appropriate
Democratic	Mass and unit	Large	Cent.	Individual plans based on objective criteria as well as soft criteria, such as participatively set goals
			Decent.	Same as centralized, but for managers use data from their sub-part of organization
		Small	Cent.	Some consideration to performance of total organization; individual plans based on objective criteria as well as soft criteria, such as participatively set goals
			Decent.	Same as centralized except sub-part performance can be used as criteria in both individual and group plans
	Process	Large	Cent.	Organization-wide plan based on objective and subjective criteria; individual appraisal based on soft criteria
			Decent.	Group plan based on plant performance, objective and subjective criteria
		Small	Cent.	Organization-wide plan based on company performance
			Decent.	Group plans based on sub-unit performance
	Professional service	Large	Cent.	Design individual plans; high input from employees; joint goal setting and evaluation
			Decent.	Same as centralized but some consideration to performance of sub-parts
		Small	Cent.	Some consideration to performance of total organization; design individual plans; high input from employees; joint goal setting and evaluation
			Decent.	Same as centralized, except that data for sub-part of organization may be relevant

Source: Lawler (1971).

in meeting their reward requirements. Such traditional practices as the blanket distinction between hourly and salaried employees will more and more come into question.

Some further trends, which do not sit easily together, may also be noted. Performance-based pay systems (where they are appropriate) are becoming more important in linking pay to performance in a motivating way. But they must be carried out in the light of modern feelings that decisions about pay should be arrived at by open and defensible processes, not by a secret personal top-down approach lacking any appeal procedure. Also, more egalitarian reward systems, which decrease the number of grade levels and set limits to the differences in rewards, go in harness with the desire of many for more open participative organizations, but may well relate less directly to performance. There are no automatic answers to these issues. 'As society changes, so must its organizations; as organizations change, so must their pay systems.'

In later work Lawler, with Christopher Worley, studied organizations that can contemplate and achieve continuous change, such as Procter & Gamble, Johnson & Johnson and Toyota. They are found to have certain characteristics, which include: tying pay to the performance of the business and therefore sharing financial information with all employees; encouraging many individuals to have contacts outside the organization, for example with customers: stressing the need to regularly change work assignments and not being afraid to eliminate jobs completely; and selecting employees who accept and seek change.

BIBLIOGRAPHY

LAWLER, E. E., *Pay and Organizational Effectiveness: A Psychological View*, McGraw-Hill, 1971.

LAWLER, E. E., *Pay and Organization Development*, Addison-Wesley, 1981.

LAWLER, E. E. *Rewarding excellence: Pay strategies for the new economy*, Jossey-Bass, 2000.

LAWLER, E. E., AND WORLEY, C. G., *Built to change: How to achieve sustained organizational effectiveness*, Jossey-Bass, 2006.

7 Organizational Change and Learning

... we contend, bureaucratization and other forms of organizational change occur as a result of processes which make organizations more similar without necessarily making them more efficient.
PAUL J. DIMAGGIO AND WALTER W. POWELL

... the real problem of strategic change is ultimately one of managerial process and action; of signalling new areas for concern and anchoring those signals in issues for attention and decision, of mobilizing energy and enthusiasm in an additive fashion to ensure that new problem areas found and defined eventually gain sufficient legitimacy and power to result in contextually appropriate action.
ANDREW PETTIGREW

Organizational defensive routines are anti-learning and over-protective.
CHRIS ARGYRIS

Today's problems come from yesterday's 'solutions'.
PETER SENGE

Fast decision-makers use, more, not less, information than do slow decision-makers.
KATHLEEN EISENHARDT

Imaginization – an invitation to develop new ways of thinking about organization and management – an invitation to re-image ourselves and what we do.
GARETH MORGAN

Organizations do change, whether for better or for worse, and writers on organizations have examined the ways in which change comes about. Some have concentrated on the factors in the organization's context and environment which appear both to impel particular changes to occur and also to set constraints on them. Others have underlined that appropriate change which assists the organization to become more effective only comes about through considerable effort on the part of the organization's managers. They have to understand the need for change and be consciously working to achieve it. In addition, modern organizations are in situations which require continuous development. They not only need to change; they have to acquire a capacity for learning.

Paul DiMaggio and Walter Powell argue that organizations change to be more like each other, since the pressures from the state, from other institutions and from professional standards require managers to conform to accepted practice. In contrast, Andrew Pettigrew underlines the specific complexity for each organization of the interacting factors of context, content and process with which managers have to grapple to execute an effective strategic change.

Chris Argyris points to the power of 'defensive routines', the psychological blocks to considering change, which limit an organization's ability to draw on the full potential of its members. He suggests ways in which they might be overcome to produce an organization more open to change and able to participate in new learning. Peter Senge is concerned to establish the characteristics of a 'learning organization', that is, one which, through a systems approach, is able to learn continuously.

Kathleen Eisenhardt advocates a strategy for change for firms in fast-changing environments called 'competing on the edge'. Gareth Morgan maintains that understanding an organization is greatly helped by applying a range of different images to it. This 'imaginization' is the key to being better able to conceive of possible changes.

Paul J. DiMaggio and Walter W. Powell

Paul J. Dimaggio and Walter W. Powell are American professors of sociology based at Princeton and Stanford universities, respectively. They are leading exponents of the particular approach to the study and understanding of organizations known as 'Institutional Theory'.

Institutional theory begins from Weber's views on the functioning of bureaucracy (see Chapter 1). Weber argues that the 'rational–legal' bureaucratic type of organizational structure has become dominant in modern society because it is the most efficient form. It is based on rationally calculating how to organize to achieve desired ends. It has a hierarchy of authority, experts who have specific areas of responsibility, and a system of rules, which together control the organization's activities. It uses the files of the 'bureau' to record the past behaviour of the organization and to capture the professionally determined best available knowledge relevant to its goals. It can therefore carry out its activities unambiguously, predictably, continuously and speedily. Since it is efficient, bureaucracy is used by governments needing both to control their staff and citizenry and to give equal protection under the law. It is also used by capitalist business firms who are in competition and therefore need to operate efficiently.

Writers in Chapter 1 of this book, like Chandler, Mintzberg and others, seek to describe and explain different types of organizational structure. But DiMaggio and Powell point out that bureaucracy has spread continuously during the twentieth century, becoming the usual organizational form. They therefore ask, not why organization structures differ, but why there is such an overriding degree of homogeneity in organizational forms and practices. Organizations of the same type in any organizational field (for example business firms in the same industry, government departments, hospitals) may have displayed considerable diversity in approach when they were first set up. But once a field becomes established there is an inexorable push towards bureaucratic homogeneity.

But, unlike Weber, DiMaggio and Powell question whether this convergence is due to the efficiency of the bureaucratic form, which leads all to strive towards it. Rather, they maintain that the convergence is a result of institutional pressures from the environment on managers in an organizational field to become more similar to one another, *whether this leads to greater efficiency or not*. This emergence of a common structure and approach among organizations in the same field is referred to as *institutional isomorphism*. This is the constraining process which forces one unit in a population to come to resemble those other units that face the same set of environmental conditions. It is important since among the major factors that organizations must respond to are other organizations in their environments. It is through these organizations that managers get their ideas about how to run organizations and obtain legitimacy for the actions which they take. Legitimate actions are those which conform to the common view; they do not have to be effective.

There are three mechanisms through which institutional isomorphism produces conformity: *coercive* isomorphism (which stems from political influence), *mimetic* isomorphism (which results from responses to uncertainty) and *normative* isomorphism (which results from the professionalization of managers and specialists). Each of these mechanisms describes a process by which ideas from institutions in the organization's environment become legitimized and adopted.

Coercive isomorphism results from pressures, both formal and informal, from other important organizations in the environment. These pressures are of various sorts. They may have the force of law as, for example, pollution-control regulations or anti-discrimination legislation. They may come from external institutions, as when government support agencies require certain accounting procedures to be in place before giving their support to charities, or when important customers require particular delivery systems from their suppliers. The pressure may come from internal authority as, for example, in the case of common control information required by the head office of a corporation from all its subsidiaries. The pressures may be persuasive in character, but they are still very real, as when standards for school curricula or new products are publicly recommended.

One result of coercive pressures may be that the conformity obtained is only superficial. Indeed, in some cases there may be a general collusion that something is being done rather than actual change taking place. For example, health and safety regulations may ensure that all organizations appoint a specialist officer, but may otherwise allow the issue to be relatively neglected throughout a whole sector. All these institutional pressures act coercively to produce a convergence in structures and procedures.

Mimetic isomorphism is based on imitation. All organizations face uncertainty, having to deal with problems with ambiguous causes and unclear solutions. This leads to what March (see Chapter 5) has identified as *problemistic search*, that is, a short-term, short-sighted, simple-minded activity to find ways of dealing with a particularly urgent problem. A common result of such searches is to copy what others in a similar situation are reported to be doing successfully, since this gives legitimization. For example, following their application in a firm generally regarded as successful, new management practices, as propagated by consultants, may then be regarded as legitimate and be taken up by many organizations.

So techniques such as job enrichment or zero-based budgeting, and new philosophies, such as 'excellence' or human resource management, quickly spread. A dramatic example of such imitation is the way in which the concept of quality circles was neglected by US managements until it proved popular and effective in Japan, and it was then rapidly legitimized and embraced by Western firms.

Such imitation may lead to a quick viable solution with less expense, but it is often undertaken when no such benefit is obvious, since being the same as the rest reduces management's feelings of uncertainty and can produce benefits in terms of image. As an example, Powell studied a public television station which, on a consultant's recommendation, switched from a functional structure to a divisional one (see Chandler, Chapter 1). Station executives were sceptical of any efficiency gains: some services had to be duplicated across divisions, for example. But they adopted the change because they wanted to give the image that the station was becoming more business-minded. Again, all these pressures to imitate foster an organizational conformity.

The third source of environmental pressures towards organizational convergence is that of *normative isomorphism*. This results primarily from the continuing professionalization of the organization's managers and specialists. They wish to demonstrate that they are fully professional and up-to-the-minute in regard to good standards, whether in information technology, accounting requirements or marketing techniques. Having had a common training, professionals are in many ways much closer to their professional counterparts in other organizations than they are to their managerial colleagues in their own. They therefore propagate common norms of legitimate practice which push all organizations to converge.

An important way in which normative isomorphism is encouraged is through the selection of the top personnel of organizations. A filtering often takes place. This might come about through the practice of recruiting high-fliers from a narrow range of training institutions, for example Ivy League business schools in the US and *grandes écoles* in France. Another filter comes from promoting to top positions only from a narrow range of specialisms, for example financial or legal. Professional careers may themselves be controlled at entry level and at key progression points. All these filters create a pool of individuals in senior jobs with very similar backgrounds, training and experience.

These similarities have been shown among superintendents in a US public school system, and among the board members of the Fortune top 500 companies. Some entrants to senior jobs are different, having managed to avoid the filters, for example black senior officials, women board members and Jewish naval officers. They are likely to be subjected to considerable persuasive pressures to gain legitimacy by acting in exactly the same way as the others. As before, the results are that the norms practised lead to organizational isomorphism.

These pressures for institutional isomorphism are so considerable, maintain DiMaggio and Powell, that the processes can be expected to continue even in the absence of evidence that the changes increase organizational effectiveness. Indeed, if organizations do become more effective, the reason is often that they are rewarded for their similarity to other organizations in their field. This can make it easier for them to transact business with other organizations, to attract professional staff and to be acknowledged as legitimate and respectable – this last being very important to public agencies in attracting financial support. But none of these factors ensures that they are actually more efficient than deviant organizations.

DiMaggio and Powell with colleagues have conducted an international survey of the changes taking place in firms at the dawn of the twenty-first century. In the twentieth century the automobile factory with its standardized assembly line represented the epitome of efficient working. Coming into the twenty-first century it is the computer which provides the ideal model, causing an emphasis on networks and flows. There is general agreement that change is occurring. The structures of business firms are becoming flatter, relying more on teamwork and less on elaborate hierarchies. This is reflected in current mimetic processes such as benchmarking, normative processes such as consultant firms with standard packages of recipes for management success, and coercive processes such as state-backed ownership networks in post-socialist Eastern Europe.

BIBLIOGRAPHY

DIMAGGIO, P. J. (ed.), *The Twenty First Century Firm*, Princeton University Press, 2001.
DIMAGGIO, P. J. and POWELL, W. W., 'The Iron Cage Revisited: Institutional Isomorphism and Collective Rationality in Organizational Fields', *American Sociological Review*, 48 (1983), 147–60; reprinted in W. W. Powell and P. J. DiMaggio (eds), *The New Institutionalism in Organizational Analysis*, University of Chicago Press, 1991; also reprinted in D. S. Pugh (ed.), *Organization Theory*, 5th edn, Penguin, 2007.
POWELL, W. W. and DIMAGGIO, P. J. (eds), *The New Institutionalism in Organizational Analysis*, University of Chicago Press, 1991.

Andrew Pettigrew

Andrew Pettigrew is Dean and Head of the School of Management of the University of Bath, England. For many years he was Distinguished Professor of Organizational Behaviour at the University of Warwick Business School, where he founded and directed the Centre for Corporate Strategy and Change. The centre has been a leader in strategic change research in Britain. In its work on understanding the process of change it takes a historical approach that is grounded in a detailed study of the context of an organization in its industrial environment.

Pettigrew maintains that strategic change is a complex, situation-dependent, continuous process. As the diagram shows, it has to be understood in terms of three essential dimensions: context (both internal and external), content (for example objectives and assumptions) and process (for example implementation patterns). Since management decision making is a political process, change is inevitably suffused with organizational politics. In major decisions, whoever is powerful among the decision group will determine the outcomes.

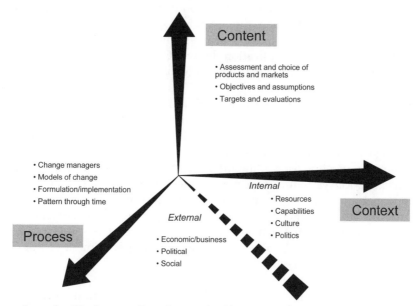

Dimensions for Understanding Strategic Change
Source: Pettigrew and Whipp (1991).

The bases of power in organizations may vary, *The Politics of Organizational Decision-Making* is a detailed study of how one decision came to be made: the acquisition of a new computer system by a British chain store. In this decision the technical manager was very powerful. One important source of his power was his ability to understand and to control the information on options which went to the board. This is an example of a common power base: the emergence of a strong specialization in a then new technology, which reduces the power of the non-specialists. But other bases of power are also available, and what they are have to be examined in each case by studying the management processes in the context in which they take place. No easy generalizations can be made in relating these to the outcome decisions (see Hickson, Chapter 1).

This focus on the processes of strategic change was continued by Pettigrew in detailed studies of change in a number of divisions of ICI, the then British industrial conglomerate. Change may be viewed as a sequence of four stages, each with its own problems.

1. *The development of concern*: this involves problem-sensing, leading to legitimizing the notion of change and getting it on the corporate agenda. It is a time-consuming and politically sensitive process, and one in which top management plays a critical role. One of the contributions that leaders of ICI such as Lord Beeching and Sir John Harvey-Jones made was to continually flag up key problems facing ICI which required it to change.
2. *Getting acknowledgement and understanding of the problems*: the building of a climate of opinion necessary for change was shown to be a long process, requiring many iterations and encountering blocks and unpredictable areas of movement along the way. Major change always affects power structures, career paths and reward systems and is therefore unlikely to be straightforward in its application. In two ICI divisions management training and development were used to equip the managers with the capacity to carry through the operational changes.
3. *Planning and acting*: it is very important in this stage to have established a desired future state of the organization around which planning can take place and commitment be generated. In one division of ICI this involved giving out clear, simple messages within a broad philosophy of downsizing and reorganization for profitability, and maintaining them without dilution.
4. *Stabilizing change*: in this stage management needs to ensure that the rewards, information flows and pattern of power and authority support the new position. Since changes are often initiated by key figures, a danger is that they last only as long as these individuals remain in their posts. A key task is thus to ensure continuity by the development and appointment of appropriate successors.

Pettigrew also examined the contribution of the various organizational development (OD) groups which were operating in the different divisions of ICI. Their success, and continued existence, varied considerably between the divisions.

One chastening lesson is not to expect too much from such OD specialists. As one supportive senior manager put it: 'using OD is in the first case an act of faith'.

In a further study with his colleague the late Richard Whipp (1954–2005), five key problems of managing strategic change were identified. Each of these is complex in itself, in addition, has to be related to the other four. The problems are:

- assessing the environment;
- leading change;
- linking strategic and operational change;
- treating human resources as assets and as liabilities;
- developing a coherent approach.

These five problem areas are examined in detailed studies of firms attempting to manage strategic change in the British vehicle, book publishing, merchant banking and assurance industries. Among the firms studied were Jaguar, Peugeot Talbot, Longman, Kleinwort Benson, Hill Samuel and the Prudential. For each area there are many factors and mechanisms to be examined, and these are different for each industry and for each firm.

When tackling the first problem, *assessing the environment*, it is not enough for companies to regard this as a technical exercise which can be left to appropriate specialists. Understanding the environment must be regarded as a multifunctional activity in which all top management participates as a continuous learning process. This is because for key firms in an industry there is a large subjective element in which their understanding, and therefore their company's activities, actually determine what the environment will become (see Weick, Chapter 4). Thus the understanding of Longman staff as to the nature of their environment led to actions on their part which altered the shape of the book trade and helped to redefine the nature of that market. Again, the change in the 1970s in the way in which the Prudential Assurance company viewed the basis for competitive behaviour in the assurance industry – away from actuarial risk towards product diversification – enabled it to redefine itself as the 'Prudential Corporation'. It was thus better placed to move forward to the structural changes necessary to operate in the changing market.

The second problem, that of *leading change*, is also complex and situation-specific, best done in a series of incremental steps in which many managers are involved. It requires building a climate accepting of change within the firm and, in addition, building the capability to mount the changes. This is quite the opposite of the 'heroic leader' notion of leading change, which is inappropriate. Thus the regeneration of the car company Peugeot Talbot required the establishment of new, open working relationships among senior management, a reworking of the relations with the parent company, a rebuilding of the confidence of the staff, shell-shocked after earlier major contractions, and the progressive elaboration of a new model programme through improved communications and structures. Such a change from survival to regeneration could not be accomplished by one person or through a single programme. It involved the emergence over a period of years of new leaders both at the top and at lower levels within the company.

The next key problem then becomes the *linking of strategic and operational change.* This is difficult because the implementation of strategic intentions over time inevitably transforms them, and what is done during implementation may overwhelm the original strategy. Indeed, often what are considered as strategies are merely the post hoc labelling of what was done: 'that worked, so it was our strategy to do it'. Great attention is required to ensure that operational aspects do not undermine the general strategy. Actionable targets must become the responsibility of change managers operating at many levels. They have to be supported by re-thought communication mechanisms and new reward systems. A major problem is that both strategic and operational change processes have to happen over the same time span and inevitably become 'political' as they press for change and meet opposition.

The problem is highlighted in the contrast between the two merchant banks studied. In the 1970s, Kleinwort Benson had begun to sense trends in its environment, to identify the need for strategic development and to foster a commitment to strategic change among senior staff. In the 1980s, these capacities allowed the firm to adopt a broad strategic position (the expansion of international banking) and to work to drive the implications of the strategy throughout the organization. It was able to learn from failures (for example the slowness of internal deliberations, which led to the failure to purchase a Far Eastern stockbroker), to make compensating changes linked to the strategy. By the time of the deregulation of the British stock market in the 1980s it was able to take relatively swift action, for example, in the acquisition of specialist firms in new activities such as 'interest rate swaps' and 'Eurobonds'.

Hill Samuel, on the other hand, did not construct a fresh corporate strategy in the 1970s: what strategy there was emerged from the amalgam of operational activities, which were continually growing and diversifying. It did not, therefore, develop a capacity to formulate and implement strategy. So in the early 1980s the linking of strategic and operational change was immensely difficult. The gap between the new ideas and the organization's capacity for change was very wide, and the new chief executive had to build up linkages personally. Over a period he had some success, but the strategic and operational linkages were still comparatively immature. Thus the senior management never resolved differences over location, and when the board offered to sell the company to a Swiss bank, the chief executive resigned. Although that deal fell through, the firm was then purchased by the TSB, a British bank.

It is vital to regard *human resources as both assets and liabilities* and to take appropriate action. The organization's members must provide the knowledge base for learning, but it is also necessary to undertake 'unlearning' when the established conceptions and skills are no longer appropriate. Shedding outmoded techniques and attitudes is not easy. Jaguar, for example, had to launch a major programme of human resource management (HRM) in the 1980s when it undertook the challenge to become a profitable, high-quality car manufacturer. It had to move away from the traditional British motor industry's conflict-focused industrial relations view of personnel management. The new HRM approach involved recruiting staff, training staff and developing the commitment of all to the firm's mission. This was done through the use of new specialisms, such as manpower and salary planning, and internal communications services. Schemes for profit sharing, employee shareholding and learning to develop new skills were established. These added up to a very demanding set of changes that needed considerable resources.

And the final problem is that of *coherence*, that is, the ability to hold the organization together while simultaneously reshaping it. Four elements of strategic thinking are required:

1. *Consistency*: ensuring that the attempts to tackle existing problems do not contain internal contradictions. For example, earlier in Peugeot Talbot's existence its then owners, Chrysler UK, tried to make it into a high-volume car producer although it had not mastered the special production techniques required.
2. *Consonance*: that the strategy should be well adapted to the environment. It should not become the victim of the organization's entrenched partial view of its competitive position, as was the case with Hill Samuel.
3. *Competitive advantage*: that the strategy aimed for should give comparative advantage in the market. For example, Longman's growth strategy included the market-led decision to add the fields of professional and business publishing to its established strengths in educational publishing.
4. *Feasibility of the strategy with the resources needed*: this was a problem that Jaguar, for example, had to beware of in its rush for change and growth.

Together with Evelyn Fenton, Pettigrew later initiated a European network of research groups to study innovating organizations and the effects of those innovations on operational success. A programme of survey questionnaires and 18 case studies was carried out. Innovations are defined as changes which develop new features of organizational design either not previously combined or completely new for that industrial sector. Fenton and Pettigrew's own studies were on two innovative professional service organizations; an engineering consultancy (the Ove Arup Partnership) and a management consultancy (Coopers and Lybrand's Pharmaceutical Network).

These were both network organizations but many of the management processes were different. In Arup there was an imbalance of integration of the groups in the network with many cliques forming, particularly affecting the selection of personnel for operational teams. They needed to optimise 'embeddedness' by emphasising a common culture and the creation of 'hubs of knowledge' that could override personal preferences in the constitution of teams. In the case of Coopers and Lybrand the success of the network in terms of growth and revenues, with its concomitant increase in task complexities, required the development of formal co-ordination mechanisms to replace informal, ad hoc arrangements.

The underlying conclusion of these studies is the recognition of the interconnectedness of all the factors involved. It is not possible to provide a general checklist of dos and don'ts in managing strategic change. Only a full understanding of the situation in each case can identify the course of the changes.

BIBLIOGRAPHY

PETTIGREW, A., *The Politics of Organizational Decision-Making*, Tavistock, 1973.
PETTIGREW, A., *The Awakening Giant: Continuity and Change in ICI*, Blackwell, 1985.
PETTIGREW, A., 'Context and Action in the Transformation of the Firm', *Journal of Management Studies*, 24 (1987), 649–70; reprinted in D. S. Pugh (ed.), *Organization Theory*, 5th edn, Penguin, 2007.
PETTIGREW, A., and FENTON, E. M. (eds.), *The Innovating Organization*, Sage, 2000.
PETTIGREW, A. and WHIPP, R., *Managing Change for Competitive Success*, Blackwell, 1991.

Chris Argyris

Chris Argyris is a psychologist who has for many years been James Bryant Conant Professor of Education and Organizational Behavior at Harvard University, where he is now Professor Emeritus. He began his career at Yale University, and his important contributions to the field have been recognized with the establishment at that university of a Chair named in his honour: the Chris Argyris Chair in the Social Psychology of Organizations.

Argyris has consistently studied the ways in which the personal development of individuals is affected by the kind of situation in which they work. Each person has a potential which, if fully realized, would bring benefits not only to the individual but also to the working group and employing organization. Unfortunately businesses and other organizations are usually run in such a way that such benefits are prevented from appearing.

This is because the typical approach of the managements of organizations and their lack of interpersonal competence prevent people from becoming mature in outlook. Employees too often remain short-sighted in their actions on the job, shirking responsibility and being uninterested in opportunities.

They develop 'defensive routines' which protect their current ways of working and inhibit them from considering any changes – even changes that would improve their present position. In their limited routine tasks they look forward to the end of the day's work, but are unable to foresee the success or failure of the whole enterprise over a period of years. To their superiors their infuriating inability to see beyond the end of their noses and their own relatively trivial work difficulties are inexplicable. They have come to accept a passive and dependent position, without initiative.

Faced with this lack of response, even among lower managers or specialists, executives are liable to become yet more autocratic and directive. Their existing strong 'pyramidal values' are reinforced. The increased use of management controls deprives employees of any opportunity of participating in the important decisions which affect their working life, leading to feelings of psychological failure. It is not they themselves but control systems (such as work study and cost accounting) which define, inspect and evaluate the quality and quantity of their performance. And as subordinates tell less and less about what is happening, as everyone pays more attention to keeping up appearances ready for the next business process re-engineering investigation or tense budget allocation committee meeting, so defensive routines come to be the norm.

These are some of the problems human beings have in relating to organizational life. Together with Donald A. Schon, Argyris has also examined some of the built-in contradictions that arise from the functioning of the organization itself, which has the paradoxical requirement of both wanting to maintain stability and also to be dynamic or changing. Thus, typically, organization members may be told: take initiatives *but* do not violate rules; think beyond the present *but* be rewarded and penalized on present performance only; think of the organization as a whole *but* do not cross into others' areas of responsibility; cooperate with others *but* compete with others when required.

The main problem is not that these contradictions exist, but that, in the usual poor state of managerial interpersonal competence, they cannot be raised and discussed as issues. Although many managers may *talk* about the openness of communication and the participative approach of their organizations (what is called their 'espoused' theory), what they actually *do* may be very different. There are very strong defensive routines built into many managements' thinking, ensuring that they resist the openness which leads to interpersonal change.

Argyris and Schon have demonstrated that the basis of many managers' actions (called their 'theory-in-use') can be subsumed under four rules of behaviour, referred to as Model I: (i) design goals unilaterally and try to achieve them, (ii) maximize winning and minimize losing by controlling the task with as little dependence on others as possible, (iii) minimize generating or expressing negative feelings in public, keep your own thoughts and feelings a mystery, (iv) be rational and objective and suppress the voicing of feelings by others, thus protecting yourself and them from facing important issues which often have an emotional content to them.

Managers who operate on Model I have a unilateral view of their world, in which they are striving to have complete control. Their aims are to defend themselves and impose on others. They thus generate mistrust and rigidity and are therefore confirmed in their Model I view that open discussion of issues is best avoided. The only learning that occurs is learning how to conform (called 'single-loop' learning) and the process becomes 'self-sealing'.

Argyris and Schon propose a Model II theory-in-use which does allow organizational learning. The norms here are: (i) take action on valid information and be open about obtaining it, (ii) take action after free and informed choice, with all who are competent and relevant taking part, (iii) generate internal commitment to the choice with monitoring of implementation and preparedness to change. Managers who operate in a Model II world are not defensive and thus they can participate in 'double-loop' learning. They look for contributions from others who are competent; they are able to confront their own basic assumptions and take part in testing them in public, which allows of their changing.

The issue then becomes: if managers operating in a Model I mode are by definition unaware of this fact since they are using defensive routines to resist change, how may they be helped to develop effective learning in Model II mode? Argyris proposes a training programme to bring out into the open these contradictions, in situations where managers' feelings of vulnerability are reduced. Managers are helped by interpersonal consultants to confront the large gap which usually exists between what is said and done in a decision-making group and what is actually felt by the members. They can then analyse the defensive routines which they habitually use to stop openness and innovation and practise taking a Model II approach in their work.

Using this approach, Argyris conducted a case study lasting over five years, as described in his book, *Knowledge for Action*. It was both a consulting and a research programme – a combination known as 'action research'. He worked with the owner-directors of a management consultancy firm to develop their Model II skills. He shows that his seminars helped them to overcome their defensive routines on many occasions (not all). Inevitably, some managers became more competent at Model II behaviour than others. Often in change programmes it is found that top managers put the need for change high in their espoused theory, but their theory-in-use stays the same. Unusually, in this case it was the senior managers who made the most progress. They are at the forefront of making the firm more capable of organizational learning.

BIBLIOGRAPHY

ARGYRIS, C., *Organization and Innovation*, Irwin, 1965.

ARGYRIS, C., *Strategy, Change and Defensive Routines*, Pitman, 1985.

ARGYRIS, C., *Personality and Organizations*, Garland, 1987.

ARGYRIS, C., *Knowledge for Action: A Guide to Overcoming Barriers to Change*, Jossey-Bass, 1993.

ARGYRIS, C., *Flawed Advice and the Management Trap: How Managers Can know When They're Getting Good Advice and When They're Not*, Oxford University Press, 2000.

ARGYRIS, C. and SCHON, D., *Organizational Learning: A Theory of Action Perspective*, Addison-Wesley, 1978.

Peter Senge

Peter Senge, a systems theorist, is Senior Lecturer and Director of the Systems Thinking and Organizational Learning Program of the Sloan School of Management at the Massachusetts Institute of Technology. He argues that, in the present-day complex world, organizations have to be able to learn how to cope with continuous change in order to be successful: that is, they have to become *learning organizations*. His concern is to describe the art and practice of such a learning organization.

It is not easy for organizations to learn because they are afflicted with learning disabilities, such as the following:

- *Excessive commitment of individuals to their own positions.* This limited view leads to people focusing only on their own role and taking little responsibility for the results produced when all the positions interact.
- *Blame always allocated externally, away from the immediate group: the enemy is out there.* It may be other departments (marketing and manufacturing blaming each other), or government regulations, or unfair competition from another country, but blaming external factors hampers learning and is almost always not the complete story.
- *The illusion of taking charge.* Being proactive rather than reactive is attractive to managers, but could simply mean fighting the enemy out there in the same way but more aggressively. Without analysis reflecting on the internal changes necessary, it may simply be disguised reactiveness.
- *Focusing on immediate events as explanations.* This precludes seeing the longer-term patterns of change that lie behind the events and attempting to understand the causes of those larger patterns.
- *Being unaware of slow, gradual processes that present greater threats than immediate events.* It is said that a frog placed in boiling water will immediately jump out but, if placed in warm water which is gradually heated to boiling, will stay and boil, since its sensing apparatus is geared to sudden changes, not to gradual ones. Senge argues that something of the kind happened to the American motor industry from the mid-1960s to the mid-1980s in regard to Japanese and German competition. Over two decades the latter's share of the market rose from near zero to 38 per cent before US manufacturers took it seriously.
- *The delusion that learning comes only from experience.* We do learn from experience, but in a complex system we can no longer directly experience the consequences of many of our important decisions. Decisions on investment

in R & D or on strategic positioning may have large ramifications over a decade or more. It is not therefore possible to learn only on the basis of trial and error.

- *The myth of top management being agreed and united.* This leads to suppression of disagreements and encourages watered-down compromises to maintain the appearance of a cohesive team. If disagreement does come to the surface it is expressed in polarized terms, with those involved finding fault and blaming each other. Thus, as Argyris (previously in this chapter) shows, real 'double-loop' learning does not take place.

To combat these considerable disabilities, Senge proposes five disciplines that organizations need to practise to become learning organizations.

The first concerns *personal mastery*. Individuals need to exercise the highest levels of mastery, not over other people, but over themselves. They need to have a good understanding of themselves and what they wish to achieve. This is the personal learning which is the basis for organizational learning, since no organization's capacity for learning can be greater than that of its members. But few organizations encourage such self-discipline, with the result that there are vast untapped resources of energy and learning potential in organizations.

The second discipline necessitates the continual challenge and review of the deeply entrenched, tacit *mental models* that members of the organization bring to all its activities. Stereotypes of customer behaviour, accepted recipes for product development and the neglect of the possibilities of discontinuous change are examples of mental models that have to be continuously reviewed in an effort to make thinking more open to a wider range of new ideas. The Anglo–Dutch Shell oil company attributes its considerable success over the last two decades in the unpredictable world oil business to its ability to challenge the mental models of its managers.

The third discipline concerns the *building of a shared vision* for the organization and its members of the future that they wish to create. A shared vision has been the key to all successful organizations: the 'value-driven' nature of excellent organizations, as Peters and Waterman put it (Chapter 4). It has to be more than the usual artificial 'vision statement', a genuine vision of what they want to achieve, which firms such as Ford, IBM, Polaroid and Apple computers have displayed.

The fourth discipline is a commitment to *team learning*: an open dialogue of cooperation in groups, rather than turf battles. Only then can the intelligence of the team exceed that of its members, rather than reduce it drastically.

The discipline which unites the others and brings all together in a pattern which can be understandable is that of *systems thinking*. This is the fifth discipline, which provides the title for Senge's book, and is the foundation for organizational learning. It is necessary to think in a systems way which is rather different from our usual focus on immediate events.

There are a number of laws of systems thinking, of which the first is 'today's problems come from yesterday's "solutions".' Often problems arise from 'solutions' which merely shift the problem to another part of the system. A solution to the problem of high stock inventory that involved drastic reductions might result in salesmen spending large amounts of their time pacifying irate customers awaiting late deliveries. The impounding by the police of a large shipment of drugs may result in an increase of drug-related crime as the reduced availability forces the price up and thus increases the crime levels of addicts desperate to maintain their supply. So other laws of the fifth discipline are 'the harder you push, the harder the system pushes back', 'the easy way out usually leads back in' and 'the cure can be worse than the disease'.

A more sophisticated understanding of the way complex systems work is required, and managers need training to encourage systems thinking. Another law of the fifth discipline is that 'behaviour grows better before it grows worse'. Treating the symptoms may bring temporary relief, but at the cost of later, larger problems. There is a fundamental mismatch between the behaviour of complex systems and our ways of thinking about them. This is because, for important issues, 'cause and effect are not closely related in time and space'. The results of a decision taken now may have effects only after some time and in a different part of the organization anyway. Thus the decision to cut the budget of the training department in a particular year may seem a sensible economy. But in the following year the result might be a large decrease in the operational efficiency of a new computer billing system through inadequate preparation.

The basic contribution of the fifth discipline of systems thinking is the art of seeing the wood *and* the trees. Managers do not often take the time to step back from the trees to see the wood and, unfortunately, when they do step back they just see lots of trees! Senge analyses the sad story of the Peoples' Express Airlines, an innovative, low-cost, high-quality airline service in the eastern US, to illustrate the necessity for systems thinking. The airline was founded in 1980 and was immediately successful, growing in five years to become the fifth largest carrier in the USA. But in 1986 it was taken over by another airline, having made a loss of $133 million in the first six months of that year.

What went wrong? Many theories were proposed, including a too great 'people orientation' by the management, lack of an adequate strategy in relation to takeovers, an innovative seat-reservation system introduced by other airlines which allowed price competition, and so on. But each of these theories is only partial. A proper analysis requires consideration of the interactions of five sets of factors (air fleet, human resources, competition, finance and policy levers), which generates a list of over 40 variables which must be considered in a system-wide way. A simulation was built at MIT which allows many of the variables to be changed to evaluate their impact on the system as a whole. Working with simulation suggests that what is required is an organization which is capable of self-analysis, for example, in understanding that you cannot innovate with dramatically new ideas in human resource policies and become a major player in the airline industry within a few years. A firm can grow too fast and so not be able to learn to understand and manage the turbulent changes involved and thus think and act systemically.

A key contribution to an organization's capacity to learn is thus the use of computer-based simulations, called 'microworlds'. These allow for 'play' in developing a more complex systemic understanding of the organization's position and what the possibilities for change are. This leads to the realization of another of the laws of the fifth discipline: 'you can have your cake and eat it too – but not at once'.

BIBLIOGRAPHY

SENGE, P. N., *The Fifth Discipline: The Art and Practice of the Learning Organization*, Century Business, 1992.

SENGE, P. N., 'Mental Models', *Planning Review*, 20 (1992)' 4–10, 44; reprinted in D. S. Pugh (ed.), *Organization Theory*, 5th edn, Penguin, 2007.

Kathleen M. Eisenhardt

Kathleen Eisenhardt took her first degree in Engineering, then came to the University of Stanford, California where she obtained her PhD in the Business School. She has continued as an academic in Stanford, and is now Professor of Strategy and Organization in the Engineering School. She also acts as consultant to firms in the high technology sector. With a number of colleagues she has conducted continuous research on how managers in organizations seek appropriate strategies and try to carry them out effectively. She has focused on strategies for firms in industries that are changing rapidly and unpredictably, and therefore where an organization must generate 'a relentless flow of competitive advantages' if it is to succeed.

With a colleague, Jay Bourgeois, Eisenhardt has studied executives making strategic decisions in firms in the fast-moving microcomputer industry. The decisions were key ones such as 'Should we develop a new product, and if so, which?' or 'Should we form a strategic alliance, and if so, with whom?' One group of companies was designated as 'fast' in that they made such a strategic decision in under 4 months. The second group was 'slow' in that they spent at least 6 months, and typically more than 12 months in making a comparable decision. These differences challenge some accepted views of effective decision making.

Eisenhardt and her colleagues found that the fast companies made greater use of real-time information than the slow companies. They found that the greater the number of alternatives considered simultaneously, the greater the speed of the decision process. In fast firms, the use by the chief executive of one experienced and well-respected older manager as a regular special confidante or counsellor was common.

In slow firms, the managers' use of 'politics' (for example withholding relevant information, controlling agendas, behind the scenes lobbying and coalition building) was found to be greatest where a powerful chief executive dominated by controlling all the decisions. Real conflict over which decisions to take occurs in all firms, but is not sufficient by itself to generate such politicking. The fast companies avoided politics by making greater use of active conflict resolution, that is, recognizing a conflict and dealing with it, rather than allowing it to linger on.

Genuine conflict – about substantive issues, not personalities – is indeed valuable in causing managers to up their game in situations of pressure. The fast firms typically used a process characterized as 'consensus with qualification'. First, the management team attempts to reach consensus by involving everyone. They focus on the facts, increase the alternatives to be considered, create common goals and use humour in the discussion. If agreement occurs, fine. If not, then the chief executive makes the choice after taking into account the views expressed, and this is accepted by all.

Perhaps the most important finding was that, in this industry, *faster* decision making is associated with *better* performance.

Together with Shona Brown, a management consultant with McKinsey and Company, Eisenhardt has developed these studies and concomitant consulting experience into a framework for understanding strategic decision making for firms in such fast-moving industries where change is incessant. The situation will not even stay the same whilst a strategy is worked out and acted upon. It is necessary to react to changes, but better to anticipate them by foreseeing the market and preparing employees, venture partners and resources in advance. Better still is to lead change by making the moves to which others have to react launching into new markets, raising industry standards, redefining customer expectations.

As Brown and Eisenhardt see it there are three testing questions for managers of such firms: *how to compete, how to change,* and *how to keep on changing*? Their answers are summarized as *balance on the edge of chaos,* and *balance on the edge of time* whilst *pacing change*. These are the features of a strategy that they term 'competing on the edge'.

Such a competing-on-the-edge strategy balances the business on the edge of chaos – between chaos and orderly structure. It operates coherently enough to be capable of organizing change but not so organized as to impede it. It balances the business, too, on the edge of time, with multiple time horizons that draw from past experience, focus actively on the present, and continually look ahead to the future. Finally, it sustains a paced change within the business, incessantly bringing forth new products or services or brands or markets.

Competing by balancing on the edge of chaos requires *improvisation* and *co-adaptation* in order to avoid toppling into chaos. Yet being on the edge of chaos is where systems can most effectively change. Systems with more structure than is found at the edge of chaos are too rigid to move. Systems with less structure are too disorganized to be effective.

Improvisation takes on the challenge of balancing sufficient organization to budget, schedule and execute efficiently, with sufficient flexibility to innovate. A telling demonstration of it is given by a continually progressing rock band, or a successful jazz band. These continually improvise as they play, but need a few minimal and semi-intuitive rules, such as who plays first, what are the permitted chords, and who follows whom, to avoid chaos. What matters most is now, the very moment of improvised playing and balancing. In their need for balanced improvisation, businesses are more like rock and jazz bands than might be thought.

Brown and Eisenhardt describe what happened to a computer corporation, which they name 'Royal', when it lost its balance and slipped into *too little structure*. Its management had decided to drive it forward into contemporary markets by adding to its long-established bureaucratic organization some new and rule-breaking sections aimed at bringing in new ideas and new business. Yet because responsibilities were unclear and overlapping, ideas were not effectively carried into action. In Royal both the new hardware section and the existing graphics section considered themselves to be in charge of the product so, whilst each was at the cutting edge in their own field, their technologies were not sufficiently compatible. The scheduling of production was held up by arguments between them. The authority and procedures to ensure coordination were lacking (cf. Burns, Chapter 2). Such ill-defined responsibilities, inoperative rules and communication which, even if plentiful are irrelevant, are all signs of too little structure.

Too much structure, off-balance on the other side, was found by Brown and Eisenhardt in another computer firm, which they called 'Nautilus'. Here there were rules and procedures for everything and a pride in keeping to them. There were detailed plans and organization charts, and minimal time-consuming superfluous communication. The consequence was that, although there was quick and efficient production of their consumer products, these were too often behind the times in such a rapidly changing market where others had the ideas first.

Balanced improvisation on the edge between too little and too much structure is hard to achieve, but one example is the American corporation Nike, based in the athletic footwear market. It has constantly outrun competitors with innovative designs and branding, and moved on into sports accessories (sunglasses, swimming goggles and so on), equipment (hockey sticks, skates and so on) and clothing. Yet it efficiently turns out products at competitive prices that are distributed globally on time. It is said to have the best logistics systems in the industry.

The challenge of *co-adaptation* is to balance the advantages of synergies between different businesses within an organization, with the degree of independence needed by each in its own market. British Petroleum's venture into minerals extraction foundered because of attempted over-collaboration between incompatibles. It looked as if there were economies to be gained from collaboration between the oil and minerals businesses, both of which were based on high-risk exploration, technically complex extraction, and sensitive relationships with governments. This was not so. Sales and earnings of minerals fluctuate in much narrower markets, and the managing of the two businesses could not be profitably interlocked.

Under-collaboration characterized a major American software firm studied by Brown and Eisenhardt. In this vigorous business with youthful personnel the policy was to employ good people and then let them 'do their own thing'. This gave full scope for the creativity needed in this industry from dedicated, hardworking staff. But potential benefits from internal cross-business collaboration were overlooked. The possibilities of sharing programs, including software code and graphics, were hardly recognized. They were no more than afterthoughts. They were no one's concern.

An effective balance of co-adaptation on the edge of chaos has been more nearly achieved by Disney. It has succeeded in a range of businesses from retailing to cable television to its famous animated movie films. The Disney brand image is carried from films into music, video and other merchandising by characters such as Pocahontas and the Lion King. Yet Disney are careful not to overdo this. They have independent film studios that avoid conspicuous links with the rest of the corporation so that what they do is distinctive.

Competing by balancing on the edge of time requires adjusting *regeneration*, drawing on the past, and *experimentation*, venturing into the future. Regeneration ensures that advantages still to be gained from past investment are fully realized. and that the lessons of past experience are not overlooked when venturing forward. The aim must be to exploit the past and to explore the new, not undervaluing either. Organizations balance on the edge of time between past and future, and competing on the edge must make the most of both.

Taking a drastic leap into new business is not the only way to go forward. Managers trying to leave past problems behind and compete on the edge are especially liable to overrate its attractions and underrate its risks. They ignore what can be gained from experience and stake too much on the unknown. Whilst there are businesses that have successfully taken such a leap, the wiser way is to blend past experience with the new, selecting from the past what is relevant to the future. One way is to include a leavening of experienced personnel with the new people who are given charge of new ventures. The other way around, new personnel can revitalize older products. All the best people should not be on the new ventures. Diversification is as much about revitalizing mature businesses as it is about winning new opportunities.

Given that warning, regeneration is nonetheless about moving into the future. McDonalds, for example, has been struggling to shake off its successful past so as to meet the challenge from newer fast foods (like tacos and pizzas) and healthier foods, as well as more variations on the hamburger. They have found it difficult to devise novelty of a kind that does not blur their strong market image and uses their strength in premises and technology. Yet regeneration demands the combination of novelty with experience to progress in an evolutionary way rather than risk the big leap.

The Japanese firm Nintendo demonstrates this. When it lost its lead in the video game sector, it came back with more advanced microprocessor electronics and joystick control that gave its games new levels of speed and visual representation. Yet to retain user loyalty it did not change its previously successful game hero Super Mario. Successful regeneration draws on the past to add something new.

Competing by pacing change is the third element in a competing-on-the-edge strategy. Change should not be left to chance or be just a response to events but it should be paced. One reason for the success of Intel, the leading semiconductor firm, is that it is a more than usually time-paced corporation. It has kept up a series of new products, innovations to existing products, and fresh manufacturing facilities. It has its own rhythm of change, synchronized with that of the marketplace. Similarly, British Airways tries to refresh its service brands at least every five years, and the 3M corporation aims for a third of its sales to be products less than four years old.

Time-pacing means changing because of the passage of time, not because of the occurrence of events. New products, new services, new markets need to come according to the calendar. A momentum of change is built up from within which is insistent, and has a degree of pattern or regularity. It may be synchronized with business rhythms such as seasonal demand, customer fashion or trade exhibitions.

So change becomes familiar and is expected. Personnel at all levels are accustomed to transitions from one product or service or market to another. Although this continual time-paced change may be stressful, the alternative is anxiety over competitors forging ahead, which can be even more stressful.

Event-pacing, the contrasting alternative, is haphazard. It is change in response to events, such as the introduction by a competitor of a new product, or changes in technology. Being reactive it is unexpected and irregular, imposing on personnel spurts of rapid disconcerting upheaval, whereas time-pacing aims at an accustomed, though urgent, rhythm of change that becomes the normal way things are done.

Competing on the edge is not always fully coherent, nor even efficient in the short term. It may take managers 'stumbling into the wrong markets, making mistakes, bouncing back, and falling into the right ones'. Despite the risks, determination to change is more important than short-term profitability, for longer-term profitability will ensue.

The strategy followed by Microsoft in the 1990s, for example, does not look like a carefully coordinated series of initiatives carried through in a planned manner. The series of competitive advantages achieved by Microsoft has occurred in a none-too-coherent way, a strategy more emergent than planned. Their ideas often come from below, as did their switch into Internet working. Some of their initiatives have failed, as did their proprietary version of the Microsoft network. There is no one big move, but incremental steps such as adding a web-page capability to Word, and a web browser to Windows 95. As well as in-house developments there are acquisitions and strategic partnerships to enable the company to remain competitive.

As Eisenhardt sees it, a firm's strategy has to constantly change so as to compete on the edge. So at the heart of a top manager's job is the ability to watch markets, products and organization structures, so as to be able to recognize patterns which point the way to the future.

BIBLIOGRAPHY

BROWN. S. A. and EISENHARDT, K. M. *Competing on the Edge: Strategy as Structured Chaos*, Harvard Business School Press, 1998.

EISENHARDT, K. M., 'Making Fast Strategic Decisions in High Velocity Environments' *Academy of Management Journal*, (1989), 32(3), 543–576; reprinted in D. S. Pugh (ed.) *Organization Theory*, 5th edn, Penguin, 2007.

EISENHARDT, K. M. and SULL, D. N., 'Strategy as Simple Rules', *Harvard Business Review*, (2001), 79, 106–116.

Gareth Morgan

Born in Wales, Gareth Morgan lives and works in Canada. He is Distinguished Research Professor at York University, Toronto, having moved there from the University of Lancaster in England. He has written books and many articles analysing organizations and management and has been consultant and seminar leader to numerous organizations.

Everyone in an organization has in mind an implicit picture of that organization, a mental image of what it is like. Morgan contends not only that an organization is seen differently by different people, but that it can be seen in different ways by any one person. If multiple images of an organization are used, much greater understanding is gained, for organizations are many things at once, so multiple images envisage more of what is going on. They can reveal new ways of managing and designing organizations that were not apparent before.

Morgan himself puts forward eight possible images of organizations: as machines, as living organisms, as brains, as cultures, as political systems, as psychic prisons, as systems in flux and transformation and as instruments of domination. The name of each image is a metaphor likening an organization to something else and, by doing so, opening up a fresh way of thinking about it.

If an organization is thought of as a *machine*, the emphasis is on the orderly arrangement of who does what and who has authority over whom. This is a mechanical kind of thinking concerned with clear hierarchy, authority and responsibility, discipline, stability and equitable treatment of personnel. It is extolled by classic management theorists such as Fayol and Taylor (see Chapter 4 for both) and analysed by sociologists such as Weber and Burns (Chapters 1 and 2, respectively). The strength of an organization seen and set up in this form is that it works well where a machine would work well; that is, where tasks are straightforward and repetitive, as in a fast-food hamburger chain or an accounts office. Its limitation is that it dehumanizes work.

However, if an organization is seen as a living *organism*, a biological metaphor, then there is less preoccupation with orderliness and more attention is given to adaptiveness. Tasks and lines of authority can be changed to realign the organization continuously in response to its changing environment. This view is extolled by Peters and by Kanter (Chapter 4 for both). It is the organic type described by Burns and one of those described by Mintzberg (Chapter 1). Its strength is that it fosters an organization which is an open, flexible system, giving full scope to human capacities, especially appropriate to competitive and turbulent conditions, as in the aerospace and microelectronics industries. Its limitations are that it can overlook its own built-in conflict potential, and that, as 'population ecologists' such as Hannan and Freeman (Chapter 2) have argued, an organization is not infinitely adaptable but can become obsolete and die.

An image of an organization as a *brain* does not mean that it has central planning teams or a research department. Rather, it presumes that intelligence is spread throughout the organization. In this the brain is similar to a holograph, in which any part can reproduce the whole and stand for it. So in all its parts the organization does not just learn, but can learn to learn better. There can be 'double-loop learning' (Argyris, earlier in this chapter) that goes further than 'single-loop learning' (which only corrects errors) into another feedback loop that questions the operating norms, the ways of working, that lead to error in the first place. Such an organization would accept uncertainty and self-criticism and be able to see further than the 'bounded rationality' postulated by Simon and March (Chapter 5 for both). Were an organization to have a rigid structure, these advantages unfortunately might not be realized. Such a structure would have opposing assumptions embedded in it. It would have specialist departments, each holding on to its own specialized information, each unable to learn from the others or to question its own ways of working.

Seeing an organization in terms of *cultures*, Morgan's fourth image, brings to attention not only its overall corporate culture, but the subcultures of its constituent sections and groups and the societal culture of which its own culture is a part. People who share a culture interpret situations and events in similar ways, sustaining their common outlook with evocative figures of speech, symbols and ceremonies. As an obvious instance, even an empty room symbolizes what is expected, having either ordered chairs and notepads or, alternatively, chairs arranged casually. This cultural view reveals the wide organizational life that is beyond the overtly rational, and shows possibilities of change. Even the relationships of an organization with its environment can be reinterpreted, rethought, and thus changed, as when a railway switches from thinking about passengers, or a hospital about patients, and each begins to think about customers instead.

The fifth image recognizes an organization as a *political system*. An organization can be autocratic or democratic, or anywhere in between. There are departmental interests, management interests and the interests of those lower down, personal career interests, and many more. All interests have a potential for conflict and for wheeling and dealing. They exploit both the legitimate authority classified by Weber (Chapter 1) and the power drawn from controlling resources and know-how analysed by Pfeffer and Salancik (Chapter 2) and Hickson (Chapter 1). The strength of this image is that it helps people to accept the reality of organizational politics and to ask whose interests are being served.

Organizations give purpose and structure to the lives of their members. Our roles become our realities, as Morgan puts it. There lies the danger. For individuals can believe they are more in control than is really the case. In this they deceive themselves, for they can be in a *psychic prison*, attributing to the organization an existence and power of its own and allowing their thinking to be confined by it. Their thinking may indeed be the result of forces in their unconscious, as psychoanalysis has shown. The strength of this prison image is that it exposes how people can become trapped in this way in a certain psychic reality and suggests to them that it is possible to break out of it. Managers can see that their organization is of their own making and take a fresh look at what they are doing.

To see an organization as in constant *flux and transformation*, a seventh possible image, is to see it as being just like everything else in the universe. There are various conceptions of how change takes place. It can be seen as brought about through one-way cause and effect or – and this is better – by mutual causality, in which 'causes' loop back upon themselves; or by 'autopoiesis', whereby the organization changes itself by changing its own environment; or by dialectical change, whereby any phenomenon generates its opposite, as when the power of the employers led to the formation of trade unions. This image warns against an organization being seen as struggling against the environment. Rather it must survive in interdependence with others in that environment.

Finally Morgan draws a picture of organizations as *instruments of domination*. He points out that the building of the Great Pyramid in Egypt was both a triumph of skill and effort and a sacrifice of the labour and lives of many to glorify a few. Organizations achieve much, but as they do so they can cripple people with accidents, diseases and stress. They can abruptly dispose of them after years of service and pollute their habitat. The strength of this image is its recognition that domination of the many by the few is intrinsic to the very concept of hierarchy which exists in virtually every organization.

Morgan shows how the problems of a small firm in the public relations industry may be illuminated by using a range of metaphors. The firm was founded by two senior partners (holding 80 per cent of the equity between them) and two junior partners. It was immediately successful, based on the client-centred, all-round competences of the founders in giving a creative service. New staff, when recruited, were encouraged to develop their overall generalist skills, as well as their specializations. While this was time-consuming and expensive, it did give great flexibility to the firm and allowed greater work interest for the staff. There was high commitment and all worked hard and for long hours. Its success allowed the firm to grow in a few years to 150 staff.

Major conflicts began when the senior partners, feeling that the demands of the organization were too great in view of their family commitments, suggested a change to a more formalized structure. Their proposals included job definitions, set procedures for the change of staff between projects, greater control over when staff were away from the office and, in general, 'more system'. The junior partners objected that the firm was successful precisely because of the present 'creative chaos' and they saw no need for change. They offered to take more of the workload from the senior partners in exchange for more equity participation in the company. But the senior partners were not prepared to relinquish control in this way. In the event, in spite of the convention that the partners operated by consensus, the senior partners installed the changes. They appeared to be accepted, but within a year the junior partners had left to found their own agency in the original 'creative chaos' style. The firm continued, but less successfully, in that its work was now regarded by some clients as 'sound but uninspiring'.

Several of the metaphors may be used to help to make sense of these developments. The *machine* metaphor would point to the increasing bureaucratization and ask what should be the appropriate level of system in view of the size and dependence of the firm. The living *organism* metaphor would focus on the potential incongruence of the organization in its environment and ask whether it has the degree of creative chaos to be successful in its market niche. The *brain* metaphor would note the loss of the holographic character of the enterprise and ask how far it is now constrained to single-loop learning. The *culture* metaphor would lead to asking how far the values of the original culture have changed, and whether there are ways of recreating some of those characteristics in the new situation.

Using the *political* system metaphor points to the considerable differences in power between the partners which allowed the senior partners to impose their own decision when real conflicts appeared. What are the limitations on the organization's processes when this degree of power can be exercised? The *psychic prison* metaphor focuses on the psychological factors shaping relationships, including the senior partners' (probably unconscious) need for dominance and the junior partners' (probably equally unconscious) need to resist.

An important benefit of using a range of metaphors is that they supply competing explanations. Proposals for change from one may be tested against another. For example, if the changes in the company were generated by the owners' unconscious need for control, then the underlying problems cannot be solved by addressing only the issues of corporate culture or learning capacity (see Argyris, earlier in this chapter).

Managers can apply these ideas, says Morgan, by *imaginization*. This is 'an invitation to re-image ourselves and what we do'. In a book with this title, Morgan illustrates what he means and how he uses images in his own work as a consultant 'to create new momentum in stuck situations'. It is a book full of lively cartoons and images, from yoghurt pots to lions. One of them 'imaginizes' an organization as a spider plant. This is a plant which throws out long trailing stems, each with a miniature on its end of the original plant. Managers seeing their organization in this way come up with ideas that they have not considered before. One would be that expansion can be by setting up offshoots instead of by increasing the size of the central plant pot. But then what financial support should these new subsidiaries receive? If the organization already has a dispersed form, this image might prompt them to ask whether the central pot is doing enough. Or too much. Are some offshoots withering and becoming a drain on the centre? And so on. Different images raise different questions and so expose problems or opportunities that might otherwise be overlooked.

BIBLIOGRAPHY

BURRELL, G. and MORGAN, G., *Sociological Paradigms and Organizational Analysis*, Heinemann, 1979.
MORGAN, G., *Images of Organization*, Sage, 1986.
MORGAN, G., *Imaginization: The Art of Creative Management*, Sage, 1993.

8 The Organization in Society

Who says organization, says oligarchy.
ROBERT MICHELS

What is occurring ... is a drive for social dominance, for power and privilege, for the position of ruling class by the social group or class of the manager.
JAMES BURNHAM

We do need to know how to cooperate with the Organization but, more than ever, so do we need to know how to resist it.
WILLIAM H. WHYTE

An organization so often ends by smothering the very thing which it was created to embody.
KENNETH E. BOULDING

The danger to liberty lies in the subordination of belief to the needs of the industrial system.
JOHN KENNETH GALBRAITH

Small is beautiful.
E. FRITZ SCHUMACHER

Organizations do not exist or operate in a vacuum. They are one sort of institution in a particular society. They have to conform to the needs and standards laid down by institutions other than themselves. The pressures of a market economy, political decisions and legal restrictions all affect organizational operations. Yet the large-scale organization is one of the dominant institutions of our time, and in its turn must exert a powerful influence on the rest of society. Many writers have taken up this theme and have tried to show how far the nature of modern organizations has changed society.

Robert Michels argues that large modern organizations inevitably produce a powerful oligarchy at the top, with far-reaching social consequences. James Burnham examines how the balance of power in society has shifted from the owners of wealth to those who manage it. For William H. Whyte also, managers are an increasingly assertive section of society; he is alarmed that their characters are being moulded by the organizations which employ them. Kenneth E. Boulding highlights the frequent conflicts between the interests of the organization and the wider interests of society.

John Kenneth Galbraith underlines the inadequacy of the market mechanism for regulating economies, pointing to the consequent frequent intervention of governments as a 'countervailing power'. E. Fritz Schumacher warns against believing that the problems of production have been solved when we are using up the resources of our planet at a rate which cannot continue.

Robert Michels

Robert Michels (1876–1936) was a German sociologist and political scientist, writing at the beginning of this century. Like many of those who were involved in the early development of ideas in the social sciences, he was politically as well as scientifically committed. He was a socialist until, as he came to the end of his life and as a result of his own theorizing, he turned towards the fascist ideas of Mussolini. His political life informed his social theories and his social theories influenced his political life.

What was it, then, that caused Michels to move from the left to the right of politics? His move derived from the contradiction that he perceived in the internal structure and functioning of organizations: the contradiction between democracy and bureaucracy. For Michels, the essential principle of organizational functioning was 'the iron law of oligarchy'. This iron law means that whenever an organization is created, it inevitably becomes controlled by a small group of people who use it to further their own interests rather than those of other organizational members. His main concern was to examine the organizational features which make internal democracy impossible and the displacement of objectives certain.

To understand how Michels arrived at his pessimistic view of organizational life, it is necessary to put him in the context of his times and to examine the kinds of organizations he was primarily interested in. Those observing and writing about society during the latter half of the nineteenth century and the beginning of the twentieth saw the rise of the large-scale organization. Not only was this becoming apparent in industrial life, but also in politics and government. The extension of voting to more and more individuals led to political parties. The beginnings of the welfare state and increasing governmental activity meant the expansion of the civil service. Michels analyses the interaction between increasing organizational scale and the growth of bureaucracy.

His particular concern is with political parties and the state. The first mass-based political parties were appearing, with the avowed aim of opening up politics – and consequently influence on the state – to a wider population than ever before. Political parties, especially those of the left such as the German Social Democratic party, were democratic in structure. But for Michels the democracy of such parties quickly became a matter of formal structures, rule-books and constitutions; the actual functioning was something different – elite domination by means of a bureaucratic organization. The emergence of a bureaucratic elite is inevitable: it is the iron law of oligarchy.

Michels suggests that as an organization gets bigger, so it becomes more bureaucratic. Political parties strive for increased membership. If they are successful and grow, they produce a larger hierarchy. They recruit full-time salaried officials and expert, professional leadership. There is a concentration of the means of communication, of information and of knowledge at the top of the organization. Because of its size and the bureaucratic mode of operation that this entails, a high level of participation is impossible in large organizations. A number of important consequences result.

Once an elite leadership and full-time officials have appeared, there is the inevitability of divergence between the leaders and the led. This is particularly the case in voluntary organizations. The role of those at the top of the organization is to present the views and aspirations of the mass of members. But with the advent of specialized personnel and a dominant elite, the gap between the top and the bottom of an organization gets wider and wider. In these circumstances leaders no longer represent the interests of the membership. So it is that an organization with a bureaucratic structure comes to be operated in the interests of its leaders who are concerned with the preservation of the bureaucracy.

Leaders wish to maintain their positions because of the prestige and influence that go with them. Salaried officials are self-interested because of the career possibilities that a well-developed bureaucracy offers. Together these constitute bureaucratic conservatism.

The processes of self-interest and bureaucratic conservatism together produce a slackening of the revolutionary ideas and fervour which Michels sees as necessary for a left-wing political organization. Indeed, such ideas become supplanted by ideologies which stress the need for internal unity, for harmony of views and ideas, and the undesirability of conflicts or tensions in the organization. Stress is also placed on the hostility of the surrounding environment, on external enemies and the danger of exposing internal difficulties and differences. With a professional leadership cut off from the mass of members, the organization becomes an end in itself rather than a means towards non-organizational ends such as equality or democracy. Because of its scale and bureaucratic nature, it serves the interests of the elite.

Although primarily concerned with the problem of internal democracy in political parties, Michels broadened his argument in two ways. First, he demonstrated the link between organizational and societal oligarchy. The leaders of organizations will be socially and culturally different from the led; indeed they will be members of the politically dominant classes, maintaining their positions through the control of organizations. In addition the expanding middle classes will be able to find security of employment through the growth of state organizations and thus enter into an alliance with the political elite as the servants of power (see Burnham, following in this chapter, for another view of the emergence of managerial powers).

Secondly Michels maintains that the iron law of oligarchy is applicable not just to political and voluntary organizations, but to all organizations subject to increasing scale because of the inherent opposition of bureaucracy and democracy. Agreeing with Weber (Chapter 1), Michels sees the development of bureaucratic structures as an inevitable aspect of organizational growth. The processes of specialization and hierarchy which are the basis of bureaucracy, are inimical to democracy because of their effects on decision making and communication.

Michels saw no way out of his cycle of despair other than through periodic revolutionary and charismatic movements. Unfortunately (from his point of view) such movements rapidly become institutionalized and subject to the processes of oligarchy. For Michels the outlook for democracy was poor, and eventually his personal answer lay in a charismatic political movement – the fascism of Mussolini.

Michels was the first to give expression to a problem that has concerned many writers for over a century; namely, can large organizations retain democratic functioning or will an inimical bureaucracy inevitably take over?

BIBLIOGRAPHY

MICHELS, R., *Political Parties*, Dover Publications, 1959.

James Burnham

James Burnham (1905–1987) was educated at the University of Princeton and Balliol College, Oxford. From 1932 to 1954 he was Professor of Philosophy at New York University. In 1955 he became editor of the *National Review*. During the 1930s he was a member of the Trotskyite 'Fourth International', but he broke his Marxist connection in 1939. His many publications are mainly on political topics.

The term 'managerial revolution' has become part of the language since Burnham made it the title of his best-known book, written in 1940. As he himself points out, his views are not particularly original, but they do constitute an attempt to formulate and argue logically about certain ideas which many people have wondered about, both then and since.

Burnham's thesis is that a declining capitalist form of society is giving way to a managerial one. The managerial revolution by which this is being accomplished is not a violent upheaval, but rather a transition over a period of time, in much the same way as feudal society gave way to capitalism. A wide range of symptoms heralded the imminent demise of capitalism as the Second World War commenced. The capitalist nations were unable to cope with mass unemployment, with permanent agricultural depression, or with the rapid rise in public and private debt. Their major ideologies of individualism, 'natural rights' of property and private initiative were no longer accepted by the mass of the people.

But there was no reason to think of socialism as the alternative. Almost everywhere Marxist parties were insignificant as a political force. The working class was declining in relative size and power. In Russia, the abolition of private property rights, which in Marxist theory should bring about a classless socialist society, neither prevented a ruling class from emerging nor promoted workers' control. Nevertheless, 'though Russia did not move towards socialism, at the same time it did not move back to capitalism'. What happened in Russia, as is steadily happening throughout the world, was a movement towards a managerial type of society. In this society it will be the managers who are dominant, who have power and privilege, who have control over the means of production and have preference in the distribution of rewards. In short, the managers will be the ruling class. This does not necessarily mean that political offices will be occupied by managers, any more than under capitalism all politicians were capitalists, but that the real power over what is done will be in the hands of managers.

In order to define who the managers are, Burnham singles out four groups of people with different functions. There are stockholders, whose relationship to a company is entirely passive. There are financiers – capitalists whose interest is the financial aspects of numbers of companies irrespective of what those companies do. There are executives, who guide a company, watch its profits and its prices. Then there are those who have charge of the technical process of producing, who organize employees, materials and equipment and develop the know-how which is becoming increasingly indispensable. These last are the managers. Of the stockholders, financiers, executives and managers, only the managers are vital to the process of production. This has been demonstrated by state ownership in Russia and by the extension of state enterprise in other nations. Moreover, even where private owners continue, they have been moving further and further away from the instruments of production, delegating supervision of production to others and exercising control at second, third or fourth hand through financial devices.

Burnham remarks on the self-confidence of managers compared with bankers, owners, workers, farmers and shopkeepers. These latter display doubts and worries, but managers have a self-assurance founded on the strength of their position. In managerial society there is no sharp distinction between politics and the arena of economics. In the state commissions, the committees, the bureaux and the administrative agencies, managers and bureaucrats coalesce. Rules, regulations and laws come increasingly to be issued by these interconnected bodies. The making of law is to be found in their records rather than in the annals of parliament. So in many nations sovereignty is gradually shifting from parliament to administrative offices.

In such an economy managers will exercise power by occupying the key directing positions. But their preferential rewards will be less in wealth and property rights than in status in the political-economic structure.

Burnham also sees the outlines of the managerial ideologies which will replace those of individualistic capitalism. The stress will be on the state, the people, the race, on planning rather than freedom, on jobs rather than opportunity, on duties and order rather than natural right.

Burnham's analysis of the overall trends in society and his projection of these into the future arouse interest to the extent that events bear him out. He was writing as the Second World War began. Much that has happened since could be construed either way, for or against his arguments. Years later, W. H. Whyte's description of the organization and *The Organization Man* is in keeping with Burnham's forecast. Is there a managerial revolution?

BIBLIOGRAPHY

BURNHAM, J., *The Managerial Revolution*, Peter Smith, 1941; Penguin, 1962.

William H. Whyte

The American writer William H. Whyte (1917–1999) was a journalist and a student of the society in which he lived. He was on the staff of *Fortune* and published articles in this and other leading magazines.

Whyte has concerned himself with contemporary trends in American society; his book *The Organization Man* is an attempt to portray vividly one such trend which Whyte himself believes may go too far. He points to the coming of an organization man (and woman) who not only works for The Organization but belongs to it as well. Such a person is a member of the middle class who occupies the middle rankings in all the great self-perpetuating institutions. Few of these ever become top managers, but they have 'taken the vows of organization life' and committed themselves to it.

Whyte argues that for an organization employee of this kind, the traditional Protestant ethic is becoming too distant from reality to provide an acceptable creed. The Protestant ethic is summed up by Whyte as the system of beliefs in the virtues of thrift, hard work and independence, and in the sacredness of property and the enervating effect of security. It extols free competition between individuals in the struggle for wealth and success. But to Whyte life is no longer like this, if it ever was. To him 'that upward path toward the rainbow of achievement leads smack through the conference room'. The younger generations of management have begun to recognize themselves as bureaucrats, even if they cannot face the word itself and prefer to describe themselves as administrators.

Such people need a different faith to give meaning to what they do, and Whyte finds in American society a gradually emerging body of thought to meet the need. He calls it the social ethic. This ethic provides the moral justification for the pressures of society against the individual. It holds that the individual is meaningless personally but that, by being absorbed into the group there can be created a whole that is greater than the sum of its parts. There should be no conflicts between human beings and society; any that occur are misunderstandings which could be prevented by better human relations.

There are three major propositions in the social ethic: *scientism, belongingness* and *togetherness*. 'Scientism', as Whyte dubs it, is the belief that a science of humans can be developed in the same way as the physical sciences have been. If only enough time and money were available, the conditions apposite to good group dynamics or to personal adjustment to social situations or any other desired human response could be discovered. Believers in scientism (who are not to be confused with social scientists) could then generate the belongingness and togetherness which they seek for all. The ultimate human need, it is thought, is to belong to a group, to harmonize with a group. But in belonging humans also need togetherness. They do not merely want to be part of The Organization, but to immerse themselves in it, together with other people, in smaller groups – around the conference table, in the seminar, the discussion group, the project team and so on.

Whyte traces the career cycle of organizational people as, guided by the social ethic, they give themselves up to The Organization. The influence of The Organization has extended into college curricula, so that by the time students are looking for their first job they have already turned their backs on the Protestant ethic. They look for a life of calm and order, offering success but not too much success, money but not too much, advancement but not too far. The Organization attempts to recruit for itself those who will fit in, those who will get along well with others, those who will not have any disturbingly exceptional characteristics. Increasingly it uses the tools of the psychologist: not only the well-tried aptitude and intelligence tests, but others purporting to reveal personality. Whyte challenges the validity of these latter tests, going so far as to write an Appendix entitled 'How to Cheat on Personality Tests': to obtain a safe personality score, you should try to answer as if you were like everybody else is supposed to be.

Once recruited, the training of potential managers emphasizes not their own work, but the exploitation of human relations techniques to manage the work of others. The successful trainee is not the one who competes successfully against others, but the one who cooperates more fully than others cooperate. What of the loss of individualism in group life? Whyte says that young people today regard this aspect of the large organization as a positive boon. Their ideal is the well-rounded person who has time for family and hobbies and, while good on the job, is not too zealous or over-involved in it. Overwork may have been necessary in the past, but now The Organization looks for the full individual. In particular this is the image held by personnel managers and business schools.

Whyte also sees the same tendencies in scientific and academic institutions. The idea of the lone genius is being displaced by that of the group-conscious research team. There is a steady increase in the proportion of scientific papers by several authors compared with those by a single author.

Though Whyte is stating a case against too great a belief in the social ethic, he realistically points out that it may never be applied as absolutely as it is preached, any more than was the Protestant ethic. Even so, the social ethic may delude individuals that their interests are being cared for when The Organization is really following its own ends. Guided by the social ethic, The Organization may suppress individual imagination and cling to a mediocre consensus. People may become skilful in getting along with one another, yet fail to ask why they should get along; may strive for adjustment, but fail to ask what they are adjusting to. It is Whyte's contention that organization man and woman must fight The Organization and accept conflict between themselves and society.

However, for some few in The Organization who start to go ahead of their contemporaries, there comes a realization that they have committed themselves: that they must go on alone to higher executive positions, that their home lives will be curtailed and their spouses less and less interested in the struggle. Such managers find themselves working 50-and 60-hour weeks, taking work home, spending weekends at conferences. They have no time for anything else. More than this, their work is their self-expression and they do not want anything else. They discover that someone on the way to the top cannot be well-rounded. The dream of a comfortable contentment just short of the top is shattered, and they talk of the treadmill, the merry-go-round and the rat race, 'words that convey an absence of tangible goals but plenty of activity to get there'.

Thus all executives contain within themselves a conflict between the old Protestant ethic and the new social ethic. Those who go ahead do so in order to control their own destinies, yet in The Organization they must be controlled and look as if they like it. Even though they want to be dominant, they must applaud permissive management. The executive may have risen by being a good team player, but now the other side of the coin becomes uppermost – the frustration of the committee room, the boredom of being sociable. Here is the basis of executives' neurosis.

BIBLIOGRAPHY

WHYTE, W. H, *The Organization Man*, Simon & Schuster, 1956; Penguin, 1960.

Kenneth E. Boulding

Kenneth E. Boulding (1910–1993) was born in England and educated at Oxford. He held a variety of teaching posts at universities in Scotland, Canada and the United States, and was for many years Professor of Economics at the University of Michigan. He was the author of many books on economics, but his work on *The Organizational Revolution* sprang from his interest, stemming from the fact that he was a prominent Quaker, in the relationship between organizations and ethical systems.

Boulding sees this 'revolution' as one of the major events of the past hundred years. There has been a great rise in the number, size and power of all organizations. More and more spheres of activity have become organized so that there are now businesses, trade unions, employers' federations, political parties, farming groups and the state, all of which are highly organized. This revolution is due on the one hand to changes in the habits and needs of people, and on the other to changes in the skills and techniques of organizing. Boulding sees the latter as the more important. Henry Ford did not mass produce motor-cars because of the demand, but because of new knowledge on how to organize and make them. Supply, not demand, was the dominant factor.

Such a growth of organizations has given rise to a large number of ethical problems. In Western societies there are certain basic values and assumptions which are drawn from Christianity. The Ten Commandments and the Sermon on the Mount are still largely the final basis for an ethical analysis of behaviour. They define morality as a matter of personal relationships, with a Christian ideal of fellowship and equality. It is on the level of personal behaviour that the application of such principles gives rise to ethical problems in organizations. All organizations create an 'in-group' made up of members of the organization, and an 'out-group' of non-members. The moral dilemma for the individual in such a situation is that the defence of the inner fellowship necessarily means the breaking of wider fellowships. To whom does the individual owe moral allegiance?

As organizations grow larger and more powerful, there is increased pressure for a hierarchy to fix the relationships and the distribution of power between people. But the presence of such a hierarchy is directly in conflict with the moral idea of equality since it tends to produce an aristocratic, highly stratified society based on status. Political democracy is an attempt to overcome this moral dilemma, making those at the top dependent on the will of the people.

The ideals of Christianity are also what Boulding calls 'familistic'. A full and intimate relationship of love and concern is the ideal human relationship. The major virtue is love, and the closest one gets to this is in the family. Such an ideal constantly comes into conflict with the necessities of organizational life. Relationships in economic organizations are based on contracts which demand only a lesser virtue, that of integrity. For large-scale organizations to exist, relationships must be pared down to the minimum, losing something vital as a consequence. The special moral problem of the businessman is balancing the equation of love and necessity. 'The business world is one in which relationships are based mainly on faith and hope, and, if it seems to be deficient in the warmer virtue of charity, it must at least be given credit for the other two.'

However, ethical problems also arise for organizations at levels other than that of personal relationships. To what extent should the leaders of any organization feel a responsibility to society as a whole? Should they advocate policies for the whole society rather than for their own special interests? What are the obligations of an organization to society? Boulding says that the usual excuse for pursuing special interests is that one is acting as a counter-pressure against other interests. The menace to society lies in the fact that certain special interests may become powerful enough to demand, and receive, privileged protection.

The heart of ethical conduct is action in the general interest. The problem is to make sure that organizations acting in such a way survive, and that those not meeting the needs and ends of society disappear. But this must be done without the use of coercion, which is inimical to the pursuit of Christian ideals. Action in the general interest is an ideal which is difficult to attain; the need is for a mechanism which will continually adjust actual to ideal.

The mechanism to achieve this is the market reacting to the laws of supply and demand. Competition and specialization, which are the mainsprings of a market economy, are prime movers in bringing together the general interest with special interests. But the organizational revolution has superimposed monopolies and large-scale economic groupings on the market economy. So the need is for a governed market economy with the principle of political representation built into it. This makes individuals responsible to others for their actions. There has been a shift from the market to representation as the adjustive mechanism. It is through the operation of social democracy that the best approximation of the ideal and the actual can be made.

BIBLIOGRAPHY

BOULDING, K. E., *The Organizational Revolution*, Harper, 1953.

John Kenneth Galbraith

J. K. Galbraith (1908–2006) was born in Canada, but lived most of his life in the US. He was an economist who spent his academic years at Harvard University. He was a supporter of John Kennedy and during the Kennedy administration served as US Ambassador to India. Galbraith has long believed in the necessity of popularizing the ideas of economics, his books being aimed as much at lay people as at professional economists.

The underlying thesis in all his work is that the nature of American capitalism has changed over the past century and that, as a result, traditional economic theories no longer apply. Classical economic theory rests on the proposition that the behaviour of buyers and sellers is regulated by the market, through which the stimulant of competition is provided. Economic power is denied to any one person or firm because of price competition. But this system depends on a large number of producers of a good or service, none of whom is in a position to dominate the market; conversely it depends on large numbers of buyers, who individually cannot affect the market. Yet this is demonstrably not the situation in modern industrial economies. Instead there is a process by which the typical industry passes from an initial stage of many firms competing, to a situation of a few large firms only – what economists refer to as 'oligopoly'.

Thus, the most important task facing modern economic theory is to analyse the place of the large corporation in the economy, and to discover what new regulatory agencies, if any, have replaced the marketplace. If the balanced power of the competitive system no longer applies, does the large corporation wield unchecked power? In *American Capitalism*, Galbraith suggests that there is a situation of countervailing power. The concentration of industrial enterprise, on which everyone agrees, produces the giant corporations which might possibly wield huge agglomerations of power both in economic and political terms. But this process brings into existence strong buyers as well as strong sellers. This is something that tends to be forgotten when the supposed 'evils' of oligopology are discussed. An example of such countervailing power is seen in the development of large retail trading chains, such as Marks & Spencer and the Cooperative Movement, who from their importance as buyers of goods are able to offset the oligopoly power of the producers or sellers of shirts, dresses and so on. Similarly, in the labour market there is the power of the union countervailing that of the employers' association. Thus, the situation is one of giants standing off against each other. Much of the increasing intervention in the economy by the state comes from the need to develop sources of countervailing power in the economy. A recent phenomenon in the US and Britain which fits the theory is the development of vocal consumers' associations.

In summary, the competitive marketplace as regulator has been replaced due to differences between the capitalistic system of today and that of 50 years ago. And today's system has its efficiencies. It is the large oligopolies which can best incur the cost of research. However, Galbraith himself points out that this system of countervailing power really only works where there is limited demand, so that the buyer has some leeway vis-à-vis the seller. In the context of unlimited demand, the balance of power shifts decisively to the seller – the large corporation. In *The Affluent Society* and *The New Industrial State*, he develops the idea of control of the market by the corporation, where a situation of unlimited demand is 'manufactured'.

Again the starting idea is the rise of the large-scale corporation, the separation of ownership from control and the results of this for a competitive market system (see Burnham, earlier in this chapter). Control of the market becomes increasingly important for the well-being of the organization because of the use of more and more sophisticated technology. The organization faces a set of technological imperatives (technology being the systematic application of scientific or other organized knowledge to practical tasks). For Galbraith there are six imperatives deriving from increased technological sophistication which have important implications for the relationship of the organization to other organizations, to the consumer and to the state.

First, the time-span between thinking of a new product and actually producing it is getting greater and greater. An example is the lead time between the initial idea for a car and its arrival on the market. Secondly the amount of capital that is committed to production increases; more investment is required. Thirdly, once time and money have been committed, there is a great deal of inflexibility; it becomes very difficult to back out. Fourthly, the use of advanced technology requires special sorts of staff, leading to the rise of the engineer, the applied scientist and the importance of technical qualifications. (As with Burnham, Galbraith sees this 'technostructure' as becoming the most important source of decision making.) Fifthly, organizations become more complex, with an increasing need for the control and coordination of specialists. Sixthly, all these imperatives together produce the need for planning.

Thus, societies require large corporations (which Galbraith names 'the Industrial System', the dominant feature of the New Industrial State) properly to acquire the benefits of new technology. But it is obvious that the imperatives outlined above involve the organization in situations of risk. There are always the famous cases of the Ford Edsel and the Rolls-Royce aero-engines as salutory reminders of what can happen when planning fails. It is only the large business organization which can find the necessary capital and employ the necessary skills to use sophisticated technology, but it still needs help in dealing with it and with the risks involved.

Organizational planning does not just mean making sure that the right materials get to the right place at the right time, internally. It also means that suppliers are reliable (producing goods, components and so on, as needed) and that buyers are there when needed. As a result, to quote Galbraith: 'Much of what the firm regards as planning consists in minimizing or getting rid of market influences.' To deal with the uncertainties involved and thus minimize the risks facing the organization, planning is required to *replace the market*. Control of the market can be done in two ways: either by direct control of the consumer, making them dependent in some way on the corporation, or by having a single customer – a guaranteed market. Both of these options involve increasing state intervention, another illustration of the changing nature of contemporary capitalism.

Direct control of the consumer can take place in a variety of ways. One of the most important is the use of advertising. This is a direct attempt to influence the demand for a product and also to create a psychological dependence on the part of the consumer. Under conditions of affluence a situation of unlimited demand can be created, with the corporation controlling the needs and aspirations of the consumer rather than vice versa. In the US the accepted view of a desirable automobile is the current model as styled in and by Detroit. A further possibility is the control of the market by size domination, a movement towards monopoly. This can be helped along by vertical integration and the use of contracts to tie buyers and sellers together, stabilizing the existence of both. The state is important in that it now carries the responsibility for regulating the level of demand in the economy, stabilizing wages and prices.

Having a single-customer guaranteed market becomes extremely important for those organizations using especially advanced, expensive technologies. In particular what happens is that the state becomes the customer and the idea of a market starts to disappear altogether. The state is in effect underwriting the cost of investment so that the line between the 'private' corporation and the state begins to disappear. This situation is typical of the aerospace industry where research, development and production are commissioned by the government. An organization such as Lockheed sells more than three-quarters of its production to the government.

Considering both the need to control demand and the role of the state in this process, there is a tendency for the corporation to become a part of the administrative arm of the state. The management of demand becomes a vast, rapidly growing industry in which the public sector is increasingly important through its control of the wage–price spiral, its setting of personal and corporate income tax, its regulation of aggregate demand and its own role as a consumer. Also the state is responsible for producing the qualified manpower (the technostructure) on which the corporation is dependent, through its financing of education.

The net result is an increasing similarity between all mature industrial societies in terms of the design of organizations and the planning mechanisms used. The heavy requirements of capital, sophisticated technology and elaborate organization, which need planning to replace the market, lead to the dominance of the large corporation. Such corporations are in turn dependent on the state. As Galbraith summarizes his position: 'Given the decision to have modern industry (in any country), much of what happens is inevitable and the same.'

BIBLIOGRAPHY

GALBRAITH, J. K., *The Affluent Society*, Hamish Hamilton, 1958; Penguin, 1967.
GALBRAITH, J. K., *American Capitalism*, Houghton Mifflin, 1962; Penguin, 1963.
GALBRAITH, J. K., *The New Industrial State*, Houghton Mifflin, 1967; Penguin, 1969 (rev. edn, 1978).
GALBRAITH, J. K., *The Age of Uncertainty*, Andre Deutsch, 1977.

E. Fritz Schumacher

Born in Germany, Fritz Schumacher (1911–1977) went to Britain in 1930 to study economics at New College, Oxford, and from there to Columbia University, New York. He later turned from the academic life to business, farming and journalism. His public service for Britain included serving from 1946 to 1950 as Economic Adviser to the British Control Commission in Germany, and from 1950 to 1970 as Economic Adviser to the National Coal Board. He was Founder and Chairman of the Intermediate Technology Development Group Ltd, President of the Soil Association (an organic farming organization), and a Director of the Scott-Bader Company.

To Schumacher the belief by economists and industrialists alike that humankind has solved the problem of production is glib nonsense. It has been solved only by the industrialized nations consuming resources at a frenetic pace. Production is using up the natural capital of our planet without which it cannot itself continue. Even supposing that there were resources sufficient for all peoples to use energy at the rate at which it is now used in the industrialized nations, if they did so the world level of thermal and nuclear pollution would be intolerable.

We must begin to evolve a new lifestyle with methods of production and of consumption that are designed for permanence, based on biologically sound agriculture and on 'non-violent technology' which does not abuse resources or people. We need 'technology with a human face'.

The fragmentary view propounded by Western economics is too narrow to see this. Its exclusive focus on readily quantifiable goods ignores the free goods from which these derive. An activity can be economic even though it destroys the environment, whilst a competing activity which conserves the environment will be made to appear more costly and therefore uneconomic.

Even work itself is seen as labour, as a cost, as a disutility, as a sacrifice of leisure. It is not seen as a desirable activity in which individuals use their faculties of brain and hand, join others in a common task, and find purpose in bringing forth needed goods and services. Virtually all production has been turned by large-scale technology into an inhuman chore where the work of brain and of hand are separated, despite the needs of a human being for both.

Technology and the organizations making use of technology ought to fit the resources of our planet to the needs of mankind. They must be of an appropriate scale: 'Man is small and, therefore, small is beautiful. To go for giantism is to go for self-destruction.'

From this critique stems Schumacher's advocacy of 'intermediate technology' and organization for the third world, and 'smallness within bigness' for the organizations of the industrialized world.

Intermediate technology should replace the 'technology of giantism'. The trend towards ever-greater size of production equipment, and of larger organizations to run it at ever-higher speeds, is the opposite of progress. Third-world poverty is a problem of two million villages to which such technologies and organizations are wholly unsuited. They result in incongruous and costly projects. A textile mill in Africa is filled with highly automated machinery to eliminate the human factor even though people are idle and even though its standards demand fibres of a length not grown locally so that its raw materials must be imported. Again, a soap factory produces luxury soap by such sensitive processes that only very refined materials can be used; these are imported at high prices whilst local materials are exported at low prices. Examples of such disparities abound.

As Gandhi said: 'The poor of the world cannot be helped by mass production but only by production by the masses.' Therefore the best of modern knowledge should be applied to designing technology at a level which is conducive to decentralized moderate-scale production that is gentle, not violent, in its use of scarce resources, and that serves human beings rather than their serving it. This intermediate technology should be a means for people to help themselves, making what their countries need rather than sophisticated products usable only by the rich populations of the industrialized world. It should enable them to work in a way fitting for themselves. Their first need is for work that brings in some reward, however small; not until they gain some value for their time and effort can they become interested in making it more valuable.

Schumacher argues that the smallest-scale technology and organization suitable for the purpose in hand should be used. He puts forward four propositions:

- Workplaces should be created where people live now, not in the metropolitan areas to which they are forced to migrate.
- These workplaces should be cheap enough to be created in large numbers without requiring unattainable levels of capital formation and imports.
- Production methods should be sufficiently simple to minimize demands for high skills either in production or in organization.
- Production should be mainly from local materials and for local use.

The intermediate level of technology may be symbolized in monetary terms. Suppose that the indigenous technology of a typical developing country is called a £1-technology, and that of developed countries is called a £1000-technology, then intermediate technology is a £100-technology.

It has been objected that using such technology is deliberately denying people the chance to be as productive as possible. Productivity should not be deliberately held down in order to limit the amount of capital per worker. People should not be prevented from increasing their wealth as quickly as possible by the latest methods. Schumacher's rejoinder is that this overlooks both the real situation, and the capabilities and needs of the people themselves. It is a mistake to assume that sophisticated equipment in an unsuitable situation will be efficient at the level projected for it in an industrialized society. Not only are the technical and administrative skills not available, but industrial estates all over the third world stand half idle because the assumed supporting communications, transport, distribution network and imported materials and components are not in fact there.

Whilst intermediate technology in the third world would require the organizing of people in small units, the giant organizations of the industrialized world cannot simply be abolished. Some goods can only be produced on a large scale. So what can be done about these giants? The fundamental task is to achieve smallness within bigness.

Bigness ensues from the constant mergers and takeovers in private industry, and from nationalization in the public sector. Individuals come to feel mere cogs in vast machines. Kafka's nightmarish novel, *The Castle*, depicts the devastating effects of remote control on an individual who gropes within the system to find what is what and who is who, perpetually mystified and confused. No one likes large organizations, yet Parkinsonian bureaucracies continue to grow.

What organizations need are both the orderliness of order and the disorderliness of creative *freedom*. Large organizations are pulled to and fro by these two needs, and in consequence go through alternating phases of centralizing and decentralizing as they give priority first to the one and then to the other. Unfortunately, administrative demands tend to bias them towards orderliness and centralization at the expense of the disorderly decentralization which allows scope for entrepreneurial innovation. Perhaps what is needed is neither centralization nor decentralization but one and the other at the same time.

This leads Schumacher to formulate five principles for running large-scale organizations which are essentially aimed at devolving them into relatively autonomous profit centres.

First is the *Principle of Subsidiarity*, or the Principle of Subsidiary Function. A higher level in an organization should never do what a lower level can do. Thus a large organization will consist of many semi-autonomous units. From an administrator's point of view this will appear untidy compared to a clear-cut monolith, but the centre will actually gain in authority and effectiveness because of the loyalty engendered in lower units (see also Tannenbaum, Chapter 5).

Accountability of the subsidiary units to the centre requires the application of the second principle, the *Principle of Vindication*. Other than in exceptional cases, the subsidiary unit should be defended against reproach and upheld: it should be assessed on a minimum number of criteria of accountability so that it knows clearly whether or not it is performing satisfactorily. In a commercial organization there would ideally be only one criterion – profitability. Numerous criteria mean that fault can always be found on one item or another, which stifles initiative.

Hence the third principle, the *Principle of Identification*. It must be possible for each unit to identify clearly its cumulative success or failure by having, not only a separate profit and loss account, but a separate balance sheet of assets. The effect of its own efforts on its own economic subsistence is then visible.

Fourthly, the *Principle of Motivation* calls for a positive approach to work. If all efforts are devoted only to doing away with work by automation and computerization, work comes to be regarded as something to be got rid of. It becomes a devalued activity which people put up with because no other way has been found of achieving required ends. They work just for the pay.

Finally there is the *Principle of the Middle Axiom* which the centre should follow if it wants to get things done, for if it uses exhortation, nothing will happen. If it issues detailed instructions, these may be erroneous because they do not emanate from the people closely in touch with the actual job. What is required is something in between, a middle axiom. This is an axiom because it is sufficiently self-evident to command consent and also clear enough for others to know how to proceed.

The incomprehensibility of large organizations to those in them is exacerbated by their forms of ownership. In small-scale enterprise, private ownership is 'natural, fruitful and just', in Schumacher's view. But in medium-scale enterprise, private ownership begins to lose its function; its contribution begins to disappear. Moreover in large-scale enterprise, private ownership 'is a fiction for the purpose of enabling functionless owners to live parasitically on the labour of others'. It 'distorts all relationships within the enterprise'.

Nationalization is a purely negative extinguishing of private rights without substituting anything positive. Schumacher describes one alternative exemplified by the Scott-Bader Commonwealth with which he himself became connected. In this polymer chemistry firm, private ownership was replaced by Commonwealth ownership. All employees became members of the Commonwealth which owned Scott-Bader Co. Ltd. as a collectivity – without individual ownership rights.

This kind of solution would be applicable only in small- to medium-size organizations. For larger organizations, Schumacher makes radical suggestions as to how a public share in the equity could be achieved. He proposes that, instead of profits being taxed, the public be issued with equity shares. In harmony with his views on the local character of industries that use intermediate technology, he proposes that these shares be held locally in the district where the enterprise is located. One way for this to be done would be to vest the shares in social councils composed of members from local trade unions, local professional associations and local residents.

To Schumacher, small is beautiful because it is the way to humane efficiency in the organizations of our time.

BIBLIOGRAPHY

MCROBIE, G., *Small is Possible*, Harper & Row, 1981.
SCHUMACHER, E .F., *Small is Beautiful: A Study of Economics as if People Mattered*, Blond and Briggs, 1973.

Name Index

Subject Index